T0339481

Understanding Chinese Corporate Governance

In a complex political and environmental global landscape, it has never been more critical for global organizations to understand the past, present, and future of Chinese corporate governance: this book is the key.

Leveraging her dual-cultural background and using a board-level practitioner's lens, Lyndsey Zhang offers insights that will help the global business community better understand Chinese companies' corporate governance practices and economic development journeys, shorten the learning curve for global business leaders and investors, and explore different economic models that better suit emerging markets. She addresses important questions such as:

- How does the Chinese government manage to retain its controlling position in Chinese companies while still making them attractive to global investors?
- What are the drivers for Chinese companies' future corporate governance improvement?
- What is China's position on the worldwide ESG and climate change movements?
- How can global practitioners feel less like "navigating in the dark" when working with Chinese companies?

This book will be an invaluable resource for anyone seeking to understand the rapidly changing world of Chinese corporate governance, including global investors, senior executives in multinational corporations, consultants, financial and political policymakers, business and law students, and researchers.

Lyndsey Zhang has extensive corporate experience working with Western and Chinese multinational companies in the automation manufacturing, clean and renewable energies, and solar technology sectors. In CFO and VP of Strategy positions with Chinese companies, and on boards of directors, she directed global expansion projects, fundraised on Hong Kong's stock exchange, managed cross-border mergers and acquisitions in European countries, and developed post-acquisition strategies for US-based corporations. A popular speaker and podcaster, Lyndsey is an Illinois-licensed CPA and holds an Independent Board Director certificate from Harvard University, as well as an MS in accountancy from Illinois State University and a BS in economics from Xiamen University. She is currently a PhD student at Henley Business School, University of Reading, specializing in ESG and corporate governance.

Understanding Chinese Corporate Governance

Practical Guidance for Working with Chinese Partners

Lyndsey Zhang

Routledge
Taylor & Francis Group

NEW YORK AND LONDON

Designed cover image: Getty

First published 2024
by Routledge
605 Third Avenue, New York, NY 10158

and by Routledge
4 Park Square, Milton Park, Abingdon, Oxon, OX14 4RN

Routledge is an imprint of the Taylor & Francis Group, an informa business

© 2024 Lyndsey Zhang

Library of Congress Cataloging-in-Publication Data
Names: Zhang, Lyndsey, author.
Title: Understanding Chinese corporate governance : practical guidance for working with Chinese partners / Lyndsey Zhang.
Description: New York, NY : Routledge, 2024. |
Includes bibliographical references and index. |
Identifiers: LCCN 2023024557 (print) | LCCN 2023024558 (ebook) |
ISBN 9781032299570 (hbk) | ISBN 9781032299556 (pbk) |
ISBN 9781003302919 (ebk)
Subjects: LCSH: Corporate governance–China. | Economic development–China.
Classification: LCC HD2741 .Z433 2024 (print) | LCC HD2741 (ebook) |
DDC 658.400951–dc23/eng/20230912
LC record available at https://lccn.loc.gov/2023024557
LC ebook record available at https://lccn.loc.gov/2023024558

ISBN: 9781032299570 (hbk)
ISBN: 9781032299556 (pbk)
ISBN: 9781003302919 (ebk)

DOI: 10.4324/9781003302919

Typeset in Times New Roman
by Newgen Publishing UK

Dedicated to the memory of my mother Lanfen Ding (1949–2005). I will never forget my childhood dreams and inspirations, particularly those inherited from my mother.

Contents

Foreword

Lyndsey has written a much-needed book namely one that informs people around the world about the state of corporate governance in one of the most important economies – China.

She points out that it was only in 1993 that China authorized the establishment of the limited liability of organizations.

She has taken us to a point of understanding the status of Chinese companies' ESG integration. This adoption of the ESG factors is truly a revolution in China.

She has pointed out that the social and regulatory systems in China are being reshaped over a five-year plan with the focus on quality. She draws attention to the key points of China's social credit system and its upcoming regulatory developments. The Chinese government seems determined to establish a trustworthy society improving people's livelihoods and eventually building a high standard for the regulation of the country's social and institutional systems.

She draws the reader's attention to key geopolitical elements that influence the Chinese corporate governance system. She highlights the ongoing developments and complexity of the geopolitical elements and the impact on the Chinese corporate governance system.

She makes some important recommendations on corporate governance for the business community in China. She discusses GUANXI, an important concept in Chinese society, which can help one not only navigate business and invest in Chinese companies but also explore other interests in China.

This book is a must read for global investors, business leaders, and anyone interested in corporate and business life in China.

Lyndsey has launched her book at a time of great uncertainty in the world and has informed outsiders about the state of corporate governance in China.

I highly recommend the reading of this book to anyone intending to enter into a business relationship with a Chinese partner or to start a new business in China.

Prof Mervyn King SC
Founder and Patron of the Good Governance Academy
Chair Emeritus of the King Reports on Corporate Governance

Foreword
A commentary

Bob Tricker*

China today is an enigma, so is China's corporate governance. Following Chairman Mao Zedong's death in 1976, his Marxist-Leninist, peasant culture was replaced by market-led reforms, the corporatization of state enterprises and, in some cases, their privatization and flotation on the Chinese stock markets, and sometimes abroad. Private property became acceptable. Private companies were created, some becoming vast and global. Over the next 40 years, hundreds of miles of high-speed railways and motorways were built, a new relatively-affluent, car-owning middle-class appeared, and China became the world's second-largest economy, with nearly 1.5 billion people, over four times that of the US.

Against that background, China needed new company law, regulation of companies, and a system of corporate governance. Initially, these were influenced by recommendations from the Organisation for Economic Co-operation and Development (OECD) and advice from the legal and accounting professions in Hong Kong. Inevitably, this experience had a Western orientation. However, the governance of China's companies soon took on unique Chinese characteristics. Governance power over corporate enterprises needed to reflect responsibilities to the people, the Party, and the State, while generating the wealth needed to fund the country's massive social change and economic growth. Then the Party leaders faced economic challenges caused, not least, by the effects of their Covid pandemic policy lockdowns, a collapse of the building market, and an aging population.

Lyndsey Zhang's book is timely. There is a great deal of interest in how governance power is exercised in China, both at the State and the corporate levels. The book takes a comprehensive look at the Chinese corporate governance system and code, with its own two-tier board structure, the governance of state-owned enterprises, and private companies not owned by the state.

A unique insight is given into the risks associated with China's corporate governance, including the fragility of investors' ownership. Another problem, familiar to many successful startup companies around the world, is the challenge of the founders' domination and succession.

Issues of audit quality, independent directors' questionable independence and objectivity, and the uncertainty of government influence and regulatory reform are also mentioned. Geopolitical tensions are recognized including the scrutiny, by both countries, of Chinese companies listed in the US. The case studies include some fascinating insights into Alibaba, Ant, and Huawei, among many others.

Part II of the book covers China's approach to the United Nation's concern for the environment, society, and governance (ESG). Described as an ESG revolution, China's approach to lowering carbon emissions and improving sustainability is driven by regulators and embraced by China's five-year plan.

Hong Kong's place as an international finance center, despite the impact of the National Security Law, and her role in the Guangdong-Hong Kong-Macau trade area is mentioned, as are links with countries in Africa and those covered by the "Belt and Road Strategy".

Lyndsey has a huge advantage in writing this book, being Chinese-American with significant experience in both Chinese and American companies. She has a bachelor's degree from Xiamen University and a master's degree from Illinois State University. A qualified US-certified public accountant, she has consulted and researched at the board level for some years in both countries and hosts the successful podcast Boardroom&Beyond. I cannot think of anyone better qualified to write this authoritative book.

The conclusion is that China is building a high-quality corporate governance regulatory system. The book's cover promises "a practical handbook for business leaders and investors", I would add "and a guide for anyone interested in China's place in the modern world".

*Bob Tricker wrote the first book with the title "Corporate Governance" in 1984, when he was a Research Fellow of Nuffield College, Oxford. He subsequently spent many years as a Professor of Finance at the University of Hong Kong.

Acknowledgments

I would like to acknowledge with gratitude the editorial contributions of Meredith Norwich and Bethany Nelson at Routledge Publishing, Dan Covic, an independent editor, and anonymous reviewers, all of whom have added great value to this book's readability.

I am most grateful to all named and unnamed interview participants and my colleagues at Chinese multinational companies, who have shared their experiences and opinions that enriched the content of this book.

I want to thank Professor Andrew Kakabadse for our enlightening conversations, and for sharing valuable feedback on the initial draft of this manuscript.

I also want to thank Professor Bob Tricker and Professor Mervyn King for writing forewords for this book, and Professor Lourdes S. Casanova, Michele Wucker, Cary Krosinsky, and John Millian-Whyte for their testimonials.

Case Studies

Chapter 1

Case Study 1.1. Alibaba's Controlling Structure
Keywords: Alibaba Partnership, Controlling voting power, Proxy voting agreement, Takeover protection, Staggered board structure
Case Study 1.2. Alibaba's Succession Planning
Keywords: Founder retirement, Succession planning, Transparent, Alibaba Singles Day, Leadership transfer
Case Study 1.3. Huawei's Rotating CEO/Chairman System
Keywords: Founder influence, Governance structure, Long-term sustainability, Rotating, CEO, Chairman, Inspiration, Long-term growth
Case Study 1.4. Huawei's "Superfluid" Organizational Structure
Keywords: Customer-centric, Business strategy, Organizational Structure, Human resource pool, Vodafone, Multiple responsibilities, Rotating, Overseas subsidiaries, Resignation and rehiring, Surgical organizational restructure, Critiques
Case Study 1.5. Alibaba's Voting Arrangements with Softbank and Yahoo
Keywords: Voting power, Proxy agreement, Major shareholder, Director nomination
Case Study 1.6. Alibaba's Founder's Commitments Alleviate Investors' Concerns
Keywords: Founder influence, Commitment, Investors, Ownership transfer, IPO, Charitable Donation
Case Study 1.7. Pinduoduo Founder's Retirement – Trend of a New Succession Plan Model
Keywords: Founder retirement, Succession planning, Leadership transfer, Relinquish super-voting rights, Agricultural technology, Rural infrastructure

Chapter 2

Chapter 3

Chapter 5

Key Recommendations

Case study: Geely/Volvo Acquisition – Mutual Learning Drives Synergy Maximization

Keywords: Founder Influence, Corporate culture, Management Style, Global Branding, Technology Sharing, Long-term success

Introduction

The Inspiration for This Book

In June 2019, I attended a one-week independent board director training at Harvard University due to my appointment as an executive board director of a newly established US subsidiary of a Chinese multinational company. Prior to that training, I had worked for three Chinese multinational companies since 2014. The one-week training was packed with case studies and became the starting point of my research of Chinese corporate governance for two reasons.

First, I learned that corporate governance does not just matter to the board of directors but permeates the entire organization, impacts the purpose of the business, the decision-making process, the interactions between board members and executives, and the relationship between the organization and its stakeholders. Moreover, a company's board governance practice is deeply influenced by its home country's culture, regulation system, and economic environment. Having worked for Western multinational companies for a decade before joining the Chinese companies, I can't help comparing the corporate governance structures and business practices between the two. As a result, I had been curious about the reason for the differences between Chinese companies and their Western counterparts, as well as the differences between those three Chinese multinational companies, each of whom had distinct ownership structures, board governance practice, and strategic approaches to expanding their business in the global market.

Second, I realized that even in one of the world's top business schools, there were no updated educational materials reflecting the upward trend of Chinese companies, who have rapidly taken leading global positions in various business sectors over the past two decades. Out of the 20-plus case studies over the week, there were only two Chinese cases: One was about Li & Fung Limited, a Hong Kong trading company, from the late 1980s to 2012s; and the other involved a brief case study of Alibaba before its 2014 Initial Public Offering (IPO) at the New York Stock Exchange (NYSE). The 2010s was the

DOI: 10.4324/9781003302919-1

golden period of Chinese companies' internationalization journey: China was the top acquirer of foreign companies in 2016,[1] and 119 Chinese companies became Fortune 500 companies (compared to 121 in the US)[2] in 2019. Twenty years ago, when I was a graduate student in a US business school, I was taught how Western companies expand into China and other developing countries, and their challenges of implementing the turnkey operation models in those countries. Today, when many companies in Western countries have to deal with Chinese parent companies (including the one I was working for at that time), their corporate mindsets still have not yet changed because the understanding of Chinese companies' governance structure and business practice continues to be very limited.

During my five years working for Chinese multinational companies, I lived in mainland China, Hong Kong, and the west coast of the US. I was exposed to three different ownership structures (privately owned, state-owned, and publicly listed), participated in numerous investment meetings and road-shows, attended meetings with Chinese government officials, worked with Chinese authorities in some RMB internationalization programs, lived in the political atmosphere and lifestyle changes in Hong Kong, and experienced post-acquisition challenges of Chinese companies' overseas acquisitions and Western subsidiaries' confusion working with their Chinese parent companies. My frontline experience with those matters later became a valuable foundation of my research for this book.

I also had opportunities to work with many Western executives in those Chinese companies and third-party consultants from Western countries. Most of them shared their common feeling with me about working with Chinese companies – as **"navigating in the dark"** aptly summarized by a German attorney friend. With my dual-background and fluent Chinese ability, I also ran into the same feeling on many occasions, just like my Western colleagues had. Inspired by some of the case studies during the one-week training, I was convinced that understanding the following topics of Chinese companies' corporate governance practices is the path to step out of the "darkness":

- *What is the corporate governance code in China? Why are some Chinese companies' governance practices so different from each other?*
- *What are the Party's roles in Chinese companies? Are all Chinese companies controlled by the Chinese government? How do Chinese State-Owned Enterprises (SOEs) govern their business?*
- *How does the Chinese government manage to retain its controlling position in Chinese companies while still making those companies attractive to global investors?*
- *What are the drivers of Chinese companies' future corporate governance improvement? In what direction is China's corporate governance development going?*

- *What are the main reasons for Chinese companies' financial fraud? What are other risks of Chinese companies' corporate governance practices for investors and business partners?*

My independent research journey that started in the summer of 2019 was driven by those questions. I began writing case studies of well-known Chinese companies (including Alibaba, Huawei, Tencent, Meituan, Wahaha) and read corporate governance books written by various scholars from the UK, US, Australia, and Hong Kong, namely, *Understanding Corporate Governance in China* (Bob Tricker and Gregg Li), *Corporate Governance: Principles, Policies, and Practices* (Bob Tricker), *Corporate Governance Matters* (David Larcker and Brian Tayan), *International Corporate Governance: A Comparative Approach* (Thomas Clarke), and *The Geopolitics of Governance: The Impact of Contrasting Philosophies* (Andrew Kakabadse and Nada Kakabadse). The pandemic outbreak in early 2020, together with the worldwide Black Lives Matter social movement and severe natural disasters accelerated the ESG movement. My research led me to topics related to the correlation between Chinese companies' corporate governance development and the accelerated worldwide ESG movement, relationship changes between China and its global partners from 2019 to 2021, and those consequential impacts on the Chinese corporate governance system.

The unanticipated pandemic outbreak has shifted the global attention away from supply chain restructuring led by the US–China trade war, to worldwide virus control, economic crisis, and the urgency of climate control action. The differences between US' and China's economic and political systems were exaggerated through those two countries' different approaches to pandemic control, economic recovery, and relationships with their global partners. On the other hand, neither the US nor China are global ESG leaders yet, but both are the largest carbon emitters. Although pressure from the public and the global community accelerated the agreement on climate action collaboration between the US and China as a remarkable achievement of COP 26 in 2021, ESG adoption and sustainable transformation will become an essential part of US' and China's mutual competition moving forward, in addition to their economic growth and political influence disagreements.

Having the world's largest economies does not automatically grant global ESG leading seats to either of those two countries. If China wants to enhance its global leading role, it has to become a sustainable leader. The questions are about *how*.

- *How do Chinese companies integrate ESG into their business practice?*
- *How would Chinese companies' corporate governance development accelerate their ESG adoption?*

- *How does the ESG revolution impact the Chinese corporate governance system?*
- *Finally, how will China's unique economic growth model and ESG model inspire future business model evolution in advanced and emerging economies in the post-pandemic era?*

While continuing to search for answers to these questions, I started to realize that reading was not enough for my independent research. I needed to hear what others think about China and Chinese companies. I then invited my LinkedIn network group for interviews. Most of the participants in those interviews were business leaders, scholars, and subject matter experts from different countries who had experience working with Chinese companies during their careers. Likewise, they were experts in either corporate governance in their home countries or ESG practices. Those individuals not only shared their knowledge and experiences during our conversations but also recommended reading materials before or after our conversations so I had plenty of opportunities to learn more. From then, I extended my research to many additional and interesting topics, namely, India's corporate governance and regulation systems and how that country's long history influenced its regulation system development; in South Africa, how each version of King Reports (South African corporate governance code) reflect social, political, and economic backgrounds of that country at the time beings; the pros and cons of Canadian oil and gas companies' corporate governance practice; the most prevailing international ESG reporting guidelines and frameworks, as well as the challenges of corporate sustainability development.

Those additional studies regarding many countries' corporate governance practices related to global sustainable development and the ESG movement helped me understand the century-long mission of sustainable development and the challenges the entire world face to balance intergenerational resource consumption and resolution of severe worldwide poverty. I am convinced that a country's governance system and business governance practice play essential roles in their contribution to that mission. I am also convinced that China has made an astonishing contribution to world sustainability development, but if nothing else, by lifting nearly 20% of the world's population out of poverty over the past 40 years! Although it's hard to judge the antecedents and consequences of China's economic growth and the country's purposeful sustainable development, the concurrent progress of both aspects deserves better recognition. Through proactive regulation reform, the Chinese government has driven the country's economy toward sustainable goals by embracing corporate social responsibility (CSR) decades ago, and welcoming the accelerated ESG movement quite recently. Today, when ESG and sustainability integration becomes front and center of the world's focus, the Chinese government's determination on that integration, while also planning to achieve 2060 carbon neutrality goals, will reshape China's social and institutional system. Therefore, I will point out those concurrent developments in this book without analyzing causes and effects.

China has taken a unique path toward its economic growth and regulation system development with a strategy of "crossing the river by feeling the stones" coined by the country's former leader Deng Xiaoping. To help readers understand Chinese companies' corporate governance practices along with regulation reforms, I carefully selected case studies from well-known Chinese companies that reflect the interconnection between business practices and different stages of the regulation reforms. In the late stage of my writing, I collected some information from some startups and small companies' real-life practices through private conversations. Although most businesses were struggling to survive the pandemic with worries and uncertainties they shared during those conversations, I was impressed by many stories shared by business leaders from these companies. The most inspiring aspect is the new generation of Chinese entrepreneurs, whose strong mindset regarding compliance, taking care of employees during the pandemic, and desire for a solid governance system, all indicate a positive trend of upcoming changes in Chinese companies. For confidential reasons, I did not use the real names of those interviewees, but their stories have been used in different chapters of this book.

What This Book Offers

To help readers better navigate different aspects of Chinese corporate governance development, this book was divided into four parts, each focusing on one theme. Also, the Takeaways section at the end of each chapter summarizes the key points of each chapter.

Part I – A Compressed Journey introduces the evolving journey of the Chinese corporate governance system, its key characteristics, and creative models developed by Chinese companies. The key point of Part I is to point out that it took 150 years (beginning in the middle 1800s) for Western countries led by the UK and US to legalize corporations, to establish current corporate governance regulatory system. China has compressed this journey into 30 years since the country legalized corporations in 1993. This section also reviews the key risks of Chinese companies' governance practices and the drivers of their development.

Part II – ESG in Action presents the most relevant topic in today's business world – environmental, social, and governance (ESG). Part II helps readers understand the status of Chinese companies' ESG integration, Chinese ESG evaluation system research, the key drivers of China's ESG adoption, and ESG-related regulatory development in China. Moreover, by reviewing numerous actions that have been taken by Chinese society (including the Chinese government, Chinese companies, and non-profit organizations) within the past few years, this section emphasizes the **ESG in Action** in China, which makes ESG adoption a revolution for China and Chinese companies.

Part III – Reshaping Social and Regulatory Systems reviews China's newly launched 14th Five-Year Plan that switches China's development strategy from high-speed to high-quality, the status and key points of China's Social Credit System, and recent and upcoming regulation developments. Although no one, including China, has ever claimed a correlation exists between sustainable development and those social and regulation system reforms, the concurrent development indicates the Chinese government's determination in establishing a trustworthy society, improving people's livelihoods, and eventually building a high-standard regulation system, and achieving its 2060 carbon neutrality goal. As a result, the concurrent progress is reshaping the country's social and institutional systems.

Part IV – The Key Geopolitical Elements of Chinese Corporate Governance discusses the key geopolitical elements that influence the Chinese corporate governance system, including China's roles in three key trade agreements, China's global positions and relationships with global partners, and the evolution of the geopolitical strategies of China and its global partners (including RMB internationalization and Hong Kong's future roles). The focus of Part IV is not to analyze those geopolitical elements or offer advice, but to highlight the ongoing developments and complexity of those elements and their impacts on the Chinese corporate governance system.

The Key Recommendation chapter is a reflection of selected topics and practical issues I have encountered during my career or that have been raised by colleagues in the global business community. Although those recommendations cannot cover all the challenges you have experienced or may encounter, my hope is that they can inspire different perspectives that may help you find solutions for your particular business needs. I also included a section in the Recommendation chapter to discuss *Guanxi*, an important phenomenon in Chinese society that can help you not only navigate business and invest in Chinese companies but also explore other interests in China.

For Whom This Book Is Intended

This book will be of interest to a few audience groups:

- **Global investors** who want to invest in Chinese companies and wish to learn what to focus on when assessing Chinese companies' corporate governance risks, and how to evaluate new investment opportunities in the Chinese market due to the recently accelerated ESG movement.

- **Business leaders (including board members and executives)** from companies who are partnering with Chinese companies in any setting, and are seeking to improve communication and relationships with Chinese partners.
- **Individuals** who are interested in obtaining board director or executive roles in Chinese multinational corporations.
- **Third-party consultants** in the fields of corporate governance, ESG, law, merger and acquisition (M&A), strategy and global tax planning, etc.
- **International financial and political policymakers** will likewise benefit from the information offered in this book.
- **Executive or master's degree students** in business, law, accounting, and auditing.
- **The entrepreneurs** who are interested in building a team with China Speed, or building companies with a corporate culture that embrace China Speed.

Notes

1 Wade Shepard, "China Hits Record High M&A Investments in Western Firms," September 16, 2016, Forbes, www.forbes.com/sites/wadeshepard/2016/09/10/from-made-in-china-to-owned-by-china-chinese-enterprises-buying-up-western-compan ies-at-record-pace/?sh=73524fea5d87
2 Lourdes Casanova and Anne Miroux, "Emerging Market Multinationals Report (EMR) 2019" Chapter 1, page 2, www.johnson.cornell.edu/wp-content/uploads/sites/ 3/2019/11/EMR-2019.pdf

Part I

A Compressed Journey

Chapter 1

Overview of Chinese Corporate Governance

In this chapter, I review

- Chinese Corporate Governance
  Chinese corporate governance code
  Chinese two-tier board structure

- Chinese SOEs
  The "China Puzzle"
  Key concerns regarding Chinese SOEs corporate governance

- Chinese Non-SOEs
  Creative corporate governance models
  Pros and cons of Chinese non-SOEs corporate governance

The definitions of corporate governance have been evolving during the past decades, along with the changes on the global geopolitical and economic environment and the demands of international companies and investors. The most suitable one, in the Chinese context, is Peter Alexis Gourevitch and James J Shinn's (2006) definition, "Corporate Governance is about power and responsibility".[1] In other words, corporate governance is how power is deployed and allocated in an organization, which includes the board, executives, and middle management. Power allocation cannot be separated from the influences and interventions of essential stakeholders such as government and regulators. Within China's one-party political structure and the high interdependence between China's economic growth and the SOEs, the way power is wielded in Chinese companies is concurrently different and similar to how power is used in Western economies, like the US and European Union.

Moreover, Chinese companies' controlling ownership structures (including SEOs and non-SOEs) have been the top concern of global investors. According to Organization for Economic Co-operation and Development (OECD) 2019 report,[2] 38% of Chinese companies' average shares are owned by public sector

DOI: 10.4324/9781003302919-3

investors (those involving state and local governments) compared with 3% of the US companies. Traditional governance pitfalls of the controlling ownership structure are the cross-ownership and pyramidal structure (multilayer chains of ownership), which allow controlling shareholders to influence boards' decisions to maximize their interest with the cost of scarifying minority shareholders' interest. Chinese companies' controlling ownership structure, which, as part of China's economy transitioning from a planned economy to a market-oriented economy, contains a lack of transparency in the decision-making process as well as vagueness of the Party's roles.

This chapter will discuss the controlling ownership structures in both SOEs and non-SOEs and their impact on Chinese companies' corporate governance.

Chinese Corporate Governance Code and Two-Tier Board Structure

In modern Western economic history, corporations (which originated in England in the 1700s) became legal business entities in the middle 1800s in the UK and US.[3] Western industrialization from the middle 1800s to the middle 1900s accelerated the international growth and ownership revolution of corporations. As a result, the conflict of interest between shareholders and managers due to the separation of ownership and control raised internal concerns and challenges for those corporations; and the corporations grew too large and their organizational structure and governance practice became too complex for policymakers to regulate and steer. Western countries' academic study of those challenges started in the 1930s, motivated by the demand of aligning the interests of shareholders and managers, and emerged to corporate governance research in the 1980s, aiming to establish a system to better govern corporations with four fundamental values (fairness, accountability, transparency, and responsibility). In 1992, the world's first corporate governance code, the Cadbury Report, was released in the UK as a best practice guide with recommendations for board structure, composition, and board directors' roles. Numerous updates have taken place after the Cadbury Report to improve board governance practices thereafter, with the latest version of the UK's corporate governance code released in 2018. In the US, the corporate governance framework has been part of the corporate laws of each state, and a set of federal regulations have been released since the early 1900s to regulate corporate governance practices. Some of the most notable regulations and laws are the taxation of corporate profit law in 1916, the Securities Acts in 1934, the Sarbanes-Oxley Act in 2002, and the Dodd-Frank Act in 2010, in addition to periodic Securities and Exchange Commission (SEC) corporate governance guidelines. Between the commencement of the legalization of corporations and today's corporate governance system in Western advanced countries, over 150 years, had elapsed.

Industrialization did not occur in modern China until the country's economic reform started in 1978. Corporate and financial market regulations eventually followed. Amazingly, the modern Chinese economy compressed the 150 years experienced by the West into only 30 years since China initially legalized corporations in 1993.

China's Corporate Governance Code

Corporations were not allowed in modern China until the first Company Law, which was promulgated in 1993 as a significant milestone in Chinese SOE reform. The Company Law established the legal foundation for corporate governance structure in Chinese SOEs.[4] Ten years later, the first Chinese Corporate Governance Code (2002) was issued by the China Securities Regulatory Commission (CSRC).[5] The 2002 Code established principles and frameworks of basic shareholder rights, information disclosures, voting mechanisms in shareholders' meetings, and primary functions and features of boards of directors of the supervisory boards.

CSRC made the first revision of China's Corporate Governance Code in 2018.[6] The new Code focused on the alignment with international standards with key changes in: establishing ESG requirements on green development and targeting poverty alleviation; encouraging institutional investors to participate in Chinese companies' corporate governance practice through voting rights; encouraging cash dividend distributions to protect minority shareholders; strengthening audit committee functions to enhance board independence; promoting board diversity to improve board effectiveness; and requiring transparent disclosure to restrict controlling shareholders' power. The new Code became an important landmark in China's corporate governance development. However, compared to most Western regulations that provide practical guidance, China's 2018 new Code is still very general. Moreover, the provisions requiring the Party's participation in Chinese companies quickly became one of the global investors' biggest concerns regarding Chinese companies' corporate governance practices.

Let's not ignore the fact, though, that despite Chinese corporations' relative infancy (from 1993 until the 2018 new Code), momentous achievements have occurred in less than 30 years! Yes, this is the most significant 30 years in China's 5,000-year history, the country has become the second-largest economy in the world, and many Chinese multinationals have also become global brands and industry leaders. But the compressed growth period has not allowed the Chinese institutional system to become as sophisticated as the Western system which has over 150 years of experience. This growth has resulted in a paradox for Chinese companies between their leading technological and market values and nascent governance practices and business mindsets.

A Close Look at China's Two-Tier Board

The corporate governance structure of Chinese companies combines elements from both the US model and the German-style two-tier board model, as explained in *Understand Corporate Governance in China* by Tricker and Li (2019). Therefore, Chinese-listed companies and SOEs normally have boards with some independent, external directors, and boards of supervisors consisting of employee and shareholder representatives. However, the chairperson and most shareholder representatives on the supervisory boards are assigned by the State-Owned Assets Supervision and Administration Commission (SASAC), which makes China's two-tier board a governance mechanism for the Chinese government to assign its people to the company. Although many private companies have created different corporate governance models, all listed China SOEs and most unlisted SOEs maintain a two-tier board structure.

Comparing Two-Tier Boards in China and Germany

The German two-tier board structure is a dual board system with a supervisory board and an executive board. Half of the supervisory board members are elected by shareholders and half represent employees. The supervisory board approves major business decisions and oversees and appoints members of the executive board, while the executive board oversees the company and makes operational decisions and provides guidance. Although the Chinese SOEs' two-tier board structure was originally based on the German style boards, the functions differ. I only started to understand the differences during my experience leading a Chinese company's overseas acquisition in Germany in 2014.

The German target company was a 200-year-old manufacturer with world-class technology and a top brand name in the industry. Unexpectedly, the most difficult negotiation during the acquisition process was not regarding purchase price, but on post-acquisition human capital arrangements with the company's union and labor representatives on the supervisory board. The fact that the share purchase agreement would not be signed without the consent from the German company's labor union representatives shocked everyone in the Chinese company's acquisition team.

"Owned by the People"

In addition to two-tier board structure, unions are quite common in most Chinese SOEs and private companies. The Chinese companies' unions are responsible for company events and some employee benefits, equivalent to the human resource function in Western companies. Employee representatives on Chinese companies' supervisory boards does not have the power to stop an acquisition deal like their counterparts in a German company.

It might not be easy to ascertain whether the idea of having employee representatives on China's two-tier board structure originated from the concept that Chinese SOEs are "owned by the people". The reality is, even in China's state-planned economy, "owned by the people" is a very ambiguous concept, which does not equate to "employee ownership" at all. In addition, the concept has led to the overconsumption of SOE assets by various parties.

While the state-planned economy in China has to a certain degree been replaced with a quasi-free market model, many people still misunderstand the concept of "owned by the people". However, the roles between Chinese companies' labor unions and those of German companies have clearly determined the functional differences between Chinese companies' two-tier boards and the German two-tier boards.

Chinese SOEs and the Key Corporate Governance Matters

SOEs are an important element in most countries, including advanced and emerging markets economies. In certain sectors like energy, minerals, infrastructure, utilities, and financial services, SOEs are the most prevalent due to many countries' strategic plans for these sectors and the amount of capital needed for these businesses.

SOEs dominate the Chinese economy and have been playing an increasingly important role in the nation's economy. In 2000, there were a total of 27 SOEs in Fortune Global 500 (FG500) companies, 9 (33.3%) of which were Chinese SOEs; in 2017, there were 102 SOEs in FG500 companies, 75 (73.3%) of which were Chinese SOEs. As China has been effectively promoting SOE reform over the past 40 years, statistics show that the total number of SOEs in China has decreased from 262,000 in 1997 to 110,000 in 2008, then increased from 2008 to 173,000 in 2016, while the total asset value under SOEs' management has continuously increased from RMB12 million in 1997 to RMB154 million in 2016.[7]

Despite this, the Chinese economy has relied primarily on the outstanding growth of SOEs over the past 40 years even though most SOEs have been inefficient due to their low productivity. This phenomenon is known as the "China Puzzle".

The "China Puzzle"[8]

China's fast economic growth along with its lagging regulation is contradictory to Western countries' growth philosophy. The "China Puzzle" refers to this exact phenomenon.

Similar to questions raised worldwide regarding the effectiveness of capitalism during the COVID-19 pandemic, research on the "China Puzzle" are challenging the Western economic growth philosophy. China has been trying to prove that the law-of-finance-growth economic philosophy is not the only path for economic success by demonstrating its own success.

To understand the "China Puzzle", we should first review the strengths and value of Chinese SOEs and their weakness due to government controlling structure.

The Strengths and Value of Chinese SOEs

Why are SOEs so important for China's economy? How did Chinese SOEs support rapid Chinese economic growth over the past decades?

- Government intervention enables SOEs to maximize their resource mobility. Most Chinese SOEs operate in essential and capital-intensive industries. The lump sum investments needed by these businesses cannot be achieved through the capital market alone.
- SOEs are valuable to maintain social stability. Chinese SOEs have been a major source of retirement pensions. During economic downturns like COVID-19, SOEs can be utilized to hire excess labor and achieve social goals by sacrificing profit.

The Weaknesses of Chinese SOEs

What are the weaknesses of SOEs that caused the low operative efficiency?

- Ambiguous ownership. Chinese SOEs are theoretically "owned by the people", which leads to non-recognition of SOEs' performance and profitability, opportunities of overconsumption of SOEs' assets, executives' enjoying on-the-job perks, and unmotivated employees in the SOEs.
- Heavy social burden. Chinese SOEs carry a heavy social burden because of their high financial cost due to a capital-intensive focus, its heavy tax burdens in order to support governments' functioning, and obligation to hire redundant labor and offer pensions and welfare to retirees on behalf of the state and local governments.
- Lack of accountability. With SOEs' heavy social burden, soft budget target, and lack of incentive for value creation, the main responsibility of SOEs executives is to solve social problems, not create business value. Therefore, CEOs are not incentivized by SOEs' operational performance; and the government cannot hold CEOs accountable for SOEs' low operation performance.

• Information asymmetry. Since most decisions are made by the state or local government, the complicated hierarchy of SOEs complicates the information transmission and decision-making process that breeds inefficiency.

The "China Puzzle" successfully facilitated China's economic growth by maximizing SOEs value and offsetting their weaknesses. The Chinese government is well aware of these weaknesses and has been pursuing SOE reform since reopening the economy in 1978. While the SOE reforms aim to enhance SOEs competitive advantage via strengthening their corporate governance, there are always concerns regarding Chinese SOEs' governance practice.

Key Corporate Governance Matters of Chinese SOEs

This section reviews some key corporate governance elements of Chinese SOEs:

Governmental Influence

As we discussed in the early portion of this chapter, Chinese companies' two-tier board structure, with the chairperson and most shareholder representatives on the board of supervisors purposely assigned by the SASAC, is designed for Chinese government officials to appoint members to the company's board. Additionally, according to the Corporate Governance Code of 2018, Party Committees are required for Chinese-listed companies.[9] Although there are no delineated responsibilities of Party Committees within these companies, the Party's influence is fundamental and imperative. In addition to listed companies, many private Chinese companies have voluntarily established Party Committees to remain "politically correct and connected". A parallel can be drawn by changes made in the governance, management, personnel practices, and public policy positions of US firms in response to the #MeToo, Black Lives Matter, and climate change movements.

Although the government authorized involvement of the Chinese Communist Party in the private sector companies remains a concern for foreigners doing business in China, foreign capital continues to flow into the country. Regardless of the ups and downs from China's COVID-19 control approaches in the past couple of years, the country's continuous GDP growth in the post-pandemic era have been recognized internationally, which further confirmed China's position as the engine of global economic recovery. As China attempts to further position itself as a global economic leader, the government's influence in Chinese companies will likely remain the same, if not greater, which is causing continued anxiety among some foreign firms and investors.

Controlling Ownership

Although China is hardly alone in maintaining SOEs, the governance practices of Chinese SOEs have caused concern among global investors for various reasons, one of which is the large percentage of government ownership (some comparison numbers are shown in Table 1.1).

As we can see from Table 1.1, US and Chinese companies are positioned at opposite ends of the spectrum of two investor categories when it comes to investor ownership, while other Western countries are in the middle of the spectrum. Obviously, institutional investors are the driving force in global corporate governance development today, but their minimal ownership in Chinese companies raises questions regarding Chinese companies' motivation to improve their corporate governance. That said, it is important to understand the progress Chinese companies have made thus far.

The ownership structure diversity reform took Chinese government 40 years to diversify SOEs' shareholder structure from 100% government ownership to the present structure, and launched various attractive initiatives such as the opening of the Chinese financial market to global investors. Corporate ownership diversification has been the primary focus of SOE reform since the 1990s, according to *Corporate Governance and Financial Reform in China's Transition Economy* by Jing Leng (2009). With China's continuous effort to reform SOEs and open its stock markets to the rest of the world, the country's corporate ownership structure is likely to gradually appear more diversified and balanced in each category to better facilitate the next phase of economic growth. Based on strategies and goals of China's 14th Five-Year Plan released in late 2020, SOEs will continue to drive China's economic development in

Table 1.1 Regional Ownership Distribution Comparison by Two Investor Categories

Countries/Regions of Companies	Chinese Companies	US Companies	European Companies	Global Average
Average share % by public sector investors (including state and local governments)	38%	3%	9%	14%
Average share % by institutional investors	9%	72%	38%	41%

Source: Compiled by author from a 2019 OECD report (A. De la Cruz, A. Medina, and Y. Tang, *"Owners of the World's Listed Companies"*, Page 11 (Table 3), OECD Capital Market Series, Paris, March 21, 2021. www.oecd.org/corporate/Owners-of-the-Worlds-Listed-Companies.pdf).

the coming decades. Details regarding China's 14th Five-Year Plan will be discussed in a later chapter of this book.

Statistical data shows that Chinese central and local governments are the largest shareholders of companies' stocks. They possess approximately 40% of the equity in Chinese SOEs and have controlling rights as the majority owner through various direct and indirect ownership formalities. In addition, the government employs a pyramid structure consisting of "cross ownership"[10] among SOEs to effectively control a large number of corporations. Confoundingly, the pyramid structure model is the primary reason for the exceedingly complicated ownership structures of most SOEs.

Moreover, the concentrated controlling structure creates conflicts of interest among controlling shareholders, minority shareholders, and executives, which is the so-called agency problem of SOEs. As the controlling shareholder, the Chinese government often requests SOEs to absorb excess labor to help reduce unemployment and to sponsor public projects, which become obstacles to the SOEs' operational improvement and investment return. Since most executives of SOEs are appointed by government authorities, those executives tend to overinvest in government projects and also consume excessive benefits.

Although the Chinese regulators are working on raising awareness to protect minority shareholders' interests and voting rights. In the 2018 Corporate Governance Code revision, provisions exist to encourage investors to participate in voting and to advocate for corporate governance policies and practices that promote cash dividend distributions.

CEO Nomination, Succession Planning, and Compensation

Boards of directors of US firms make decisions regarding the CEO's recruitment, succession planning, and compensation. Because US companies tend to tie a significant portion of CEOs' compensation packages to company performance, CEOs tend to be highly motivated. According to data from June 2013 to May 2014, 47.4%[11] of compensation packages for CEOs of the top 100 US companies are related to company stock price, according to *Corporate Governance Matters* by David Larcker and Brian Tayan (2016). In China, CEOs and most executives of Chinese SOEs are selected by the Chinese government and can be rotated to other SOEs by government authorities, not the board. These SOE executives rank in a hierarchy within the Chinese government. Unlike in US firms, where CEOs enjoy highly remunerative compensation packages, including stock options, the CEOs of Chinese SOEs have their salaries aligned with government officials of the same rank, and stock options are definitely not part of the equation.

According to 2019 Fortune Global 500 rankings, 23 of the top 25 Chinese companies are SOEs, which means that a majority of China's top CEOs are not incentivized to maximize company performance. Given that, a CEO is not just the head of a company but also its most important leader, the differences in how CEOs are selected and motivated in Chinese companies determined these companies' different governance and operations.

Obviously, there are other differences in corporate governance practices between US and Chinese companies, including information transparency and disclosure, decision-making processes, and shareholder voting rights. However, those and other differences emerge from the three primary differences noted above.

As Chinese firms become more prominent in the global market, and the country's economy becomes an even greater part of the global economy, one can reasonably expect that Chinese corporate governance practices will continue to evolve, improve, and close the gap with Western countries. While Chinese SOEs may remain dominant in the domestic economy, with SOEs increasing in number (as well as the percentage rate of shareholders), and given the SOEs' growing commitment to international regulations concerning climate change and ESG standards, the corporate governance practice and business mindset of SOEs will gradually reflect international standards. As a result, the entire landscape of Chinese corporate governance development will change, facilitating rapid adoption of improved corporate governance practices and ESG performance.

Ineffective Boards Independence and Boards Functions

Since 2003, government regulations require that at least one-third of each company board must consist of independent directors. A relevant question, though, is whether independent directors play effective monitoring and advising roles in the SOEs. The generally agreed answer to this question is presently mixed. Chinese companies' board independence has been improved over the past two decades with no doubt, while independent directors are less likely to vote against any proposals from SOE boards. Also, many independent directors on SOE boards are professors and influential celebrities, who might not have the requisite business experience to monitor and guide an SOE's growth.

When this book was written, a new practice appeared within some local governments for authorities to rotate former SOE executives to non-executive directors' roles. These non-executive directors are still enjoying government official rankings, and their former executive experiences will improve boards' monitoring and advising functions, although they won't be able to offer independent opinions at all. This new practice, together with Chinese SOEs' further participation in the global business community and regulators' commitment to building higher corporate governance practices, may be a new trend of Chinese SOEs' corporate governance reform that will improve the effectiveness and professionalism of SOE boards' functions.

Information Transparency Issue

Lack of transparency has been one of the top concerns of China's SOEs. Traditionally, SOEs' controlling shareholders intended to keep the information opaque (especially negative information) mainly for political reasons, creating a company culture that people were unwilling to share with outsiders primarily to avoid unnecessary trouble.

With Chinese regulators' efforts to establish high-standard economic regulations and enforce audit firms' independence, public information disclosure requirements for companies will likely benchmark Western standards. Encouraging free conversation and business-sharing practices requires business culture changes that will take some time. With a new development philosophy including openness and sharing initiated in China's 14th Five-Year Plan released in late 2020, the hope is that the new philosophy led by the government will stir business mindset changes for SOEs' leaders who can drive SOEs' business culture changes.

Chinese Non-SOEs and the Key Corporate Governance Matters

In addition to Chinese SOEs, which have driven the country's economic growth in the past three decades, the rise of Chinese non-SOEs is notable due to their success in the global market. As in most emerging markets, China's corporate governance development started under the tutelage of Western countries, then moved into a self-development phase, and has become a fluid learning system. With few regulatory restrictions, Chinese non-SOE companies have created many new, different, and often innovative governance models. Leading companies like Huawei and Alibaba have demonstrated the advantage of their unique governance models, which achieved massive growth and international recognition.

Creative Corporate Governance Models of Chinese Non-SOEs

Alibaba's Partnership Governance Structure. With Alibaba's first IPO at NYSE in 2014, institutional investors were concerned about the company's extreme insider-controlled governance model that limited investors' influence on business operations. What does Alibaba's governance structure look like? Let us delve into our Case Study 1.1 for some details.

Case Study 1.1   Alibaba's Controlling Structure

Alibaba designed Alibaba Partnership to ensure the mission, culture, and value of its business for the long term. Alibaba Partnership is a dynamic group with a fluctuating number of members (30 before the 2014 NYSE IPO and 37 in 2019). Alibaba Partnership holds one class of shares and controls over half of the candidates for directors. A five member Partnership Committee within the Partnership is the core controlling group that determines the nomination of directors and future partners and the annual cash bonus pool for all partners.

Alibaba's governance structure has multiple layers of takeover protection[12]: (1) A super-majority provision: any change to Alibaba Partnership's nomination requires 95% voting approval at the shareholder's meeting; (2) Proxy voting agreements: Alibaba reached agreements with its biggest strategic partners, Softbank and Yahoo, to ensure that voting power of these two shareholders will not escape the control cycle; (3) A staggered board structure: at each annual shareholders meeting, only one-third of the directors can be replaced.

In Western countries, the takeover protection governance structure has been outdated since the mid-2010s, and many companies have reversed their takeover protection structure. The number of S&P 1,500 companies with staggered board structures declined from 896 in 2004 to 477 in 2014,[13] according to data summarized in David Larcker and Brian Tayan's book *Corporate Governance Matters* (2016). If we consider two elements simultaneously – the number of S&P 1,500 companies that had takeover protection governance structures before 2010, and the short history of Chinese companies' global growth – it is not difficult to assert that a takeover protection governance structure is a popular protocol for early-stage companies. Whether the protection structure in Chinese companies will fade over time along with the maturity of these companies remains to be seen. The answer will depend on the matureness of Chinese companies' governance practices over the next few decades.

Despite the trouble Alibaba and its founder, Jack Ma, have experienced since late 2020, the company has demonstrated considerable corporate governance development. While recognizing Alibaba's creative governance model, we should not neglect another remarkable success that also resulted from this model – Alibaba's Succession Planning (please see Case Study 1.2).

Case Study 1.2   Alibaba's Succession Planning

Alibaba has a transparent and thoughtful succession plan. The company begin succession planning almost since its inception in the early 2000s. Daniel Zhang, Jack Ma's successor, has been with Alibaba since 2007 and has served as Alibaba Group CEO since 2015. Given his financial background, Zhang was highly praised by Ma for his analytical mind and an intuitive grasp of innovative and creative business models. Zhang was also well known for successfully running Alibaba's e-commerce platforms, Taobao and Tmall, where he created the magic of Alibaba's Singles Day shopping event. His contribution to Alibaba paved the way for him to take over the leadership role of Jack Ma. In 2008, when Ma announced his retirement and Zhang stepped up as chairman, the leadership transfer was highly praised by Western financial media outlets. The smooth transfer of power ensured the continuity of Alibaba's core values.

In a September 2018 Forbes article named "What Jack Ma Taught Us about Good Corporate Governance This Week",[14] high praise was given to Alibaba's Partnership structure as "the most powerful thing that will drive Alibaba for generations". The Partnership allows Jack Ma's lifelong membership with the Alibaba Partnership and plays a vital role in Alibaba's succession planning. "Alibaba is a leader in terms of governance and its succession planning", the article concludes.

Huawei's Rotating CEO/Chairman Governance Structure. Huawei's governance model is new and creative in a different way, having evolved from a perfectionist culture with leaders who are unafraid to make bold reforms (see Case Studies 1.3 and 1.4).

Case Study 1.3   Huawei's Rotating CEO/Chairman System[15]

In 2011, Huawei implemented a rotating CEO/chair system with the three CEOs taking turns as the CEO for six months at a time. The functioning CEO oversees Huawei's operations and crisis management and chairs the meetings of the Executive Committee. The three rotating CEOs are from different company departments. During each of their turns as CEO, they are also responsible for their daily responsibilities as deputy chairman, while the other two act as the functioning CEO/chair. The rotating CEO system incorporated the chairman's position into the rotation in 2018.

Huawei's rotating CEO/chairman system was designed by its founder, Ren Zhengfei, to build an effective and mechanical governance structure to serve Huawei's long-term sustainability. The idea was inspired by two animal kingdom stories: (1) A buffalo herd story from "Flight of the Buffalo" by James A. Belasco and Ralph C. Stayer. In this book, the authors use buffalo herds' stories (buffalo herds follow chief buffalos, and once the top buffalo is killed, the entire pack will end up in chaos and die) to inspire and encourage organizations to a new leadership structure with employee empowerment; and (2) "The Flight Pattern of Migratory Birds" which explains the rotation of bird flock leaders to ensure the success of a long migration. The allegories of these stories describe Ren's desire for Huawei's journey to be like one of the migratory birds. He also applied the US presidential term limit concept to the company's leadership arrangement plan.

It's worth mentioning that Huawei's CFO, Meng Wanzhou, the daughter of Huawei founder Ren Zhengfei, was named chairwoman in the rotating role in April 2022, while also remaining CFO and deputy chair, identical to the two other CEOs/chairs. Upon her appointment, Huawei publicly re-emphasized its goal to fine-tune the corporate governance structure for its long-term survival and growth.[16]

Case Study 1.4   Huawei's "Superfluid" Organizational Structure

In addition to the rotating CEO/Chairman structure, Ren Zhengfei designed a superfluid organizational structure to maximize its customer-centric business strategy. This organizational structure placed all of Huawei's most talented experts in a human resource pool, enabling the team to be deployed worldwide at any time. This organizational innovation is the foundation of Huawei's commitment to serving ever-changing customer needs. To understand how this organization's innovative structure enabled Huawei's success, consideration also needs to be given to those who function within it. Below are three key components that demonstrate some pros and cons of this structure:

1 *The "superfluid" organizational structure*

The Vodafone Spain project is an excellent example of how Huawei utilizes its "superfluid" organizational structure as a competitive strategy. In 2006, Vodafone had difficulty delivering a reliable mobile phone signal for Spain's newly completed high-speed rail network. Huawei rapidly assembled a team of professionals with expert knowledge and abundant ancillary resources to develop and test a high-speed packet access network expansion solution. The project was successfully completed within two months. Huawei's quick resolution enabled Vodafone to serve all of the major cities in Spain. Vodafone senior managers lauded Huawei's efficiency, which resulted in Huawei sharing a significant market share with Vodafone Spain. During the same time, Huawei's competitors, Ericsson and Nokia, were still preparing initial proposals.

2   *The concept of rotating middle and senior managers every three years exposes them to multiple responsibilities and encourages a superfluid culture.*

As one of the biggest Chinese multinationals, the rotating positions for these managers can be reassigned worldwide. Employees' families, though, are not included. There is nothing comparable to that in Western companies. Most employees rotating to overseas positions can visit their families only during the Chinese New Year celebration. Huawei might appear extreme with its three-year CEO rotating term, but the same policy applies to most Chinese companies' overseas employees. Rotating employees are comfortable with the company's business operations, which helps build Huawei's corporate culture at overseas subsidiaries and facilitates cooperation between headquarters and its subsidiaries.

3   *Two surgical organizational restructures in Huawei's 30-year history.*

During a 1996 annual review, all Huawei marketing managers were asked to submit a work plan report and a resignation letter. The company would either approve the report or accept the resignation. In 2007, Huawei conducted a resignation and rehiring exercise to optimize its organizational structure and requested 7,000 employees resign. A total of 6,581 were subsequently rehired for more suitable employment positions.

Huawei's organizational restructures in 1996 and 2007 brought a sense of urgency, energized its employees, and established the tone of Huawei's corporate culture that promotes dedication, encourages competition, and recognizes employee contributions. According to Tian Tao and Wu Chunbo's "The Huawei Story" (2014), an executive of Motorola China once commented on Huawei's dramatic organizational restructures, "Only Huawei dared to do it, and it had succeeded".

Regardless of its success, the Chinese and foreign media criticized the experiment.

Huawei's "superfluid" organizational structure[17] demonstrated its efficiency with many projects such as Vodafone Spain. However, the rotating system did not consider the quality of life of employees and their families. In addition, with rotating employees filling most management positions, few management positions remained for non-Chinese employees in overseas countries. Moreover, Huawei's dramatic organizational restructuring caused many people to lose their jobs. With today's ESG movement, employees' well-being and workforce equity and inclusivity worldwide are critical factors for evaluating a company's social performance. Multinationals like Huawei need to reconsider their strategy to strengthen their industry-leading positions in the global market.

Since 2012, the US government and some American democratic allies have imposed a series of restrictions on Huawei due to concerns that the company is too close to the Chinese government and that its equipment could be used to spy on other countries and companies. These measures have introduced uncertainty into Huawei's future. Nevertheless, the company's performance is a testament to China's economic reform. Huawei's success is not coincidental since some strategies such as the surgical organizational restructuring were concurrent with the particular stage of China's economic reform when the strategies were executed.

Founder Controlling Structure and Its Sustainability

The founder controlling structure is investors' paramount concern regarding privately owned Chinese companies. The founder controlling structure often comes with dual-class shares, where one share class controls the company's voting power. However, the founder controlling structure is common in nearly all companies' early stages, including companies in more developed economies. American giant tech companies Facebook and Google both have founder controlling structures with dual-class shares. Perhaps the most significant difference is the institutional investor's average share percentage in Chinese companies versus their counterparts in the US. Data below collected at the time this chapter was written can better explain the differences (Table 1.2).

Table 1.2 Share Structure Contrasts – Alibaba vs. Facebook

	Alibaba Group Holding Ltd (NYSE: BABA)	Facebook Inc. (NASDAQ: FB)
Insiders (major) shareholders	43.8%	10.7%
Retail investors	40.1%	26.9%
Total share percentage by institutional investors	16.1%	62.4%

Source: Compiled by the author.

As I explained in Case Study 1.1, Alibaba's Controlling Structure describes the authoritarian nature of its founder that detrimentally impacts potential investors' influence on company's board governance, business development, and decision-making. However, considering Alibaba's success over the past two decades, it is worth examining the advantages and disadvantages of Chinese companies' founder controlling structure.

Dictatorship and Voting Rights

As we see from Table 1.2, the institutional investors shared percentage in Alibaba (16.1%) is significantly less than Facebook's (62.4%). However, 16.1% is greater than other Chinese companies that average 9%, as listed in Table 1.1. In fact, the extreme controlled structure examples of companies like Alibaba are not indicative of only the investors' share and founders' voting power structures, but also its exclusive board nomination rights and voting power through voting arrangements with major shareholders (as illustrated in Case Study 1.5.).

Case Study 1.5   Alibaba's Voting Arrangements with Softbank and Yahoo

In addition to the Alibaba Partnership that enables exclusive control over half of the company's board positions, Jack Ma and another founder, Joe Tsai, also signed a voting agreement with two additional major shareholders, Softbank and Yahoo. Below are three essential aspects of the voting agreement:

1 Softbank has the right to nominate one director upon the condition that it owns at least 15% of Alibaba's common shares.
2 An Alibaba Partnership and Softbank coalition agree to support the nomination of each party's director – provided Softbank owns at least 15% of Alibaba's common shares.
3 Softbank and Yahoo grant voting powers to Jack Ma and Joe Tsai through proxy agreements.

At the time of Alibaba's IPO in 2014, Softbank and Yahoo owned a combined total of 56.5% of Alibaba's shares (Softbank 34.1%, Yahoo 22.4%), while Jack Ma and Joe Tsai owned 8.8% and 3.6%, respectively.[18] However, the voting agreement detrimentally limited the influence of Softbank and Yahoo in Alibaba's boardroom. When this chapter was written, Softbank owned 25%, while Yahoo had sold most of its Alibaba shares.

Despite its autocratic rule, Alibaba was an investor's darling as the largest Chinese e-commerce company until the Chinese government's scrutiny starting with the suspension of Alibaba's affiliate company Ant Group's IPO plan in late 2020. Just like Facebook and Google, investors wanted a piece of these companies' growth, regardless of the controlled structure limitations. Plus, as we all know, shareholder engagements from most institutional investors have never reached the level expected by the public, even with recent years' shareholder activism movements in the West. According to my interviews with institutional investors and proxy agencies in North America with thousands of companies in their portfolios – many institutional investors simply do not have enough resources for the shareholder engagement even with their American portfolio companies. Most of them rely heavily on proxy agency recommendations for their voting rights.

Of course, because of language and cultural barriers, it is difficult to communicate with Chinese companies and attend annual general meetings (AGM). Shareholders' engagement with Chinese companies is still also at a minimal level. Regardless why bother if the portfolio company financially performs well?

Long-Term Value Creation

During my recent interview with Professor Andrew Kakabadse regarding board leadership, the professor raised concerns about the lack of balance between compliance and stewardship of corporate board functions today.[19] He also shared his opinions regarding the importance of boards' in-depth understanding and engagement in company business.

In founder controlling companies, the founder's commitment is an essential measurement that rational investors believe in value creation that offsets the disproportional controlled structure imbalance. Successful entrepreneurs usually possess great passion for their businesses, so, therefore, are willing to devote all their effort to grow the company. A disproportionately controlled structure allows founders to actively participate in management, ensuring company strategies continuity even if the founder's share percentage is reduced over time.

In Alibaba's case, Jack Ma has identified Alibaba's core values – customers first, teamwork, embracing change, integrity, passion, and commitment, all of which are consistent with his personal values. Alibaba's investors expect to benefit from the current structure as long as Ma continuously molds Alibaba in his entrepreneurial vision to build an online global empire. And with the Alibaba Partnership structure, Ma's control and influence will remain during his lifetime, regardless of his retirement status.

The Founder's Commitment

If the founder controlling structure concerns global investors, how do companies like Alibaba reassure the market and persuade investors to continue funding them, given their extreme insider controlling system? Case Study 1.6. offers an answer.

Case Study 1.6   Alibaba's Founder's Commitments Alleviate Investors' Concerns

With the founder controlling structure, primary concerns raised by investors are conflicts of interest and related party transactions. To address these concerns, Jack Ma has promised to donate all of the personal distributions he receives to the company and charity from the following two self-dealt transactions:

1 *The ownership transfer of Alipay[20] to Jack Ma's wholly owned company Ant Financial Services in 2011 is a controversial example since the transfer appeared to be a self-dealing transaction. To address concerns raised by the Alipay transaction, Ma committed in Alibaba's first IPO prospectus to reduce his interest in Ant Financial Services to the degree commensurate with his interest in Alibaba Group and agreed to refrain from capitalizing on proceeds of the company's share reduction.*
2 *As a major shareholder of Yunfeng Capital, which co-invested with Alibaba in Youku Tudou and Citic 21CN, Ma committed in Alibaba's first IPO prospectus to donate all his interest in Yunfeng Capital to the Alibaba Foundation, a charitable non-profit organization.*

Obviously, in the first chapter of Alibaba's success, Jack Ma's charisma and his commitment to not taking economic benefit from controlling interest of his businesses helped to engage investors, build trust, and preserve faith in the market.

Smooth Leadership Transfer

Concerns regarding the founder controlling structure are always connected to leadership transfer as part of succession planning. Alibaba's smooth leadership transfer in 2018 with transparency and long-term planning established a splendid example of succession planning. The leadership transfer of Pinduoduo in 2020 indicated the trend of a new succession planning model and the rise of social entrepreneurship[21] that may inspire future generations of Chinese entrepreneurs – Unlike Jack Ma, Pinduoduo's founder gave up his super-voting upon retirement as discussed in Case Study 1.7. below.

Case Study 1.7   Pinduoduo Founder's Retirement – Trend of a New Succession Plan Model.

The Shanghai-based company was founded in 2015 and has been listed on the NYSE since 2018. Pinduoduo is a platform focused on agricultural and low-price consumable products, with a next-day grocery pickup service launched during the pandemic. In 2020, Pinduoduo overtook Alibaba Group to become China's largest e-commerce platform with 788.4 million annual active buyers. The company's 2021 annual revenue is reported as 2,441 billion yuan ($383 billion), an increase of 46% from the 2020 annual revenue of 1,668 billion yuan ($262 billion).[22]

Current CEO Chen Lei was appointed as chairman. Lei is a founding member of Pinduoduo and has been in the position since July 2020. The leadership transition plan between Pinduoduo's chairman and CEO is similar to Alibaba's from Jack Ma to Daniel Zhang in 2018. However, unlike Ma, who still controls Alibaba through Alibaba Partnership, the current CEO, Huang Zheng, will relinquish his super-voting rights in the company upon retirement. Zheng will then explore his interest in food science upon retirement and recently donated $100 million to Zhejiang University to support biomedical science, agriculture, and food research.

On March 17, 2020, Pinduoduo's stock price fell 8% when Huang Zhen announced his retirement. Experts, though, believe Zheng's retirement indicates Pinduoduo's confidence in future growth without the founder's influence, and significant changes in company operations are not anticipated.

As a result of Chen Lei's solid planning, a firm foundation exists in the company. Given Pinduoduo's accomplishments in rural product quality and continuous investments in agricultural technology and rural infrastructure, the company's future seems promising after Huang Zheng's retirement.

Although both Alibaba's and Pinduoduo's leadership transfers upon founders' retirement were considered successful, the latter initiated a new succession plan model for Chinese companies that is in line with the global trend in the rise of social entrepreneurship. Important factors that contribute to the differences between these two companies' corporate governance models and the two leaders' business mindsets are the 16-year age differences between these two entrepreneurs and their companies: Jack Ma (born in 1964) founded Alibaba in 1999, and Huang Zheng (born in 1980) started Pinduoduo in 2015. The Chinese economy and China's regulation reform made fundamental improvements between 1999 and 2015 (Appendix 1, Regulation Reform Timetable). The age difference between these two founders distinguishes their personal values and business vision. And the 16-year age difference between these two companies determines their remarkable corporate cultures, corporate governance practices and development paths, and probably the futures of these two giant e-commerce companies.

Takeaways

- **China's Corporate Governance Development** – The Compressed Journey.
- **The "China Puzzle" – China's SOEs' strengths and weaknesses**, key corporate governance matters, and important roles in China's economic growth.
- **Privately owned, company founders' controlling structures**, their pros and cons, and the challenges and trend of the new succession plan model.
- **The challenges Chinese privately owned companies** confront and what differentiates them from privately owned/family-owned companies in the West.

Notes

1 Peter Gourevitch, *"Political Power and Corporate Control: The New Global Politics of Corporate Governance"*, Page 2 (Chapter 1), Foreign Affairs (Council on Foreign Relations), Princeton University, January, 2006, November 1, 2020. www.researchg ate.net/publication/24117949_Political_Power_and_Corporate_Control_The_New_ Global_Politics_of_Corporate_Governance
2 Adriana De la Cruz, Alejandra Medina, and Yung Tang, *"Owners of the World's Listed Companies"*, Page 11 (Table 3), OECD Capital Market Series, Paris, March 21, 2021. www.oecd.org/corporate/Owners-of-the-Worlds-Listed-Companies.pdf
3 Gerry Grant (2003), "The evolution of corporate governance and its impact on modern corporate America," *Management Decision*, 41, 923–934.
4 Leng Jing, *"Corporate Governance and Financial Reform in China's Transition Economy"*, Page 44 (Chapter 3), Hong Kong University Press, 2009. www.amazon. com/Corporate-Governance-Financial-Transition-University/dp/9622099319
5 The CSRC was established in 1992 as a government body to regulate the new stock market. The CSRC is the equivalent government authority to the Securities and Exchange Commission (SEC) in the US.
6 Jamie Allen, "New Code of CG for Listed Companies in China", ACGA, 2018, March 18, 2021, www.acga-asia.org/advocacy-detail.php?id=149&sk=&sa=
7 Karen Jingrong, et al., "State-Owned Enterprises in China: A Review of 40 years of Research and Practice," Page 4 (Table 1), February 15, 2020, March 21, 2021. https://reader.elsevier.com/reader/sd/pii/S1755309119300437?token=91E751 28C185D0ED722A47589D2611801E1FCAFD44CBF7511FF78D1B 63784EBBC6681AEE3584563 68A97389103A01BC7

8   Karen Jingrong, et al., "State-Owned Enterprises in China: A Review of 40 years of Research and Practice," Pages 2–3, February 15, 2020, March 21, 2021. https://reader.elsevier.com/reader/sd/pii/S1755309119300437?token=91E75128 C185D0ED722A47589D2611801E1FCAFD44CBF7511FF78D1B63784EBBC 6681AEE358456368A97389103A01BC7

9   Jamie Allen, "New Code of CG for Listed Companies in China," ACGA, 2018, March 18, 2021. www.acga-asia.org/advocacy-detail.php?id=149&sk=&sa=

10 Cross ownership refers to different SOEs becoming shareholders of each other.

11 David Larcker and Brian Tayan, "*Corporate Governance Matters*", Page 228 (Table 8.5), Pearson Education, 2016. www.oecd.org/corporate/Owners-of-the-Wor lds-Listed-Companies.pdf

12 Yu-Hsin Lin and Thomas Mehaffy, "Open Sesame: The Myth of Alibaba's Extreme Corporate Governance and Control," https://brooklynworks.brooklaw.edu/cgi/view content.cgi?article=1219&context=bjcfcl

13 David Larcker and Brian Tayan, "*Corporate Governance Matters*", Page 328 (Figure 11.3), Pearson Education, 2016.

14 Hendrik Laubscher, "What Jack Ma Taught Us About Good Corporate Governance This week," Forbes, September 10, 2018, April 4, 2020, www.forbes.com/sites/ hendriklaubscher/2018/09/10/what-jack-ma-taught-us-about-good-corporate-gov ernance-this-week/#15b04e19fa2b

15 Tian Tao and David De Cremer, "Leadership Innovation" Huawei's Rotating CEO System," November 20, 2015, March 18, 2021. www.europeanbusinessreview.com/ leadership-innovation-huaweis-rotating-ceo-system/

16 www.reuters.com/business/media-telecom/huawei-cfo-meng-wanzhou-named-dep uty-chairwoman-2022-04-01/

17 Peter J. Williamson, Xiaobo Wu, and Eden Yin, "Learning from Huawei's Superfluidity," Ivey Business Journal, May/June, 2019, March 23, 2020. https://ivey businessjournal.com/learning-from-huaweis-superfluidity/

18 Alibaba Group Holding Limited SEC Report, Principal and Selling Shareholders section, September 15, 2014. www.sec.gov/Archives/edgar/data/1577552/0001193 12514341794/d709111df1a.htm#toc

19 Boardroom&Beyond podcast interview with Prof. Andrew Kakabadse in February 2021. https://boardroomandbeyond.com/board-leadership-the-emerging-challenges-for-corporate-boards-and-board-chairs-a-conversation-with-professor-andrew-kak-abadse/

20 Alipay is the mobile payment platform launched by Alibaba in 2004 as an escrow account to bridge the trust between online buyers and sellers, which became the main competitive advantage of Alibaba's e-commerce business, given the fact that credit cards were not widely used in the early 2000s. Alipay later became the core business of Ant Group. A case study of Ant Group will be examined in Chapter 5.

21 Huang Zheng decided to move into a new position in food and life sciences R&D according to this news article. www.scmp.com/tech/big-tech/article/3126018/pinduo duo-founder-colin-huang-says-he-stepping-down-chairman-focus?module=perpe tual_scroll&pgtype=article&campaign=3126018

22 Pinduoduo company website: https://investor.pinduoduo.com/news-releases/news-release-details/pinduoduo-announces-fourth-quarter-2021-and-fiscal-year-2021

Chapter 2

Chinese Companies' Key Corporate Governance Risks

In this chapter, I review

- Inside Share Pledging Risk
  Motivations of CEO share pledging
  Inside share pledging risk mitigation
  Disclosure requirements between the US and China

- Variable Interest Entity (VIE) Structure
  VIE legal uncertainty and risks
  Regulatory reform on VIE structure

- Other Corporate Governance Risks

Risks and opportunities go "hand in hand". Although we all understand the importance of risk mitigation, eliminating risks is not a good option since "avoiding 'bad' risks at all costs presents a countervailing risk: that we will fail to take 'good risks'", according to Michele Wucker, the American author and policy analyst specializing in the world economy and crisis anticipation, and taking the "good risks" often leads us to opportunities. In her new book, *You Are What You Risk*,[1] Ms. Wucker contends that active risk-taking is healthy and beneficial when expectations are established, and challenges are not only expected but also conquered.

Most CEOs I worked with emphasized that businesses should take calculated risks, which means company executives need to be aware of risks for the specific business they are running and be able to measure the maximum damage of these risks and the potential opportunities as a result of taking these risks. Some risks are explicit, some are hidden, and some are more harmful than others. Traditionally, we categorize business risks as economic risk, compliance risk, financial risk (including fraud risks), operational risk, competitive risk, and political risk if operating in other countries. With the fast growth of digital business, increasing discussions regarding business purpose and the worldwide

DOI: 10.4324/9781003302919-4

ESG movement, reputational risk, data security risk, and corporate governance risk all become vitally important to businesses.

Corporate governance risks are risks associated with the governance system including the decision-making process, mechanisms for checks and balances, and minority shareholders' interest protection. Corporate governance risks often are systematic risks with these phenomena: opaque board decision-making processes, failure of board directors' fiduciary duties, and hidden related party transactions. Moreover, most corporate governance risks are not explicit, which makes the risks difficult to be identified and calculated.

What are the most critical corporate governance risks of Chinese companies that we should be aware of, while exploring opportunities with these companies? Let us zoom in on this chapter for some insights.

Insider Share Pledging Risk

Share pledging refers to companies that use a percentage of company stocks as collateral to obtain loans with an agreed stock price at the time of pledging. In practice, the lender will force sales of the pledged shares when the stock price drops to a certain level. The forced selling will cause panic in the stock market, which leads to a further decline in the share price and potential destabilization of the equity market. During the 2008 financial crisis, forced share selling due to margin calls caused further stock price drops for companies with insider share pledging, which exposed serious share pledging risks for investors. Therefore, share pledging has been widely considered a serious corporate governance risk.

Insider share pledging refers to company insider shareholders who use their shares as collateral with a third party in exchange for cash. Due to the fact that a higher percentage of companies in emerging markets are dominated by family-controlled companies, and most emerging market countries do not have systematic securities laws, insider share pledging is more prevalent in emerging markets than in advanced countries.

What then are the motivations for CEO share pledging?

CEO Share Pledging Motivations

A 2019 US study summarized motivations of CEO share pledging in three categories,[2] and the disclosure requirement for US companies:

- **To double the CEO's influence in the company.** A CEO's confidence about the firm's future performance and their desire to increase voting power in the company are the top drivers in this scenario. CEOs normally use cash from share pledging to increase their ownership in their firms despite exposing the company to additional risks.

- **To access additional cash.** Pledging allows CEOs to access additional cash while retaining voting rights without selling their shares. Founders/CEOs are often motivated by this type of monetizing pledge. In addition, the inside pledging disclosure requirements are not as restrictive as those for stock transactions. US companies are required to disclose share pledging in their quarterly proxy statement, while stock transactions by founder/CEOs must be disclosed within two business days.
- **To mitigate risk of personal wealth.** Driven by negative inside information and an uncertainty of a firm's future, CEOs might choose to pledge shares and invest the proceeds in other assets to decrease personal wealth risks. CEO share pledge disclosure is only required for the quarterly proxy statement instead of the two-business day mandate if CEOs enter hedging transactions with their shares.

The study identified that CEO share pledging occurs more often in companies led by founders; with high levels of CEO ownership; experiencing considerable stock price appreciation; led by CEOs with long tenure; with a history of poor liquidity; or with larger boards of directors.

Regardless of the motivations and reasons for CEOs share pledging, insider share pledging could cause a disaster to company stocks and expose outside shareholders' interests to great risk.

Risk Mitigation of Insider Share Pledging

If share pledging is a corporate governance risk, can corporate governance practice improvements help mitigate the risk? The following are a few corporate governance factors that could reduce share pledging opportunities and the challenges of these mechanisms.

- **Shareholder engagement.** Many studies today recommend increasing institutional ownership as a path for mitigating share pledging risks, with the assumption that institutional investors are willing to influence companies' decisions using their voting powers, and investors are willing to implement effective monitoring systems to identify early signs of share pledging risks. However, effective monitoring demands have a cost, and investors might have different agendas and strategies that impact their cost expectations. The underlying message is that shareholder engagement allows investors to understand the business, therefore, be able to sense the motivations of share pledging and identify early signs of potential risks.
- **Independent board directors' roles.** Share pledging often occurs in controlling structure companies. A well-designed system of checks-and-balances system with independent board directors can help mitigate share pledging risks. Having a board comprising a majority of independent board directors

has become worldwide corporate governance practice for decades and many countries have made this practice a part of corporate governance regulation. However, in most emerging market countries, the understanding and effectiveness of independent board directors' roles are limited primarily due to the controlling corporate culture and lack of talent. Therefore, most independent directors are still considered "outsiders" who are not involved in critical decisions. A large percentage of Chinese companies' independent directors come from academic (approximately 40%) or government backgrounds with little business experience, according to Xin Tang, professor at Tsinghua University School of Law and former member of the China Securities Regulatory Commission. There is room for improvement to ensure that independent voices can be heard in boardrooms, and independent opinions are necessary for important business decisions as part of corporate governance practices. Moreover, an independent director's independence should be evaluated by whether or not the director is able to offer independent opinions, not merely by the formality of the relationship to the business.

- **The corporate repurpose revolution.** Worldwide corporate repurposing discussions were also intensified by the 2020 COVID-19 pandemic. Corporations are under pressure to repurpose their businesses to consider stakeholders' interests and environmental issues. In the end, a cumulative mindset change is driven by top leaders (board chairs, founders, and CEOs). Since insider share pledging motivations are mostly related to personal interests, would corporate leaders' mindset change effectively reduce share pledging transactions? I believe the answer will be revealed in the coming decades.

CEO Share Pledging Landscape in the US

Modern companies often offer various stock packages to align CEOs' personal interest with share price, which motivates CEOs to drive firms' financial performance. Company share ownership is a long-term compensation element to retain good CEOs. Studies of S&P 1,500 companies in 2018 show that 83% of S&P 1,500 companies require CEOs to own shares, while 45% of these CEOs' total compensation packages included various stock plans.

Of interest, the infamous 2003 WorldCom debacle[3] revealed that company's then CEO, Bernard Ebbers, owned an estimated 11 million company pledged shares valued at $286 million, for which the company's board reluctantly decided (more precisely, the board was "hijacked") to extend a loan because of their fears that the company's stock value would significantly decrease in case of forced sales. When this scheme was discovered, US regulators realized the substantial risk that corporations would encounter with these types of transactions, which led to the SEC 2006 share pledging disclosure requirement for company executives and boards of directors.[4]

Notwithstanding the SEC disclosure requirement and the financial crisis, American companies' CEO share pledging became substantial over time. American proxy advisory firms ISS and Glass Lewis issued statements in 2012 and 2015, respectively, to address their concerns regarding insider share pledging risks and related companies' governance weaknesses. In 2015, the SEC amended share pledging disclosure requirements to broaden its scope of shareholder transactions and to include requirements for the details of the pledging transactions.[5] Due to pressure from the proxy advisory firms and the substantially rising number of American companies adopting anti-pledging policies between 2007 and 2016, the CEO compensation structure between base salary and performance-driven incentives has changed significantly over the past few years.

In the US, academic and professional studies continue to explore the effect and impact of anti-pledging policies on companies' investment decisions and company value. Although the SEC does not prohibit company share pledging yet, its risks and the impact on companies' stock prices are a vital concern of shareholders and are closely monitored by proxy agencies and regulators.[6]

Chinese Companies Founders and CEOs' Share Pledge

Although share pledging is a worldwide practice, companies' share pledging risks in China are considerably more dangerous than in other countries due to the size of China's economy and the immaturity of Chinese securities market and regulation system. Statistics show that Chinese companies' share pledging amount was RMB 4 trillion ($620 billion) in October 2018, which represents 10% of the total Chinese A-shares market capitalization at the time of the analysis.[7] Since China presently has the second-largest stock market in the world, such a huge amount of share pledging could place the Chinese market at substantial risk, which could significantly impact global stock market.

The Luckin Coffee scandal discovered in early 2020 is a good example of how a Chinese company was exposed to share pledging risks.

Case Study 2.1   The Luckin Coffee Scandal and Founder Pledge

Luckin Coffee opened its first store in January 2018, made its IPO debut on Nasdaq in May 2019, quickly grew its business from 2,370 to 6,500 stores, then suddenly crashed in April 2020 after financial fraud was revealed. As a typical insider controlling founder firm, the founders' group controlled in excess of 50% of company shares, over 60% of the voting power, and 49% of company shares were pledged as loan collateral. As a result, the founders' pledges significantly jeopardized the business and investors' interests.

Additionally, both the chairman and CEO held board committee chair positions that compromised the independence and objectivity of the board committees. Upon admitting to sales fraud of $310 million USD (42% of 2019 revenue) in April 2020, Luckin's stock price plunged 91%.

In May, the company fired its CEO and COO as part of an internal investigation into the sales fraud. In June 2020, the investigation discovered that the chairman instructed employees via company email to commit sales fraud. The chairman is currently facing criminal charges in China. Consequently, Nasdaq suspended Luckin's stock trading on June 29 and delisting procedures followed. In July 2020, Luckin replaced the entire board of directors with five independent directors with professional backgrounds in management, corporate finance, law, and governance. As of May 2021, Luckin is still trading on Nasdaq with only 14% of its initial stock value at the time the fraud was discovered in April 2020. Although Luckin's business continues, considerable time is needed to repair its reputation.

Since the Luckin founders pledged 49% of their company shares as loan collateral, when stock price dropped due to the company's financial fraud and the chairman defaulted on the loan, Luckin's lending companies were forced to sell the founder's pledged shares, which amplified the disaster. And the forced sale caused further decline in Luckin's stock price.

Luckin's share pledging criteria were consistent with CEO pledging firms' schemes: companies led by founders, high CEO ownership, and considerable stock price appreciation. Luckin's share pledging is no different from companies from other countries as far as the share pledgers' motivations, the creditors' reactions when stock prices fall, and the harm that caused stock prices to further decline are concerned. However, most Chinese companies' investors, board directors, and executives, are not as sophisticated as those of US companies, in terms of their understanding and awareness of insider share pledging risks (that probably nourished share pledging abuse opportunities), and the potential damage that companies may face.

In addition to share pledging, the Luckin case also revealed the company's significant board oversight weakness – the ex-chairman governed the Nomination and Corporate Governance Committee, while the ex-CEO chaired the Compensation Committee, both of which jeopardized the independence and objectivity of board functions. Is it possible impartial board oversight could have prevented Luckin's share pledging failure? The answer is not certain. However, an objective, fully functioning board may have prevented this scandal by monitoring and scrutinizing the company's operations policies and procedures, including its share pledging policy.

In my opinion, the question that truly matters is: Will Luckin's share pledging risk and the catastrophic result lead to Chinese regulatory improvements, just like WorldCom's CEO's share pledging disaster led to the SEC's regulation reform?

Variable Interest Entity (VIE) Structure

Over the past three decades, the variable interest entity (VIE) structure has been a widely used business practice for Chinese companies to access overseas capital. As of October 2018, 92% of Nasdaq-listed and 64% of NYSE-listed Chinese companies made use of the VIE structure. This practice has been an unsolved mystery in the global market. But because its impact on the market is not as visible as other hot Chinese business topics like related-party transactions and auditor independence, the VIE structure remains as a hidden risk.

Establishing a VIE structure is not cheap; maintaining a VIE structure can be very costly. However, for many Chinese companies expanding their business in the global market, establishing a VIE structure becomes a "must have" regardless of the actual necessity. I had the opportunity to participate in some of these orchestrations during my career from 2014 to 2017 when working for various Chinese companies to help their "going global" strategies. Because of my corporate finance background, I always cared about a multinational company's tax structure whenever adding new entities to that organization. One VIE structure can cause a complex tax structure by adding a few new entities to the organization, while some Chinese companies have multiple VIEs in their organizations. All these complexities could lead to potential tax burdens for the entire internationalization operation. Moreover, eliminating these complexities afterward, though, could be even more costly.

I remember that I could not understand why decision makers of these companies never cast doubt on the complicated organizational structure caused by VIEs, which may or may not be utilized in the future. Despite the sizable amount of service fees for attorney firms and secretary services to maintain the structure during a VIE's lifetime, few individuals seem to consider the hidden dangers of potential future tax burdens and tax planning complexities.

On the other side, I was constantly confronted with challenges when attempting to convince some company executives about the necessity to seriously consider global tax structure planning before executing overseas acquisition transactions. I also wished that the same routine as the VIE structure would have been established as part of Chinese companies' overseas acquisition strategies, which would have saved these companies millions of tax dollars in their post-acquisition operations.

So, what is the beauty of VIE structures that made Chinese companies so obsessed with them? And what are the potential risks for investors and founders? I discovered the answer after considerable research.

VIE Structure and Its Legal Uncertainty

A VIE structure is a unique business structure in which investors do not have direct ownership but have a controlling interest in the entity through special contracts. The contracts specify the service and purpose of the agreements and the percentage of profits allocated to each party but do not provide direct voting rights to the controlling party. Almost every listed Chinese company that can be purchased outside of China is listed through a VIE structure. Through this structure, investors do not actually own any part of the actual underlying Chinese company. The VIE structure comprises the following (see Figure 2.1).

In the case of overseas-listed Chinese companies, a VIE refers to a company that is incorporated in China and owned by individuals who are Chinese citizens (usually the founders). The Overseas Listed Offshore Entity (OLOE) is typically a shell company domiciled in the Cayman Islands. An OLOE often incorporates

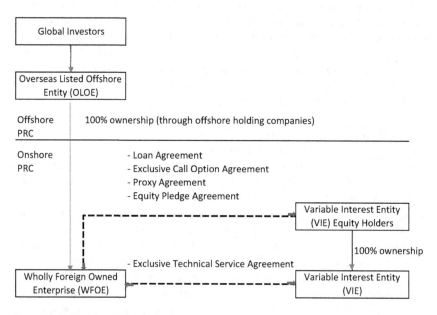

Figure 2.1 The Simplified VIE Structure.

Source: Compiled by the author.

a Wholly Foreign Owned Enterprise (WFOE) in China that holds material assets and conducts operations on behalf of the overseas-listed company. An OLOE generates revenue mainly through its ownership of WFOE, and the WFOE captures profits of the VIE through a series of contracts between the WFOE and the VIE. The contacts (loan agreements, technical services agreements) give WFOE the rights to the VIE's residual profit. Additionally, the VIE and its owners will sign a power of attorney or proxy agreement to grant the WFOE voting rights at the VIE shareholder meetings. Technically, OLOE shareholders do not own the VIE but have contractual rights to the VIE's profit and will be able to conduct voting rights through its WFOE. An OLOE can operate its business through more than one VIE. We often refer to the entire set of relationships as a "VIE structure".

VIE structures normally contain a dual natural arrangement: On the control side, the business' VIE is controlled by OLOE through various agreements. The OLOE is listed overseas, which technically has no voting rights with the VIE. On the operational side, the VIE is owned by a Chinese domestic company (WFOE) that has contractual control over the VIE through the OLOE. The VIE structure circumvents the regulator's restrictions on foreign ownership – when a company uses a VIE structure to work around the approval process for foreign capital access, the company intentionally evades these regulations and enters a "gray area" of Chinese contract law. Therefore, VIE structure exposes all related entities and their owners to considerable legal risks.

Investors' Fragile Ownership

When investing into a company with VIE structure, investors are only shareholders of an offshore holding company (OLOE) that excludes investors from decision-making processes unless agreed upon. The most prominent example is the Alipay spin-off controversy between Alibaba and its partners, Yahoo and Softbank,[8] in 2011, when the Chinese government tightened regulations on online payment businesses. Alibaba decided to transfer ownership of its online payment platform, Alipay, to a private company owned by founder, Jack Ma.[9] Unfortunately for them, Yahoo and Softbank were not part of the decision because of Alibaba's VIE structure, and their dispute has become a warning to global investors.

Case Study 2.2   Alibaba Alipay Case Ownership Transfer Case – VIE Structure and Its Risk to Shareholders

E-commerce started in China in early 2000. Foreseeing a fast-growing e-commerce business opportunity in the Chinese market, eBay entered the market in 2002 upon acquiring Eachnet, a Chinese C2C marketplace. However, the limited use of credit cards in China and eBay's dependence

> *on PayPal as the only allowed direct payment method caused a severe lack of trust between buyers and sellers in e-commerce transactions. Because of a better understanding of the Chinese market and consumers, Alibaba launched the mobile payment platform, Alipay, in 2004 with an escrow mechanism to ensure that buyers would make payments upon receiving promised goods. The innovation of Alipay became a powerful engine for the growth of Alibaba's e-commerce business and helped Alibaba successfully conquer its foreign competitor eBay. In 2006, eBay closed its Chinese operations and exited the market. However, during the four years of eBay's operations from 2002 to 2006, Chinese e-commerce users more than doubled from 59 million to 138 million. Alipay was later transferred to Ant Finance and became the core business of the latter company.*
>
> *On March 31, 2011, Yahoo and Softbank were notified that two relevant transactions were pending: Alipay's ownership transfer would take place in August 2011, and the financial statement deconsolidation of Alipay was effective in the first quarter of 2011. The decisions of both transactions were made without the knowledge or approval of Alibaba Group's board of directors, where Yahoo and Softbank both held seats. After the announcement about losing Alipay in May 2011, Yahoo's stock price dropped significantly.*
>
> *Alipay's ownership was transferred to another domestic company, the majority of stock for which was held by Jack Ma. The reason for Alipay's transfer was a result of China's new regulation that forbade foreign ownership of online payment companies. However, the tricky part of the transaction was Alibaba's VIE structure that excluded Alibaba Group's partners, Yahoo and Softbank, from being involved in the decision of such a significant transaction. As part of Alibaba's VIE structure, Alipay was obligated to distribute its revenue to Alibaba Group while Alipay was valued at RMB 330 million at the time of the ownership transaction. Forfeiting Alipay's revenue caused a substantial drop in Yahoo's stock price.*

Jack Ma claimed that the Alipay ownership transfer transaction demonstrated his intention to follow Chinese regulations by terminating the VIE operation. However, the exclusion of its business partners to take part in the decision-making process significantly impacted the magnitude of losses in Yahoo's stock value, which provides strong evidence of the risk that the VIE structure may create for investors.

Chinese Government's Regulatory Approach to VIE Structure

China has been taking a gradualist approach[10] to economic reform and corporate governance development over the past 30 years. The approach has proved to be successful in contrast with the Russian "rush approach",[11]. According to *Corporate Governance and Financial Reform in China's Transition Economy* by Leng Jing, countries utilizing a gradualist strategy tend to lack well-functioning or updated regulations, which means regulatory development always lagging. It appears obvious that Chinese regulators are concurrently using the same strategy to fix VIEs as they steadily and continuously relax foreign investment restrictions and improve the overall standard of its regulation system.

Since VIE naturally favors founders, some VIE agreements include conditions to mitigate risks associated with a founder's personal status (such as marriage status change), to protect investors' interests. However, whether or not these VIE agreements are legally protected by Chinese law is questionable, which is the largest vulnerability of VIE. According to current Chinese law, a contract written to avoid regulation requirements is void and the courts will not enforce it. The special contracts enabling global investors' controlling interests of VIEs are technically not valid.

Since the middle 2000s, Chinese regulators have attempted to address the VIE issues with notable regulatory improvements listed below:

In 2006, the former Ministry of Information Technology issued a memo to request all Chinese telecom companies get its approval before applying for an overseas listing[12];

In 2009, the Chinese publishing authority issued a direct regulation to attack online gaming companies using VIE structures;

In 2011, some unconfirmed research data implied the China Security Regulatory Commission intended to attack the overseas IPOs of internet companies that had VIE structures;

In 2015, regulators attempted to amend the Foreign Investor Law to address the VIE issue, but the relevant revision was withdrawn later[13];

In 2019, the new Foreign Investor Law was enacted but regulators did not address VIE issues as expected by the market, which created much apprehension regarding Chinese regulators' approaches to close the VIE loophole;

In 2020, the new antitrust law enforcement guidelines were enacted, and the regulators instituted additional scrutiny of mergers and acquisition transactions associated with a VIE structure, focusing on the restriction of foreign ownership in certain technology sectors, while not completely eliminating the VIE structure;

In January 2022, the CSRC issued a set of "Draft Rules" to propose a new filing system for all Chinese companies including those with VIE structures, which signals the Chinese government's acknowledgment of the VIE structure. Once in effect, the "Draft Rules" will become a regulatory milestone that affirms the legal status of VIE-structured overseas-listed companies.[14]

At the time of this writing, many practical requirements still remain to be seen, such as the treatment of new VIE-structured companies' filing with those that pre-exist, and the potential of regulatory relaxation for Hong Kong H-share listing compared to other overseas listings. The Chinese government's intention to regulatorily solve VIE structure issues echoes with other corporate governance regulation reform.

Although the most recent regulatory proposal aims to legalize the VIE structure, which significantly reduces the legal uncertainty risk of VIE-structured companies, global businesses and investors should not ignore other potential risks caused by the complicated VIE structure.

Other Risks

The Founder Controlling Company's Key Person Risk

Many large Chinese companies are controlled by the founders. Although some of these companies have successfully grown within the global market and become industry leaders, their governance models and decision-making processes still function as if they are early-stage companies. That means, the most important company decisions are made by the founders without a systematic decision-making process. The advantage of this centralized control and decision-making system is efficiency, which allows companies to grow rapidly. In addition to the functional disadvantages including the lack of a checks-and-balances mechanism and a lack of independent objectivity, there are two factors that cannot be overlooked: the significant impact on companies caused by a key person's absence and a key person's poor reputation.

The following case study of JD.com, the second-largest e-commerce business in China, reveals the impact on company value and stock price due to the founder's poor personal behavior.

Case Study 2.3   JD.com Founder's Poor Reputation Impacts Company's Stock Price

JD.com was founded by Liu Qiangdong in 1998 and is the second-largest Chinese e-commerce company. The company has been listed on Nasdaq since May 2014 and secondarily listed on Hong Kong Stock Exchange (HKEX) since July 2020. The significant differences between JD.com and Alibaba are JD inventories of various products and processes to fill its orders with a much lower operating margin, while Alibaba is an e-commerce paid listing platform for third-party sellers. JD's operation model allows the company to better control its product quality and delivery schedule.

In September 2018, Liu Qiangdong was arrested in the US after being accused of raping a Chinese student at the University of Minnesota, where Liu was taking doctoral business administration courses. Although Liu denied any misconduct and was released with no charges 3 months after the arrest, JD's stock price hit an 18-month low during the week of Liu's arrest, resulting in a $7.2 billion loss (16% of its market share) caused by investors' fears that JD.com would significantly lose consumers due to Liu's arrest. A November 2018 report showed that the company's customer base declined dramatically, as projected.

As the controlling founder, Liu Qiangdong has heavily weighted voting rights, tight control of the company, and is the primary decision maker on the company's board of directors. Jiu's case raised many questions about JD's corporate governance risks regarding:

- *Succession planning – who is the company's immediate successor?*
- *The decision-making process – who has the authority to provide major decisions if/when Liu is unable to lead the company?*
- *Minority shareholders' interest protection – what options are available for minority shareholders who have limited voting rights?*

JD.com founder's case may be an egregious example, but the corporate governance risks exposed by companies like JD.com should serve as a warning call for investors and other companies. While many might believe tightening regulatory compliance requirements can help eliminate corporate governance risks, for Chinese companies such as JD.com, the best approach to avoid corporate governance risks and business risks due to a critical person's wrongdoing or inability to perform leadership roles is not to enhance compliance, but to improve board oversight including optimizing board committee functions and decision-making process.[15] At the moment, institutional investors' influence in Chinese companies is still limited due to their tiny share percentage, and many obstacles (e.g., the language barrier) that limit investors' voices. Over time, though, investors' engagement and their outspokenness via voting rights should have an impact.

Audit Quality and Audit Information Transparency

All foreign companies listed in US stock markets are required to have their financial statements audited by an independent firm, while most of these multinational companies are audited by firms in their own country. Under the Sarbanes-Oxley Act, the Public Company Accounting Oversight Board (PCAOB) has established formal cooperative arrangements with foreign audit regulators, which allows the PCAOB to conduct an inspection of audit firms in these countries. However, although this practice is not just for Chinese multinationals, an equivalent arrangement has not yet been established between the PCAOB and the Chinese regulators. Therefore, regardless of the fact that many Chinese companies listed on the US exchange are audited by the "Big Four" accounting firms, without Chinese regulators' authorization, companies conducting business in China cannot yet relinquish their audits to the PCAOB. The Big Four auditors had been compressed between the US and China after spending nearly three decades building their operations in the Chinese markets.

In the Luckin Coffee case, Ernst & Young Hua Ming LLP, a member firm of Ernst & Young LLP (EY) in the US, has been Luckin's auditor. Although EY did not audit Luckin's 2019 financial statements at the time the scandal was revealed, EY issued a "comfort letter" to investment banks in early 2020 to underwrite Luckin's stock and bond sales, despite EY's denial of irresponsibility.[16]

At the time this book was written, an agreement was signed between the PCAOB and Chinese authorities to prevent Chinese companies from being delisted from the US stock exchanges. However, the details of the communication between both countries have not been revealed, and further cooperation arrangements that are in line with both countries' legal and regulatory requirements are still in negotiation. While China has national security concerns, PCAOB aims to conduct on-the-ground audit inspections by the November 2022 deadline. Consequently, time is ticking!

Board Independence and Objectivity

Today, most Chinese companies have established a Western-style board structure with independent board directors. It's worth pointing out two traditional characteristics in Chinese companies' governance system and business practices that are invisible, inherited, and unlikely to evaporate from Chinese culture: a patriarchal culture and nominal board. A patriarchal culture implies valuing the considerable depth of familial-like relationships, and nominal boards allow controlling shareholders to manipulate company board decisions. Because of these two features, the most important decisions are still made by one individual without a transparent decision-making process with a checks-and-balances mechanism, regardless of the company size. Moreover, most Chinese companies choose to breed home-grown talent for critical positions instead of hiring professional executives selected from the marketplace. In recent years, increasing numbers of Western executives are taking positions in Chinese companies, and more overseas-listed Chinese companies hire local independent directors to make company boards appear more professional and independent.

But most Western executives are not in the "core cycle" (individuals who have been following the founder since the company's early stage), and most independent board directors are viewed as outsiders or consultants without access to core information or are prohibited from participating in important decisions. The dual existence of the patriarchal culture and nominal board feature are the obstacles to Chinese companies' board independence and objectivity.

Luckin Coffee is a typical patriarchal company, where former chairman Charles Lu and former CEO Jenny Qian held 30.53% and 19.68% of company shares and voting rights of 36.86% and 23.7%, respectively in each category. In addition, before jointly founding Luckin, Qian was COO of another public company founded by Lu. The patriarchal culture, combined with Lu's and Qian's control of the board committees, eliminated any possibility that Luckin's company board directors could perform properly according to the company's corporate governance documents.

Related Transactions

Using intragroup transfers and loan guarantees to shift resources among related parties are the most common transactions of its kind for companies across the world, as are disclosure requirements for related transactions. What creates opportunities for related transactions that are hidden in Chinese companies are these companies' complicated organizational structures, most of which resemble a maze and are also difficult to understand. Many of these complexities not only prevent investors from monitoring related transactions but also cause these companies unnecessary tax burdens or troublesome and expensive restructuring costs during their global growth. While the motivation of the complicated organization structure may be either sinful or innocent, it's worth paying additional attention should an opportunity arise.

Luckin Coffee is also an excellent example, although the details of Luckin's fabricated sales in 2019 were not revealed. It is likely, however, that Luckin's complicated supply chain linked to its founder and then-chairman, Charles Lu, almost certainly explains the reason. Although investors will not be able to access the company's internal information, Luckin's 558% third-quarter and 400% fourth-quarter sales revenue increases in 2019 should have been viewed as early warning signs and been questioned by investors whose interests may be jeopardized, as well as by independent board directors who tied their personal reputations to the company and could be held liable for the company's misconduct.

Regulation Reform Predictability

Several recent regulatory actions taken by the Chinese government in the past couple of years raised significant concerns regarding the predictability of Chinese regulation reform. For example, the newly released Data Security and Personal Information Protection Legal Framework, which affected most overseas-listed tech companies; and the newly released education tutoring restriction rules, which fundamentally reshaped the business models of Chinese companies in education services. The sudden issuance of these two regulations has resulted in stock price fluctuation of companies in both sectors that shakes international investors' confidence due to the unpredictable regulation uncertainty (details of recent regulation reforms will be discussed in later chapters of this book).

Some of the key corporate governance risks to Chinese companies will diminish while improvements of corporate governance practices and government regulations continue. However, some remnants may remain as Chinese companies' unique identities. Has my exploration of Chinese companies' key corporate governance risks helped you adopt a different risk appetite when considering an investment or a career opportunity? I hope the discussion in this chapter brings awareness and stirs some consideration regarding these key corporate governance risks.

Takeaways

- **China's inside share pledging risk,** with which China's lagged regulation system is the main reason that makes Chinese companies' CEOs' share pledging transactions riskier than those of US companies. However, there is hope that catastrophic cases such as the Luckin Coffee scandal will lead to corresponding regulation reform in China.
- **The most significant VIE structure risk is its legal uncertainty.** Although it's unlikely for the Chinese government to suddenly terminate the VIE compact, financial market regulation reforms in both China and its global partners are aiming to eliminate the VIE structure for the dual purposes of improving the regulation system and protecting investors' interests.
- **Founders' personal risk.** The best approach to mitigate corporate governance risks caused by founders' personal risk is to **improve corporate governance functions and processes**.

Notes

1   Wucker, Michelle, *You Are What You Risk*, Pegasus Books, 2021. www.amazon.com/You-Are-What-Risk-Navigating/dp/164313678X

2   In this research paper, the author explained behaviors and motivations of three groups of CEO pledging as "doubling-down CEOs", "monetizing CEOs", and "hedging CEOs". Kornelia Fabisik, "Why Do US CEOs Pledge Their Own Company's Stock?" November 11, 2019, April 4, 2020, https://ideas.repec.org/p/chf/rpseri/rp1960.html

3   Barbara Powell, "WorldCom, Ex-CEO Ebbers in Loan Dispute, 2003," Midland Daily News, May 14, 2021, May 30, 2021. www.ourmidland.com/news/article/WorldCom-Ex-CEO-Ebbers-in-Loan-Dispute-7103182.php

4 Siqi Wei, "Inside Share Pledging, Managerial Risk-Taking, and Corporate Policies," Page 4, May 1, 2021, June 1, 2021. https://cba.lmu.edu/media/lmucollegeofbusines sadministration/responsivesite/research/paper_4.pdf

5 Paul Hastings, "The SEC's Proposed Disclosure Rules for Hedging Transactions by Directors, Officers, and Employees," 2015, May 14, 2021. www.paulhastings.com/insights/client-alerts/the-secs-proposed-disclosure-rules-for-hedging-transactions-by-directors-officers-and-employees

6 Siqi Wei, "Inside Share Pledging, Managerial Risk-Taking, and Corporate Policies," Pages 5–6, May 1, 2021, June 1, 2021. https://cba.lmu.edu/media/lmucollegeofbus inessadministration/responsivesite/research/paper_4.pdf

7 Evelyn Cheng, "China Talks Up the Stock Market Lurking Concerns about Share-Backed Loans," CNBC, 2018, May 14, 2021. www.cnbc.com/2018/10/24/china-sto cks-share-pledge-loans-pose-risk-to-equity-markets.html

8 Gregory J. Millman, "Alibaba's IPO Puts VIE Structure in the Spotlight," The Wall Street Journal, September 22, 2014, April 10, 2020, https://blogs.wsj.com/riskan dcompliance/2014/09/22/alibabas-ipo-puts-vie-structure-in-the-spotlight/

9 Maurice Sanchez, "Alibaba-: Case B: Jack Ma Takes Alipay," Yahoo!, 2011, May 1, 2021. www.readkong.com/page/alibaba-yahoo-case-b-1303530

10 China's "gradualist approach" refers to a constantly experimental and correcting economic reform process. Regulators will issue interim regulations to guide the economic reform through different stages with progressing evolution focus in order to transform from a planned economy to market economy with continuous correction and improvement on the regulatory system, industries' standards, and business practice. China's gradualist approach to SOE reform will be discussed in Chapter 3.

11 Russia's "rush approach" is a top-down reform package consisting of programs designed to destroy all existing economic structures and replace them with a Western-style market economy. Russia's "rush approach" led to political conflict during firms' privatization and eventually led to economic reform failure in the 1990s.

12 Fang Zhou and Brett Zhang, "VIE Structure – A Long Untold Story," Financierworldwide.com 2018, May 1, 2021. www.financierworldwide.com/vie-structure-a-long-untold-story#.YI1LFy2cbUZ

13 Paul Gillis, "VIEs in the New Foreign Investment Law," Seeking Alpha, March 15, 2019, April 4, 2020. https://seekingalpha.com/article/4249013-vies-in-new-foreign-investment-law

14 www.ropesgray.com/en/newsroom/alerts/2022/January/China-Puts-VIE-Structured-Overseas-Listings-under-Regulatory-Spotlight

15 Alexandra Ma, "One of China's Richest Men Was Arrested in the US on Sexual Misconduct Allegations," Insider, September 3, 2017, April 15, 2021. www.business insider.com/jdcom-ceo-liu-qiangdong-arrested-in-us-on-sexual-misconduct-allegati ons-2018-9

16 Jing Yang, "Ernest & Young Says It Isn't Responsible for Luckin Coffee's Accounting Misconduct," 2020, May 1, 2021. www.wsj.com/articles/ernst-young-says-it-isnt-responsible-for-luckin-coffees-accounting-misconduct-11594909084

Chapter 3

What Is Driving China's Corporate Governance Development?

In this chapter, I review

- Three Common Characteristics
  Government influences
  Creative models with quick decision-making
  The vernal years

- Domestic Drivers and Opportunities
  Global branding strategy
  Leadership transfer
  Regulation reform
  Political influence

- Primary Drivers in Global Context
  US regulatory scrutiny of US-listed Chinese companies
  US–China political tussle

I met many Westerners who moved to China after China joined the WTO in 2000. Some of them were senior executives at the Chinese subsidiaries of Western multinational companies, such as Amazon, and Apple; some of them were representatives from Western third-party consulting firms providing legal or other consulting services to help their Chinese clients' overseas expansion. Although I speak fluent Chinese and understand Chinese culture, I later found I shared the same business mindset as those Westerners. The most significant misunderstanding with Western business philosophy is the expectation that China's growth, or any country's growth, would follow the path of the West, one proven as a great success in the twentieth century. This misunderstanding, I later found, is the root cause of many struggling moments and miscommunication between Western companies and professionals with their Chinese counterparts.

After three years of dedicated research, I realized that China's thousand-year-old culture and different political and economic environments determined the

DOI: 10.4324/9781003302919-5

unique path China had to take to grow its economy and improve its global position. I also learned that China and Chinese companies' desire to establish a "China Model" is concurrent with an emerging determination to capitalize on its continued success toward increasing China's global position. This decision will drive the country's nonstop growth over the coming decades and is a catalyst for the creativity of Chinese companies to earn recognition in the global market. Moreover, China's success testifies that, given the differences in many economic growth elements such as culture, demographic characteristics, and regulatory environment, the Western models might not be suitable for emerging markets countries. Although the "China Model" still has room for improvement, the rise of the "China Model" suggests the emerging trend of diverse economic growth, corporate governance practice, and business practice models for emerging markets countries.

However, to build a "China Model" with worldwide recognitions, China needs to improve its domestic institutional system to align with international standards. Moreover, China must overcome the challenges to engage in ever-changing global business environments and geopolitical provocations, including those involving the US. Facing these domestic and international challenges is likely to become the most powerful driver of China's corporate governance development.

Common Characteristics of Chinese Companies' Corporate Governance Practices

Although the flexibility of the Chinese regulation system provided opportunities for creative corporate governance models as discussed in previous chapters, there are a few common characteristics of those models and practices that will most likely serve as the foundation for the "China Model".

Government Influence

Chinese SOEs and listed companies are required to establish Party Committees, and many established private companies have voluntarily established their Party Committees to remain politically correct and connected with the government. In Chinese SOEs, the chairperson, most members of the boards of supervisors, and most executives are assigned by the SASAC. Members of the Party Committee are from different business positions within the organization. A Party Committee is not an operational function, but a communication channel between government and a business, which enables the government to understand the business and provide support to a business. China's recent political reforms officially authorized the Party Committees' corporate governance roles on monitoring and ensuring regulation and legal compliance in Chinese companies. In SOEs, the Party Committees are also involved in important business decisions to ensure that a company's growth aligns with government's strategy.

During an interview with Professor Lourdes Casanova, the professor shared her opinion regarding the key reasons for Chinese multinationals' successes compared to multinationals from other emerging markets. Given her years of research experience with multinational companies from emerging markets such as Latin American countries and Asian countries, Professor Casanova concluded that the Chinese government's financial and regulatory supports, including low-interest rate funding and tax breaks, enhance companies' (SOEs and private) capability of technology innovation and make them more resilient in the global marketplace. In the recently published book *Innovation from Emerging Markets: From Copycats to Leaders*, co-authored by Professor Casanova and her emerging markets research group, various case studies were analyzed and ultimately arrived at the same conclusions.

The government's support leads to easy access to capital, other resources, tax breaks, and a sophisticated mechanism of checks and balances that enhance internal control. Although one could argue that government support distorts market order and creates unfair competition, who does not want governmental funding support? Since companies are generally subject to governmental audits or reviews when government funding is used, such a scenario helps improve those companies' internal control systems. Moreover, aligning with government strategy reduces regulation compliance risks and promotes good relationships with stakeholders, including authorities, banks, and local communities, all of which are also vital. For an emerging markets country such as China that does not have a well-structured financial regulation system, the government's intervention somehow works as a supplement to improve business practices.

However, government intervention has been the biggest concern for global investors, mainly because of a lack of transparency regarding the government's role in a business' decision-making process. With the official authorization of the Party's monitoring roles that are required to be reflected in company bylaws and organizational charts, both the Party and the companies are making adjustments at the moment, and we should expect further clarification on this topic in the coming years. For the time being, instead of clamoring over whether government intervention in companies is necessary, perhaps it is more important to consider and evaluate whether government intervention impacts the integrity of business decisions or disturbs compliance with international standards.

The government's assignment of executives to SOEs also causes concerns regarding their professionalism and motivation for business success, especially in Chinese multinationals which require an international vision and global business experience to lead a company in the global marketplace. Moreover, in Chinese SOEs, the CEO's compensation amount must align with government-mandated salary limits. At the same time, company boards do not have the power to decide on Chinese SOEs' executives' compensation, which could also affect the efficacy of board oversight.

Creativity and Quick Reaction Capacity

Growing alongside China's regulation reforms that have been constantly subjected to trial and correction while taking this adventurous journey without practical guidance, many Chinese companies developed creative governance models and business practices both of which enabled quick reactions to regulation changes. Most notable are Alibaba's partnership controlling structure and Huawei's rotating CEO system with its "superfluid" organizational structure. Both companies' corporate governance models have contributed to their companies' success. Still, areas for debate and potential future improvement exist for Alibaba due to its extraordinary control of keeping investors' influences at a minimum, and Huawei's "superfluid" organizational structure that unfortunately became questionable in terms of employees' well-being consideration.

Investors should keep their collective eyes on those creative governance models to verify that essential governance functions are sufficiently outlined, a mechanism to protect investors' interests is invoked, and that business practices comply with both Chinese regulations and international standards. While language barriers and other inconveniences may be present, investors should be highly encouraged to participate in AGM and other shareholder meetings to understand and engage with a business and not be reluctant to raise their voices with respect to any concerns.

Chinese companies' quick reactions to global business uncertainties seem suitable for today's ever-changing business environment due to the COVID-19 pandemic and worldwide disaster interruptions. However, the impact of these "knee-jerk reactions" on a company's long-term sustainability will need to be further examined, given the complexities of today's global business environment.

The Vernal Years

Most Chinese companies are young (merely 30–40 years old) since their incorporation, and the concept of shareholding companies was introduced only as recently as the 1990s. Therefore, most Chinese companies are still operated or are highly influenced by the founders' generation. These founders are dedicated and have substantial emotional and financial investments in their companies, having secured the success of their business by including an efficient decision-making process and less bureaucracy that enhances investors' confidence despite regulatory uncertainties. This notably contrasts with some corporate governance concerns from more developed countries' corporate governance practices today since their boards can suffer from a "disconnect" with the business, making board oversight less effective and less efficient. For example, Alibaba's Jack Ma's personal engagement and commitment helped retain investors' confidence despite the company's VIE structure.

However, because of Chinese companies' young ages, even if some of them are proliferating domestically and internationally, their corporate governance practices are still in the early stages, similar to Western startups that lack comprehensive board procedures, well-established board functions, and sound decision-making and succession planning processes. The Luckin Coffee and JD.com case studies are good examples. In both cases, the founder/chairman made most of the decisions, and a well-functioning monitoring and enforcement mechanism was missing.

In addition, the absence of a sophisticated internationalization strategy that includes a global talent strategy reveals another weakness of young Chinese companies. This tendency is typically reflected by a lack of understanding of host countries' business practices and regulations, while they also overemphasize the "China Model". The main reason for this scenario is the limited numbers of business leaders with professional career track and international business experience. Although some Chinese multinationals started to hire Western board members and executives, the absence of a talent recruiting strategy and these companies' governance models and leadership styles often lead to challenges to recruit and retain qualified talents. Despite having a dual cultural background and bilingual skills, navigating the decision-making process and understanding many business behaviors are still challenging for me. I can only imagine the challenges for Western executives working for Chinese companies, which lead to difficulties for Chinese companies seeking to hire and retain business leaders who have international experience.

According to Christine Raynaud, a former director of the European Chamber of Commerce in Hong Kong and business owner in China, Western companies have historically internationalized by deploying their home country's model to overseas subsidiaries. The internationalization model is no longer applicable due to an increasingly complicated global business environment underpinned by proliferating regulations and competition from domestic market players. Those challenges apply to Chinese companies seeking to become multinationals, who will need to understand, respect, and legitimize a host country's culture and business practices and empower local management to succeed. Highly centralized management styles and the lack of international business experience among senior executive teams are the challenges for both Chinese companies and seasoned global Western executives. In addition to facing difficulties with those leadership styles and governance models when working for Chinese companies, Western executives are not entirely trusted. They are often treated as external consultants despite executive titles or board directorship roles. Relying on her experience advising Western and Asian companies' global talent strategies since the 1980s, Ms. Raynaud suggests that China's education system and Chinese multinationals should establish comprehensive international talent development strategies as part of their global business growth plans.[1]

It takes time to establish a sophisticated board process and global internationalization strategy and to overcome related corporate governance challenges. The learning process may be painful and costly for Chinese multinationals until their higher standard corporate governance practices are established and implemented. What is driving Chinese companies' government practice development then?

Key Domestic Drivers

Paralleling Chinese companies' perpetual growth domestically and internationally are some concomitant challenges that may occur during that growth, possibly revealing these companies' corporate governance weaknesses that must be quelled in order to capture future corporate governance improvement. Seeking solutions for these challenges will identify corporate governance improvement opportunities and allow these companies to realize that improving their corporate governance practice and conquering obstacles simultaneously can make them more competitive in the global marketplace.

Global Branding Challenges

Despite many success stories, some Chinese companies have overlooked the key elements of corporate governance while chasing growth and expansion. These corporate governance weaknesses eventually became obstacles to their global growth. Specifically, one of the primary challenges for Chinese companies is global branding.

Although there is no research yet establishing a direct relationship between a company's corporate governance practice and brand value, it is understood that high-standard corporate governance practices significantly increase a brand's valuation.[2] Since BrandZ and Brandirectory began ranking the top 100 and 500 most valuable brands in the early 2000s, many international brand valuation firms have been testing brand valuation models and identifying factors that influence brand value. According to Cornell University's annual Emerging Markets report,[3] some Chinese brands have shown steady rank improvements on both BrandZ's and Brandirectory's lists from 2009 to 2018, while other Chinese companies have struggled with brand recognition because they have failed to view corporate governance practice improvements as a part of their global branding efforts. Consider Haier as an example: As the largest home appliances and consumer electronics manufacturer in the world and one of the first Chinese multinational companies, Haier planned to build their brand upon entering the global market in the 1990s and made sizable investments in a branding strategy. However, the price of Haier's white goods was at the lower end compared to its counterparts in North America, Japan, and South Korea. Haier struggled to achieve top-tier global brand rankings until the late 2010s,[4] unlike their Chinese peers, Lenovo and Huawei, who have successfully positioned themselves as price leaders across most product categories and have enjoyed higher brand rankings since the middle 2010s.

Case Study 3.1   Corporate Governance Weaknesses of Haier's Rendanheyi Model

Haier spent ten years designing, experimenting, and implementing the Rendanheyi model, known by the slogan "making everyone a CEO" by dividing the entire organization into semiautonomous microenterprises to encourage superior service-oriented employee performance while promoting the idea of "zero distance" to the customer. The model provides authorization for business, recruiting, and compensation decision-making responsibilities to microenterprise leaders, connects the largest part of an employee's compensation to performance, and creates an entrepreneurial corporate culture, significantly improving the company's net profit of Haier's China operations.

However, Haier was not able to implement the Rendanheyi model in its acquired subsidiaries due to the following weaknesses of the model:

1 ***The model's lack of consideration for other societies' cultures and its inherent inability to appreciate host countries' regulation systems and business practices.*** *Haier's implementation of the Rendanheyi model led to a 25% domestic workforce reduction in 2016. The company acquired its subsidiaries, GE Appliances, from the US in 2016 and Sanyo White Goods from Japan in 2011. In the former case, the model failed due to stringent labor laws prohibiting massive layoffs; in the latter, a disavowal of Japanese social history and understanding of the country's shareholders.*

2 ***Lack of a long-term sustainable strategy.*** *The compensation structure under the Rendanheyi model created conflicts between the microenterprises' desire for short-term profit and Haier's long-term corporate strategy.*

Haier designed and refined their Rendanheyi organizational model in approximately the same amount of time as Toyota took to create their "Lean Manufacturing" model, but so far, Haier has failed to enjoy the same kind of global success. Toyota's Lean Manufacturing model has been widely replicated by global manufacturers and has successfully helped worldwide companies enhance their operational efficiency and save costs, establishing Toyota as a global industry leader for decades while contributing to its consecutive No. 1 Global Auto Brands position.

Haier's Rendanheyi model has successfully improved the company's corporate culture and increased its domestic operations profit, but its limited application slowed its global scaling strategy and prevented the company from maximizing the business value they expected from the model. Also, the company's failure to consider the model's legal and social implications restrained it from being recognized as a good corporate citizen and industry leader in the global marketplace. Although its brand's value has increased since 2018, enabling the company to become a top-tier global brand in 2019, Haier decided to establish the Rendanheyi Silicon Valley Center in Menlo Park, California in 2020 to improve and promote the model and inspire ongoing innovation. The Rendanheyi model will continually improve over time and eventually align with international standards.

Leadership Transfer Challenges – Founder Generation Retirement

In Western countries, it is not difficult to recognize those companies that have nearly or over 100-year histories. Some of those companies have become industry leaders or famous multinationals, such as JP Morgan Chase (founded in 1799), DuPont (founded 1802), and Macy's (founded in 1858), all of which are lucrative businesses managed by professionals. Some are still controlled by small-size founder families, whose members have transferred their businesses in perpetuity, which has enabled their success despite various (and sometimes detrimental) problems.

With PR China's establishment in 1949 and the tumultuous political and economic reforms afterward, Chinese private companies became officially "legal" no earlier than the early 1980s. Most successful Chinese companies are still managed or overseen by the founders' generations, although many of these founders are close to or already at their retirement age. Leadership transfer upon a founder's retirement has become one of the top challenges for many companies. Moreover, the leadership transfer challenges revealed these companies' corporate governance weaknesses. These companies have been searching for solutions by experimenting different approaches over the past two decades. The case study below demonstrates the corporate governance weaknesses and challenges due to the founder's retirement from Wahaha Group, the largest beverage producer in China. The lessons learned by Wahaha Group will hopefully present opportunities to improve their corporate governance practices and develop useful strategies to overcome these challenges.

Case Study 3.2   Wahaha's Corporate Governance Weakness Revealed through Its Leadership Transfer

Hangzhou Wahaha Group (WHH) was founded in 1987 as a local SOE owned by the Hangzhou Shangcheng District. The company has been led by Zong Qinghou since its establishment. In 1996, WHH signed a joint venture agreement with Singapore-based Jinjia Investments Co., a joint holding company formed by Groupe Danone, a French multinational food products company and Peregrine Investment Holdings, a Hong Kong-based investment company. In a WHH joint venture holding structure, foreign partners hold 51% of the stock, and Chinese partners hold 49% (39% by WHH and 10% by employees). With the formation of the joint venture, Zong Qinghou became an important minority shareholder, board chairman, and CEO of the holding company, as well as five additional joint venture companies. The WHH joint venture holding company's board then comprised four members: Zong Qinghou as chairman, two members from Danone, and one from Peregrine. During the 1998 Asian financial crisis, Peregrine collapsed. Groupe Danone confiscated Peregrine's shares in Jinjia Investments Co. and replaced Peregrine's board seat on the WHH board, and as a result, became WHH's majority owner with 51% of the shares.

While Danone owned the majority of WHH's shares, they were interested in remaining a shareholder only without being involved in WHH's operations. Nevertheless, its embedded board presence and financial interest led to frequent clashes between them and Zong Qinghou, the most significant of which occurred in 2007 when both parties warred over a trademark dispute. The following are a few corporate governance weaknesses revealed during the trademark battle as described in a Forbes article at that time:

- *With the WHH JV agreements, Danone agreed not to be involved in JVs' operations as majority owner (of 51% ownership).*
- *Zong Qinghou operated the WHH joint ventures and made important decisions without consent from the board.*
- *Zong Qinghou was able to create many non-JV companies selling WHH JV products.*

> • *Zong Qinghou's family members held critical positions in the WHH Group.*
>
> *These elements accepted WHH JV's corporate governance weaknesses regarding board structure and process, decision-making, compliance, and transactions involving family members, all of which were revealed at the time of the trademark ownership battle. Chinese companies' corporate governance development over the past two decades has brought significant improvements. However, the primary challenge presently facing WHH Group and Zong Qinghou is the company's succession plan regarding Zong Qinghou's retirement.*
>
> *In 2007, Zong Qinghou's only child, Zong Fuli, became president of one of the company's subsidiaries. Contrasted to her father, who was not interested in attracting additional capital to WHH, Zong Fuli was more open-minded so Qinghou began delegating authority to allow his daughter's ascension to CEO. However, an acquisition failure with a Chinese candy company in 2017 has stalled the leadership transfer. In recent interviews with the media, the 76-year-old founder mentioned that preparing for a management succession includes establishing a decision-making structure and the creation of more executive positions in the decision-making process. Zong Qinghou has also commented that the challenges facing the 30-year-old company are a "sickness". In mid-2020, WHH announced its plan for a Hong Kong IPO.*

The WHH's founder's retirement case study represents the challenges many Chinese companies are currently or will soon encounter via generational inheritance or selection. The most important point to ponder from WHH's case is that its founder, Zong Qinghou, after nearly a decade of promoting his daughter to take over the company's leadership, has recognized the importance of building an organizational structure and a feasible decision-making process, as well as a professional management team as salient parts of succession planning. Since Zong Fuli is anticipated to take over the helm of WHH, the newly established structure and succession process will enhance her and WHH's long-term success. Therefore, WHH's journey while seeking a comprehensive succession plan solution has become the impetus of its corporate governance development.

Becoming a listed company requires more compliance and board oversight, including optimizing a board's structure and process. WHH's IPO plan indicates Zong Qinghou's desire for new governance models to cure the company's "sickness", another driver needed for its corporate governance development.[5]

WHH was not the only company going through succession planning challenges due to a founder's retirement. Wangda Group, another well-known

Chinese multinational with business across various sectors, was experiencing the same challenges but differently. In the case of Wangda Group, the founder's only child did not want to take over leadership roles.[6] Founders' mindsets changed during that process, and with the trend for these Chinese companies to converge with the corporate governance practices of their contemporaries in more developed countries, will better prepare corporate governance practices to sustain these companies' competitiveness in the international marketplace. At the same time, some young entrepreneurs' retirements from Chinese companies and transferred company leadership position to partners – such as Huang Zheng's retirement from Pinduoduo and ByteDance's Zhang Yiming's resignation from the CEO role – not only provided pertinent examples of the different succession plans of traditional Chinese entrepreneurs but also indicated the modern mindset of the younger generation Chinese entrepreneurs with consideration of social responsibility and companies' long-term sustainability, which will accelerate the momentum for Chinese companies' corporate governance development in the future.

China's Continuous Regulation Reform and Enhancement of Regulation Enforcement

With the fast growth of Chinese e-commerce and digital businesses over the past few decades, regulators have been trying to correspond with a similar pace of new and various business models. The ultimate goals of these new regulations are to prevent systemic failures, establish an effective monitoring system, prevent fraud and other crimes, and eventually provide continuous improvement guidelines for companies' corporate governance practices.

Like most emerging market countries, the Chinese regulatory system was unfortunately well known for its lack of enforcement mechanisms. Therefore, some companies did not take the new regulations seriously and subsequently paid enormous costs for their neglect. One of the most notable examples is Ant Group's IPO incident that occurred at the end of 2020.

Case Study 3.3   Ant Group IPO Incident

In the summer of 2020, Ant Group (Ant) was on the verge of releasing its highly anticipated IPO – the world's largest with a $312 billion valuation – and was seeking to raise $34.4 billion for dual listings in Shanghai and Hong Kong. Despite the tension between the US and China, many American tier-one investment banks and institutional investors had taken part in this iconic transaction with other global players. Fewer than two days before Ant's shares were to begin trading, China's regulators *suspended Ant's IPO. The news shocked the financial world and left many people speculating about what happened and what the future held.*

Ant (originally "Ant Financial" until June 2020) was launched by Alibaba in 2012 as a microloan solution provider for Chinese small businesses (hence the applicable name "Ant"). In 2012, the thresholds for small and middle enterprises (SMEs) receiving loans from Chinese banks were about $1 million, which disqualified financing possibilities for most Chinese SMEs. Ant filled this need to extend an average loan size of RMB8,000 (about $1,200), with the lowest financed amount available of RMB324 ($50). Ant grew its lending business to individual consumers in 2014. In 2019, the least credit limit offered by Ant was RMB45 ($7).

Because of the vast amount of consumer data generated by small businesses on Alibaba's platform and Alibaba's advanced algorithms, Ant was able to analyze borrowers' profit margins, transaction histories, and affordability, then simultaneously determine a borrower's finance terms, such as loan amounts, interest rates, and payback periods. The quick process enabled Ant's microloan business to operate with a default rate of only 1% (much lower than the worldwide average of 3.9% in 2018, according to S&P Global Ratings). In contrast to the complicated application process and documentation required for receiving traditional bank loans, Ant offered a user-friendly financing process by offering customers the ability to apply via a smartphone and receive cash if their applications were approved. The entire process took roughly three minutes, and no personal bankers were involved. (Of interest, Ant also sold insurance, investment products, and financial technology to enterprises.)

To pave the way for its IPO, Ant significantly expanded its international business in 2019 by acquiring the London-based payment company, WorldFirst, to establish a European foothold, invested aggressively in Asian and South American countries, and established payment channels with 35,000 merchants in the US. The large transaction volume from Alibaba's e-commerce platforms (Taobao and Tmall), combined with the growth of overseas consumer activities driven by Chinese tourists and students and the wide acceptance of Alipay by overseas merchants, made Ant the largest fintech in the world and precipitated its Asian IPO in January 2020.

In early November 2020, Chinese regulators halted Ant's IPO. In late December, regulators ordered Ant to return to its roots as a payment service provider and revamp its insurance and money management businesses, which were both in need of regulatory compliance. Moreover, regulators mandated Ant improve its corporate governance procedures due to Ant's proclivities to "cut corners" that allowed the company to skirt regulation compliance, culminating in a weakened company board that

> *impaired its functions and responsibilities. Regulators also launched an antitrust investigation into Alibaba, which owned one-third of Ant Group.*
>
> *Ant purposely positioned itself as a technology company for higher IPO valuation due to technology companies' having higher price-earnings (PE) ratios than finance companies. According to PE ratios of Chinese main banks' stock indexes, Ant's valuation would only be $33 billion as a finance company vs. $312 billion as if valued as a technology company before its 2020 IPO application, based on the same reported net assets.*
>
> *In February 2021, Ant agreed to restructure as a financial holding company directly under the auspices of China's central bank. At the time of this writing, Ant was ordered by Chinese regulators to take the first step of the restructuring plan by setting up a consumer finance company to take over its consumer credit business.[7] The consumer finance company is a joint venture with six other shareholders, including two state-owned financial institutions and one of China's largest distressed assets management firms. Setting up the new company was deliberately designed to cease Ant's current consumer lending models and establish a new consumer finance business under regulatory supervision.*

The timing of the suspension was dramatic, but regulatory reforms that led to the decision have been decades in the making. Let us take a brief look at the regulations that affected Ant Group's IPO suspension.

Online Payment and Mobile Payment

While Ant has been the largest fintech in the world since early 2019, the company has tried to position itself as a technology company to obtain higher valuation status, as well as to minimize the regulatory pressure from China's new online and mobile payments regulations from the following:

- The Measures for the Administration of Online Payment Business of Non-Bank Payment Institutions, issued by the People's Bank of China (PBOC) in 2016,[8] requires non-bank payment platforms to standardize the processes for client registration, creditworthiness evaluation, risk management implementation, client data usage notifications, and data privacy protection.
- In 2018, the PBOC established the Online Settlement Platform for Non-Bank Payment Institutions as a centralized clearinghouse. All mobile payment transactions must be settled at the centralized clearinghouse.
- China's new rules for financial holding companies issued in September 2019 and effective November 1, 2019, require large companies possessing two or more financial businesses with 85% or higher debt-to-asset ratios to register

with authorities and secure at least RMB5 billion ($731 million) for their financial businesses (e.g., online payment and lending).[9]

After suspending Ant's IPO, China's regulators determined that Ant was not a technology company.

Antitrust Laws

Immediately after rescinding Ant's IPO, the State Administration for Market Regulation drafted a series of new antitrust laws in November to stop anti-competitive practices of internet-based businesses while also protecting consumers. The new anti-monopoly rules applied to China's internet giants Alibaba, Tencent, Pinduoduo, JD.com, and Meituan. Although these large companies have been praised during the COVID-19 pandemic for minimizing the disruption to Chinese society, the use of an exclusivity agreement between one of Alibaba's e-commerce platforms and the food delivery service company Meituan transgressed these new antitrust laws, prompting regulators to forcefully respond. The Chinese government started its investigation of Alibaba because of the company's suspected monopolistic conduct in December 2020 and issued a record-high fine of $2.8 billion for violating antitrust laws in April 2021. By enforcing these laws, the Chinese government intervened in a timely way and prevented other Chinese multinationals from operating outside the law.

These were some of the reforms that were front and center resulting in Ant's suspended IPO. Perhaps more important than the story behind Ant's IPO suspension is to understand the underlying purpose of the antitrust law enforcement in two primary aspects.

Narrowing the antitrust enforcement gap between China and the US. Due to a huge consumer market and a burgeoning middle class over the past few decades, Chinese multinationals have learned to grow their domestic companies before expanding into the international marketplace, leveraging the domestic market for further global growth. The Chinese regulators have incurred suspicion from the global business community for allowing unfettered growth of Chinese companies at home due to the country's flexible regulation system. With this suspension, China has shown its willingness to enforce its antitrust laws. This mirrors what we are seeing in the US, as big tech companies such as Google, Facebook, and Amazon face greater scrutiny and antitrust investigations.

Improving the quality of China's economic environment. China's antitrust enforcement is sure to impact other Chinese internet giants such as Tencent, Meituan, and JD.com and may possibly damage China's economy and investors' interest and faith in Chinese companies for the time being. However, over the long term, a well-regulated economic environment is essential, especially as China's economy transitions to the digital era and plays a greater role in the global economy. Since China suspended Ant's IPO and penalized Alibaba's monopolistic behaviors to demonstrate its commitment to higher regulatory standards, it may have come just in time not only to prevent systemic and credit risks, but also to sustain and strengthen Chinese companies and the country's entire economy.

Chinese Government's Political Reforms

In Chapter 1, I choose Peter Alexis Gourevitch and James J, Shinn's corporate governance definitions to define China's corporate governance – "Corporate Governance is about power and responsibility", which I believe best implies the close relationship between China's corporate governance evolution and its political system development.

Some scholars believe that China is moving toward a "politicized corporate governance" system.[10] Without judging and debating whether a country's corporate governance regulations have automatic ties to its political policies and further elaborating how these connections may be different due to a country's political system, for the purpose of this book, I thought it will be helpful to understand some recent political reforms in China that have affected and will further influence China's corporate governance development in the future.

Anti-corruption Reform

The People's Republic of China's Supervision Law issued on March 20, 2018 established the Communist Party's Central Commission for Discipline Inspection (CCDI), a political institution and the Party's primary investigative and disciplinary body. The new Supervision Law defined corruption as a duty-related violation that includes "bribery, abuse of power, neglect of duty, power rent-seeking, funneling, practice of favoritism and falsification, and waste of state assets". CCDI is assigned to all investigations, and criminal offense-related corruption cases will be transferred to traditional legal institutions after a CCDI's investigation.[11]

China's anti-corruption reform will have a direct impact on Chinese SOEs' corporate governance practice in a few aspects: enforce legal compliance and accountability; enhance the Party Committees' monitoring function including a type of whistleblower utility on behalf of the Party; prevent wrongdoing from SOEs' directors and executives assigned by government authorities; eliminate undesirable related-party transactions; and ensure CSR including ideological education. In addition to the four basic corporate governance functions (accountability, monitoring and supervising, strategy, and policy making) defined by Professor Bob Tricker,[12] these elements will effectively enhance Chinese SOEs' corporate governance functions and improve transparency and reduce minority shareholders' risks from related transactions, and more importantly, compensate for the "weakness" of SOEs' board that does not have authority to nominate company executives and decide executives' compensation.

Although there are debates regarding the vagueness of the lines between political anti-corruption and regulation enforcement due to the involvement of the corporate structure as channels for the Party's anti-corruption investigation, and the potential loss of investors if corruption cases eventually become criminal prosecutions,[13] research data has already proved significant and positive responses on stock market performance due to China's anti-corruption work.[14]

Formalizing Party Committee's Corporate Governance Roles in Chinese SOEs

The guiding opinions jointly issued by the Central Committee of the Communist Party of China and the State Council on Deepening the Reform of SOEs in 2015 detailed SOEs' obligations to establish a Party Committee and the corporate governance roles of the Party Committee. Party Committee roles in Chinese companies have been considered opaque and therefore been one of the top concerns of global investors. The anti-corruption reforms that officially formalized the assigned corporate governance oversight role by Party Committee authorities will help clarify and adjust the expectations and procedures of the Party Committee, corporations, and investors.

In addition, with China's 2018 updated Corporate Governance Code that requires Party Committees for all listed companies, the number of Chinese companies which have adopted Party Committee's governance involvement according to the company's bylaws and organizational charter amendments has been increasing according to statistics in 2021.[15]

Although Party Committee's roles in privately held listed companies are not as clear as in SOEs, the trend indicates that their roles will focus on monitoring and ensuring regulatory compliance and private businesses' assistance with anti-corruption reform and related investigations, if applicable. Party Committees' roles at the moment are not involved in privately held listed companies' decision-making process.[16] Will Party Committees' roles evolve in the future? The answers will be revealed in the coming decades.

Major International Drivers

The globalization process over the past few decades significantly improved worldwide economic exchange but created complicated commercial relationships between some countries and the rest of the world. With Chinese companies increasingly participating in global business activities, the demands for these companies' corporate governance practices from the rest of the world are rising too. The following are two prominent external drivers that will likely have quick and significant influences due to their persuasive impact on Chinese companies.

US Scrutiny of US-Listed Chinese Companies

Perhaps April 2020 was the darkest month for US-listed Chinese companies. Less than one week after Luckin Coffee admitted to its $30 million financial scandals, two other Chinese companies were reported for inflating sales revenue figures – the online education company, Tomorrow Advancing Life (TAL) Education Group, who admitted to employee misconduct, and the video streaming company, iQIYI, who denied accusations of two activist short sellers after an internal review was performed. Regardless of the investigative outcomes of these incidents, the coincidence of all three having occurred in such a short period troubled global investors who already had serious doubts regarding Chinese companies' corporate governance practices. The April incidents exceeded the US stock market's tolerance limit, leading to consequential scrutiny of US-listed Chinese companies in the following months. US stock exchange regulator then initiated a series of legal and regulatory changes targeting China-based, US-listed companies. The following are a few highlights and consequences for these Chinese companies.

Tightening Reporting and Disclosure Requirements

On April 21, 2020, in a joint statement by the US SEC and PCAOB, directors of both organizations addressed their concerns regarding the reporting and disclosure quality of US-listed companies operating in emerging markets, particularly in China, due to the SEC and the PCAOB's inability to enforce US disclosure standards for listed companies. The directors also urged that the risks of these US-listed emerging market companies should be carefully evaluated and disclosed to investors. On May 18, 2020, Nasdaq offered three proposals to the SEC suggesting additional listing criteria for companies operating in countries with regulations restricting US regulators' access to company information. China is one of these countries. Upon approval of these three proposals, Nasdaq will evaluate new listing applications based on additional criteria or improved measurements of applicant companies' financial numbers, due-diligence efforts, and organizational structures.

The increasing pressure from the US caused Chinese companies' "homecoming wave" in 2020. Game developer NetEase and online retailer JD.com entered secondary listings in Hong Kong in 2020, with more companies to follow. In 2021, Sina Corporation, one of the first Chinese internet IPO companies in the US since 2000, led fellow companies to delist their companies' stocks from the US stock market and "go private."[17]

Holding Foreign Companies Accountable Act (HFCA Act)

On May 20, 2020, the US Senate passed the Holding Foreign Companies Accountable Act (HFCA Act) as an amendment to the Sarbanes-Oxley Act of

2002 Act (SOX Act). According to the amendment, certain US-listed companies are required to certify that those companies are either not owned or controlled by a foreign government or permit the PCAOB to inspect these companies' audit firms for three consecutive years. The failure to meet either one of these two requirements disqualifies a company from trading its securities at any securities exchanges within the SEC's jurisdiction and will result in delisting from US stock markets. On June 4, 2020, the US White House issued a presidential memorandum that recommended US financial markets participants to react accordingly should Chinese companies fail to meet transparency and accountability requirements of US regulations.

The HFCA Act and the White House's enforcement memo are obviously targeting the stalemate that US and Chinese regulators are encountering regarding the PCAOB's lack of access to Chinese companies' information. As many of the US-listed Chinese companies are SOEs in energy, transportation, communication, and pharmaceutical industries, Chinese securities law has been prohibiting any documents and materials of Chinese companies from being disclosed overseas, which has stymied China-based US public accounting firms from obtaining audits of overseas securities, as these audits may involve sensitive information. Compliance with the HFCA Act will force Chinese companies to violate Chinese securities law. As a result, the HFCA Act will cause significant numbers of Chinese companies to be delisted from the US stock markets. As this chapter is being written, three Chinese state-owned telecommunications companies, China Mobile Ltd., China Unicom, and China Telecom Corp, are expecting to be delisted from the NYSE after their appeals were rejected by the NYSE due to national security consideration.[18]

New Disclosure Requirements for Chinese Companies' IPOs in the US

On July 30, 2021, the US SEC publicly announced its plan of new disclosure requirements for Chinese companies' IPOs in the US. The new requirements include a registration statement for Chinese VIEs to provide detailed information regarding the relationship between a shell company and a China-based company, and the possible uncertainty of the impact on the validity of a contractual arrangement resulting from future Chinese government action (please see details regarding VIEs operation and risks in Chapter 2); the proof of Chinese authorities' permission for overseas IPOs; and the possibility of not being able to provide audited documents required by PCAOB per the May 20, 2020, SOX amendment (which could lead to US stock exchange delisting).[19] On August 17, 2021, the US SEC chairman publicly emphasized the mandate by declaring "full and fair disclosure of what US investors are investing in is actually a shell company in the Cayman Islands or another part of the world" in reaction to Chinese regulators recent regulation reform that targets tech and after-school tutoring companies.[20]

Many Chinese companies, led by Tencent-backed and popular podcast app Ximalaya, Ant-backed, bike-sharing platform Hello, Taobao-backed media and data cloud service platform Qiniu, and many other companies are still seeking IPOs in the US stock market for various reasons. Until this time, only Chinese companies who do not use VIE structures (VIE is required by SEC for full disclosure) and do not manage sensitive data (companies dealing with sensitive data are not allowed by Beijing to list overseas) have an opportunity to seek a US IPO. These newcomers will be compelled to receive official approval from Chinese regulators upon improving their reporting and disclosure standards in order to comply with US regulations.

The Political Tussle between the US and China

The geopolitical tussle (including "economic decoupling") between the US and China since the start of the current US–China trade war has been exacerbated by the HFCA Act, which explicitly pushed the political battle to the US stock market. As a result, a series of US governmental actions following the HFCA Act extend the geopolitical contest to global financial markets. Without digging too deeply into politics, I hope the highlights below help establish some understanding and consideration.

Political Intention of the HFCA Acts

US regulatory scrutiny of Chinese companies' reporting and disclosure quality inevitably contain political involvement. Considering the HFCA as an example, in addition to tightening securities regulation compliance, the Act requires additional information to be inspected by PCAOB, including the names of Chinese Communist Party members who serve on a Chinese company's board of directors or its affiliated entities, and a company's legal documents and texts that contain the organizational structure regarding the Party's involvement in a company. These requirements explicitly crossed the line separating economic from political policies.

US Political Involvement in the Global Financial Market

Paralleling the HFCA Act and beginning in May 2020, a series of interactions between the White House and SEC occurred that escalated political involvement in financial markets: On May 4, the SEC formed the Staff Roundtable on Emerging Markets to examine the risks of investing in emerging markets (including China); on May 12, 2020, the US government publicly pressured the federal retirement funds administrator to cancel its investment plan in Chinese stocks[21]; on July 24, 2020, the President's Working Group on Financial Markets program was issued to protect US investors from significant risks from Chinese companies and pressed the SEC to take action to promote and enhance risk disclosure of investment in China; on August 10, 2020, the SEC issued its Statement on SEC Response to the Report of the President's Working Group on Financial Markets[22]; in November 2020, a presidential executive order was issued to reduce US investments in certain Chinese companies due to national emergency considerations; and on January 11, 2021,[23] a blacklist naming 44 Chinese entities was established.[24] This list is likely to be growing in number since then.

In addition to pressuring the NYSE to delist certain Chinese companies, the blacklist has also impelled global index providers to expel Chinese companies from their indices. As the time this book is being written, FTSE Russell and S&P Dow Jones Indices have removed dozens of Chinese companies (including Semiconductor Manufacturing International Corp.), while Hangzhou Hikvision Digital Technology Co. was removed from FTSE Russell and Luokung Technology Corp. was removed from S&P. More similar activity to include a broader range of industries is anticipated in the near future.[25]

US–China Technology Competition[26]

The US–China political contest is also reflected by the two nations' technology competition that was initiated in the early 2010s, when Chinese Huawei and ZTE were classified as untrustworthy due to potential security threats to US national security. The tension was escalated over the years until the US' 2021 Secure Equipment Act that aimed to prevent Huawei and its Chinese peers from obtaining new equipment licenses from the US government in 2022, which also included $1.9 billion USD toward removal of Huawei's equipment from US networks.

US–China technology competition has caused Huawei undoubtable economic suffering, global brand value deterioration, and forced the company to diversify its business lines with further a commitment to embark on chipmaking its own technology development. Consequently, serious questions have been raised regarding the cost and efficacy of the US government's effort due to broad usage of Chinese-made telecommunication equipment across Department of Defense facilities and US commercial airlines. Moreover, concerns are currently being raised about the US lagging behind China in the race toward 5G deployment.[27] Has the US achieved its intended goals of banning Huawei? The answer is two-fold.

Initially, Huawei being banned by the US has served as a warning call for China and other Chinese companies regarding the nation's technology self-reliance. In their book, *Innovation from Emerging Markets: From Copycats to*

Leaders (2021), Professor Casanova and Professor Miroux discussed Chinese companies' significant investment in technology innovation over the past decade. Since the early 2000s, Huawei has gained empathy and support from many Chinese companies and further stirred increasing nationalism in Chinese business and the public. Secondly, China's 14th Five-Year Plan made technology self-sufficiencyresi one of its development priorities. The sum of these two elements will enhance Chinese companies' sensitivity regarding technology development and IP protection. Details regarding China's current Five-Year plan will be discussed in a later chapter of this book.

Therefore, the tightening scrutiny that Chinese companies are facing at US stock exchanges and technology challenges they have to overcome to compete with their global peers are parts of these two countries' ongoing political tussle. In the long term, these struggles will accelerate the development of China's regulation system and enhance technology self-reliance of the country and the Chinese companies.

Should these domestic and international drivers perform well, Chinese companies' corporate governance practices will evolve in the coming years and hopefully become more transparent and compliant with international standards. However, due to the unique features of Chinese companies' corporate governance practices discussed in earlier chapters, we should also expect and honor China's corporate governance development to have its own path instead of following any models from more developed countries. With the rise of emerging markets and the different economic environments within emerging markets countries, the trend of developing suitable economic growth models and governance practice models for emerging markets is rising too. Further research and debate regarding the geopolitical impact on multinationals' corporate governance development need to be based on three elements: political policy changes in the home country (e.g., China's political policies directly affect the Party's roles in Chinese companies); political policy changes in host countries (e.g., the US regulatory scrutiny of US-listed Chinese companies); and the changing geopolitical landscape in the global market. For the time being, the increasing compliance requirements of both countries, and the trend to enhance corporate governance functions and improve transparency from all these economic and political reforms, are powerful drivers for Chinese companies to improve their corporate governance development in the decades to come.

Some Westerners describe their experiences while working with Chinese companies as "navigating in the dark". After three years of research, I believe the so-called darkness mainly comes from a lack of understanding of Chinese companies' corporate governance structures, decision-making processes, and business practices, while also appreciating the layer of opaqueness that shrouds the Party's roles in Chinese companies. These are the root causes of many corporate governance practice differences in Chinese companies compared to their counterparts in advanced countries. Although the realities and research confirm that the Party's roles won't fade under China's current political system, their roles in a company may become better defined and transparent along with China's continuous regulation and political reform. I hope the discussion in this book will shed some light for you to step out from the "darkness".

Takeaways

* **Three common features** of Chinese companies' corporate governance practice.
* **The demand for Chinese companies to overcome their global growth hurdles and the evolving challenges** in domestic and international markets will drive those companies' corporate governance improvement.
* Some **Chinese political policy reforms interface with China's corporate governance regulation development,** causing improvements in defining and documenting the Party's roles in Chinese companies.
* **Global partners' political policy changes and global financial market landscape changes** are exerting powerful influences on China's corporate governance development.

Notes

1 Boardroom&Beyond podcast interview with Christine Raynaud in October 2020. https://boardroomandbeyond.com/what-international-skills-make-future-business-leaders-at-board-level/
2 B. Gidwani, *"The Link between Brand Value and Sustainability"*, October 2013, The Conference Board. https://brandfinance.com/wp-content/uploads/1/the_link_between_brand_value_and_sustainability.pdf
3 Lourdes Casanova and Anne Miroux, "Emerging Markets Multinationals Report (EMR)", 2018–2020, Emerging Markets Institute, Johnson School of Management, Cornell University. www.johnson.cornell.edu/emerging-markets-institute/research/emerging-markets-report/
4 Brand Finance. *Global 500 Ranking.* https://brandirectory.com/rankings/global/2018/table
5 Zhang Xia, "Food and Beverage Producer Hangzhou Wahaha Considers Going Public, Says its Chairman," Yicai Global, 2017, May 3, 2021. www.yicaiglobal.com/news/food-and-beverage-producer-hangzhou-wahaha-considers-going-public-says-its-chairman
6 Allen Young, "Does China Face a Family-Owned Business Succession Crisis," *CKGSB*, May 23, 2018. https://english.ckgsb.edu.cn/knowledges/china-family-firms-face-business-succession-crisis/
7 Cheng Leng, "China's Ant Group to Restructure under Central Bank Agreement," Reuters, 2021, May 8, 2021. www.reuters.com/business/view-chinas-ant-group-restructure-under-central-bank-agreement-2021-04-12/
8 Zoe Liu, "The Great Leap Forward: China's Digital Payment System (Part II)",. August 21, 2018. www.ccpwatch.org/single-post/2018/08/21/the-great-leap-forward-chinas-digital-payment-system-part-ii

9   Stella Yifan Xie, "China's New Financial Rules to Cover Jack Ma's Ant Group", September 13, 2021. www.wsj.com/articles/chinas-new-financial-rules-to-cover-jack-mas-ant-group-11600013259

10 Tami Groswald Ozery, "Illiberal Governance and the Rise of China's Public Firms: An Oxymoron or China's Greatest Triumph?" *SSRN*, Page 52, June 24, 2021. https://papers.ssrn.com/sol3/papers.cfm?abstract_id=3616513

11 http://www.npc.gov.cn/npc/xinwen/2018-03/21/content_2052362.htm   [https://perma.cc/ZS95-SVLM]

12 Corporate Governance (4th ed.) Pages 179–180.

13 Tami Groswald Ozery, "Illiberal Governance and the Rise of China's Public Firms: An Oxymoron or China's Greatest Triumph?" *SSRN*, Page 63, June 24, 2021. https://papers.ssrn.com/sol3/papers.cfm?abstract_id=3616513

14 Ding Haoyuan, et al., "Equilibrium Consequences of Corruption on Firms: Evidence from China's Anti-Corruption Campaign," Working Paper No. 26656, *National Bureau of Economic Research*, January 2020. www.nber.org/system/files/working_papers/w26656/w26656.pdf

15 Lauren Yu-Hsin Lin and Curtis J. Milhaupt, "Party Building or Noisy Signaling? The Contours of Political Conformity in Chinese Corporate Governance," *SSRN*, January 27, 2020. https://papers.ssrn.com/sol3/papers.cfm?abstract_id=3510342

16 *"The CCP Opinions on Strengthening the United Front Work of the Private Economy in a New Era"*, The State Council, P.R. China, September 15, 2020. www.gov.cn/zhengce/2020-09/15/content_5543685.htm

17 Megan Cattel, "Sina Goes Private after 21 years on Nasdaq," SupChina, May 9, 2021, June 3, 2021. https://supchina.com/2021/03/24/sina-goes-private-after-21-years-on-nasdaq/

18 Ross Kerber, "Three Chinese Telecom Companies to Be Delisted by NYSE," Reuters, 2021, May 8, 2021. www.reuters.com/business/media-telecom/three-chinese-telecom-companies-be-delisted-by-nyse-2021-05-07/

19 Paul Kiernan, "SEC to Set New Disclosure Requirements for Chinese Company IPOs," *Wall Street Journal*, July 30, 2021. www.wsj.com/articles/sec-to-set-new-disclosure-requirements-for-chinese-company-ipos-11627651546?page=1

20 Tang Ziyi, "US Stocks Regulator Pauses IPOs of Shell Companies Used by Chinese firms", Caixin Global, August 17, 2021. www.caixinglobal.com/2021-08-17/us-stocks-regulator-pauses-ipos-of-shell-companies-used-by-chinese-firms-101756439.html

21 Anne Tergesen, "Trump Administration Tells Federal Retirement Plan to Avoid Chinese Stock", WSJ, May 12, 2020. www.wsj.com/articles/trump-administration-tells-federal-retirement-plan-to-avoid-chinese-stocks-11589322094

22 "President's Working Group on Financial Market: Report on Protecting United States Investors from Significant Risks from Chinese Companies," July 24, 2020. https://home.treasury.gov/system/files/136/PWG-Report-on-Protecting-United-States-Investors-from-Significant-Risks-from-Chinese-Companies.pdf

23 Tami Groswald Ozery, "Illiberal Governance and the Rise of China's Public Firms: An Oxymoron or China's Greatest Triumph?" *SSRN*, Pages 79–80, June 24, 2021. https://papers.ssrn.com/sol3/papers.cfm?abstract_id=3616513

24 Jodi Xu Klein, and Robert Delaney, "US adds nice Chinese firms, including Xiaomi, to military blacklist", South China Morning Post, January 15, 2021. https://www.scmp.com/news/china/article/3117814/us-adds-chinese-oil-giant-chinese-national-overseas-oil-corporation

25 Samuel Shen, Tom Westbrook, and Sanjana Shivdas, "S&P Dow Jones Indices and FTSE Russell dump dozens of Chinese Companies", The Standard, July 9, 2021.

www.thestandard.com.hk/breaking-news/section/2/176413/S&P-Dow-Jones-Indi
ces-and-FTSE-Russell-dump-dozens-of-Chinese-companies

26 Congressional Research Service, January 2022, "U.S. Restrictions on Huawei
Technologies: National Security, Foreign Policy, and Economic Interests", www.eve
rycrsreport.com/files/2022-01-05_R47012_65c5c54827b8fef912a19079f10e144b3
b88d009.pdf

27 Valerie Hernandez, September 2022, "Have the Huawei Bans Achieved the US'
Intended goals?" https://internationalbanker.com/technology/have-the-huawei-bans-
achieved-the-us-intended-goals/

Part II

ESG in Action

Chapter 4

The Rise of the ESG Movement in China

In this chapter, I review

- ESG Adoption in China
  MSCI China ESG rating scores
  E, S, and G factors in the Chinese context

- Chinese ESG Rating Systems
  Beautiful China ESG 100 Index
  ESG rating system in the Chinese context

- ESG Revolution in China
  ESG regulation reforms with a different approach
  Green finance transformation and collaboration with international
    organizations
  New carbon trading market and energy spot trading platform

ESG, as the measurement and reporting system of sustainable development, has been integrated into business strategy and practice since the early 1990s. Since then, international organizations, regulators, and companies have been taking action to encourage, guide, and implement ESG adoption.

International organizations have issued different sets of frameworks and standards for investors and corporations to provide guidance on sustainability reporting to measure and analyze corporate ESG performance. The three most notable standards are the Global Reporting Initiative (GRI) issued in 1997, the Sustainability Accounting Standards Board (SASB), which commenced in 2011, and Task Force on Climate-related Financial Disclosures (TCFD) released in 2017. Many countries have also released their own guidelines and regulations accordingly. With an increasing amount of ESG discussion in the global business world today, more regulations are coming soon. An increasing number of businesses are working on integrating ESG factors into their business strategy and operation.

DOI: 10.4324/9781003302919-7

ESG integration was accelerated in 2020, driven by the COVID-19 pandemic, the Black Lives Matter movement, and worldwide wildfires. Moreover, global supply chain disruption also raised worldwide concerns regarding health and safety, diversity and inclusion, climate change, and business purpose. At the same time, the number of ESG investors has been growing fast over the past decades. Since the United Nations launched its "Principles for Responsible Investment" (PRI) in 2006, being a PRI signatory has been widely recognized as a requirement for obtaining the status of a responsible investment company, as confirmed by the dramatic increase in the number of PRI signatories – from 63 in 2006[1] to 4,900 firms as of March 2022,[2] with the total amount of assets under management (AUM) increasing from $6.5 trillion to $121 trillion in the same period of time. The top ten asset management firms worldwide are PRI signatories with a combined AUM of over $30 trillion.

However, due to the broad range of E, S, and G factors, a lack of unified ESG implementation and measurement frameworks, and the complexity of ESG adoption within particular business contexts, the progress of corporate ESG adoption is still the concern of the global business community as of today. For a long time, ESG was focused on businesses' reputations and was thus managed by companies' public relations or marketing departments. Although the direct correlation between ESG performance and company financial performance is still being studied, a 2018 KPMG research report shows that poor ESG performance exposes companies to environmental, legal, and reputational risks that impact their financial returns.[3] Because of worldwide ecological, economic, and demographic changes, ESG-related matters such as climate change, workplace diversity, executive compensation, ESG adoption is no longer optional but part of business strategy.

How did Chinese companies adopt ESG? What is the status of the ESG movement in China then?

ESG Adoption in China

When the worldwide ESG movement emerged in the early 2000s, most Chinese businesses had already integrated CSR into their business strategy and were well aware of environmental regulatory compliance. The rise of China's middle class also gave a boost to CSR and ESG, as those citizens became more cognizant of their societal position and demanded better living conditions, safer products, and a healthier environment. This middle-class pressure also led to changes in corporate behavior. As a result, Chinese companies – and the government – have been increasingly required to ensure the safety and quality of commercial products, while also having to respond to public outcry over environmental destruction and pollution.

MSCI China ESG Rating Scores

Owned by MSCI Inc., a leading American finance company and global provider of equity, fixed income, hedge fund, and stock market indexes, MSCI ESG Indexes' broad international coverage makes it the most popular tool for global institutional investors with international portfolios. Overseas-listed Chinese companies have participated in MSCI's ESG rating system since 2015, followed by companies listed on China's mainland stock exchanges Shanghai Stock Exchange (SSE) and Shenzhen Stock Exchange (SZSE).

MSCI's "Corporate Governance in China" report issued in September 2017 laid a framework for future Chinese ESG evaluation research. The 2017 report summarizes Chinese corporate governance practices through a global investor's lens. The report highlights three fundamental realities of Chinese corporate governance – VIE structure,[4] state involvement, and controlling ownership. This report points out the VIE structure's legal uncertainty and unequal voting power risk. It reveals the shallow corporate governance scores that MSCI gave leading Chinese companies with VIE structures, like Alibaba and JD.com. The report then reviews a significant percentage of Chinese SOEs, lists the corporate governance weaknesses of SOEs, and details China's incremental SOE reforms. The report also documents the various controlling ownership structures of Chinese companies and corresponding corporate governance risks. It concludes that Chinese companies' corporate governance scores cluster around the median of emerging markets (EM) peers and VIEs, while SOEs have obvious governance risks.

The MSCI China ESG Index was launched in March 2018. In June 2018, when China's A-shares officially became part of the MSCI EM Index and MSCI Global Index, around 200 A-share listed companies have been evaluated by MSCI's rating system. The number of Chinese companies participating in MSCI's evaluation has increased from 152 in 2017 to 717 in 2022, displaying consistently improved ESG rating scores among the top ten weighted constituents in the Index (see Table 4.1). The MSCI ESG rating system builds and maintains companies' positions and reputations. Chinese companies participating in the ESG evaluation are working on improving their scores because they understand that higher ESG scores are welcomed by global investors.

Viewing ESG Factors within the Chinese Context

Without further investigation regarding precisely how ESG was initiated by the Chinese government and companies, it's fair to say that the government and those businesses have been seriously engaged in the global ESG movement over the past decade, with different approaches to embrace E, S, and G factors.

Table 4.1 ESG Performance Trends of Top Ten Weighted Constituents of MSCI China ESG Leader Index

Rank	Issuer	Sector	2021 Portfolio Weight	2016	2017	2018	2019	2020	2021
1	Tencent Holdings LI (CN)	Communication Services	23.34%		BBB	BBB	BBB	BBB	BBB
2	Alibaba GRP HLDG (HK)	Consumer Discretionary	17.92%		B	BB	BBB	BB	BBB
3	Meituan B	Consumer Discretionary	8.39%				AA	A	AA
4	China Construction BK H	Financials	5.35%	BB	BB	BB	BBB	A	A
5	Baidu (HK)	Communication Services	3.50%				CCC	BB	BBB
6	NETEASE	Communication Services	3.15%			B	BBB	BBB	A
7	BYD CO H	Consumer Discretionary	2.73%			A	BBB	BB	BBB
8	Wuxi Biologics	Healthcare	2.72%			A	A	AA	A
9	China Merchants Bank H	Financials	2.16%	BBB	BBB	BBB	BBB	BBB	A
10	LI Auto A ADR	Consumer Discretionary	1.73%	n/a	n/a	n/a	n/a	n/a	n/a

Source: Author's based on data from MSCI data on June 30, 2022, retrieved on July 9, 2022.
Note: MSCI China had 717 companies, and MSCI China ESG Leader Index had 166 constituents as of June 30, 2022 (MSCI, "MSCI China ESG Leaders Index (USD)", June 30, 2022. www.msci.com/documents/10199/78514cc5-a16d-493a-9774-af1012aa0420).

"E" is heavily regulated now due to the Chinese government's commitment to carbon neutrality by 2060, which will be a major driver in the adoption of ESG practices in China over the coming years. In addition to the climate change urgency and severe pollution issues, energy transformation has received great attention in China. Chinese environmental protection laws started in the early 1970s[5] and have been developing since the middle 2010s.[6] With the emergence of the climate change battle over the past several years, China is one of the pioneering countries that have mandated environmental factors disclosure by enacting regulation reform in 2021, while also encouraging the disclosure of social factors (details of China's ESG regulation reform will be discussed later in this chapter). Further regulatory reforms focusing on "E" factors to encourage and guide energy transformation are coming.

"S" is part of Chinese companies' DNA, stressing the concept of "owned by the people", revealing the dominant role of Chinese SOEs and their intimate nature of exercising social responsibilities on behalf of the government. However, there are many social issues raised that Chinese companies have needed to confront in recent years, such as labor law consideration, workplace safety and work-related injury compensation, and the relationship with labor unions of those companies' overseas operations (details will be explained with SinoHydro-Ghana Bui Dam Hydroelectricity Project case study in a later chapter of this book). The recent improvement in Chinese labor protection laws has addressed some of those "S"-related issues, such as gender equality and Chinese employee legal rights protection. During the worldwide pandemic, some Chinese companies followed a new norm and established a hybrid working model that allows employees to work from home for certain days of their choice. While China's 14th Five-Year Plan has been focusing on improving people's livelihoods, the continuing ESG revolution, and diversity and inclusivity matters, most of those explicit "S"-related issues have been addressed in some form and will be measured by prevailing international standards toward further improvement.

The importance of "G" needs to be emphasized to ensure the success of ESG integration and Chinese companies' further growth in the global market. With the Chinese government's commitment to building a high-standard regulation system, many regulatory reforms have enhanced China's corporate governance (G) development infrastructure, such as antitrust law enforcement, intellectual property (IP) protection laws, and shareholder interest protection (I will discuss details in Chapter 7). However, compared to "E" and "S" factors, the direct impact of "G" on society and company/individual is not explicit, and the measurement of "G" is difficult to be quantified. And more importantly, "G" is highly influenced by many other societal factors as discussed in the early chapters of this book. However, the importance of "G" in the success of ESG implementation should always be noted and emphasized.

At the same time, it's worth mentioning that the focus of E, S, and G factors in China today are not much different from more developed countries mainly due to the urgency for adopting behavioral changes to tackle environmental degradation, climate change, and humanity. However, regardless of the prioritization differences of E, S, and G factors in the global ESG movement, the effectiveness and high quality of "G" are core elements of ESG implementation during any given stage in China and elsewhere.

Chinese ESG Evaluation Systems and Future Development

China's self-developed ESG rating systems are still in their infancy. However, Chinese firms' continuous efforts toward exploring different ESG models to align with global ESG standards are auspicious signs. As the disruption caused by the COVID-19 pandemic opened opportunities for ingenuity and creativity, those same disruptions may uncover unseen possibilities with ESG evaluation development as well.

In addition, it's worth stating the influential effort on future ESG rating system development from some notable non-government organizations, as the impact from those organizations indicates the broad acknowledgment and acceptance of ESG integration in Chinese society.

Chinese ESG Rating Systems

Chinese ESG evaluation research started in the middle 2010s following the development of global ESG ratings. The most elemental ESG evaluation system in China is "Beautiful China ESG 100 Index", which was launched jointly in August 2019 by the International Institute of Green Finance (IIGF) Institute at the Central University of Finance and Economics a key Chinese research university under direct administration of China's central government authority, and Sina Finance, a media platform providing global financial market coverage and commentary in Chinese. This index comprises the top 100 ESG performers from China's stock markets (35 companies from the SSE, 42 companies from the SZSE, and 23 companies from the HKEX). Beautiful China ESG 100 Index's ESG rating system was developed solely by IIGF and considers Chinese characteristics including China's economic development status and industrial distribution and economic and environmental regulation development stages while incorporating an in-depth understanding of China's markets (since IIGF is directly administrated by China's central government authority). In addition to basic ESG factors, Beautiful China ESG 100 Index's ESG rating system added negative and risk elements that consider violations and lawsuits regarding E, S, and G measurements, respectively, and uses A (excellent),

B (good), C (qualified), and D (needs improvement) to categorize ESG evaluation results. Beautiful China ESG 100 Index reports the top ten companies of the Index without publicly disclosing each company's ESG rating scores (see Table 4.2).

It's worth mentioning that stabilized progress has been made on Beautiful China ESG 100 Index since I started to track the index's top ten portfolio-weighted companies in June 2020. Of the top ten companies reported in the June 2020 list, only one company (Ping An Insurance) appears on the June 2022 list above, while eight of the June 2021 top ten companies are still showing on the June 2022 list (please see Appendix 2 for details). The progress indicates the early stage of the Beautiful China ESG 100 Index's ESG rating system.

Another leading Chinese ESG rating firm is SynTao Green Finance (STGF), an independent consulting firm promoting sustainable finance in China. In December 2017, STGF and Caixin Media, a privately owned Chinese media group providing financial and economic news, jointly launched the China ESG50 Index (SGCX ESG50 Index), the first equity index incorporating the ESG performance of listed companies in the mainland Chinese stock market. STGF has been publishing its monthly "Landsea China ESG Development Index Report" since then with regular updates. STGF and Moody started a strategic partnership in October 2019 with the expectation of developing effective ESG methodologies that consider both global ESG standards and Chinese characteristics. After China's COVID-19 pandemic outbreak in early 2020, STGF published "ESG Evaluation for SSE 50 Index Constituent Stocks on Epidemic Control" on February 24, 2020. In this report, STGF developed an ESG Epidemic Control Valuation model (ESG-ECV) with indicators of "S" to assess how companies manage corporate social responsibilities, and "G" to measure the timeliness of corporate actions against the pandemic and quality of relevant information disclosure in response to the coronavirus outbreak in China. The ESG-ECV system graded all SSE 50 companies using five performance levels and 9 companies received the highest level score.[7]

XinHua CN-ESG System, which launched in December 2020, closely aligns China's ESG evaluation with global ESG evaluation standards. XinHua CN-ESG System was jointly launched by Ping An Insurance (Group) Company, one of the largest financial service companies in the world, and Xinhua News Agency's China Economic Information Service, one of the largest economic information service organizations in China, under guidelines from MSCI ESG Ratings and the Dow Jones Sustainability World Index.[8] Built with cutting-edge technology and comprehensive indicators designed for Chinese companies, XinHua CN-ESG System provides real-time analysis and ESG scores for companies. With Ping An's leading role in ESG engagement, its leading position in Beautiful China ESG 100 Index, and China Economic Information

Table 4.2 Top Ten Portfolio Weighted Constituents of Beautiful China ESG 100 Index

Rank	Code	Issuer	2022 Portfolio Weight	Sector
1	0941.HK	China Mobile Ltd.	17.96%	Telecommunication
2	601318.SH	Ping An Insurance (Group) Co.	8.98%	Finance
3	601012.SH	Longi Green Energy Technology Co. Ltd.	6.50%	Information Technology
4	00294.SZ	BYD Company Ltd.	6.48%	Consumer Discretionary
5	000858.SZ	Wuliangye Yibin Co.	6.20%	Consumer Discretionary
6	2388.HK	BOC Hong Kong Holdings Ltd.	5.69%	Finance
7	1109.HK	China Resources Land Ltd.	4.15%	Real Estate
8	0960.HK	Longfor Properties	3.42%	Real Estate
9	002129.SZ	TCL Zhonghuan Renewable Energy Technology	2.13%	Technology
10	300124.SZ	Shenzhen Inovance Technology	2.11%	Technology

Source: Author's based on data from Sina Finance, June 21, 2022, retrieved on July 9, 2022 (Sina Finance, "Beautiful China ESG 100 Index June 2022", June 21, 2022. https://finance.sina.com.cn/esg/investment/2022-06-21/doc-imizirau9702062.shtml).

Service's state backing and broad range of services, XinHua CN-ESG System rose quickly and contributed to China's ESG evaluation and reporting standards improvement.

In April 2021, Chinese Securities Index Co., LTD. (CSI) launched a series of ESG-themed indexes, including the CSI 500 ESG Index and CSI 800 ESG Index. CSI, a joint venture between the SSE and the SZSE, was established in 2005 as the leading index provider in China and has approximately 4,000 indices under its management. The CSI 500 ESG Index is designed to cover only the top 80% of performers, which will help establish ESG performance benchmarks and promote ESG performance improvement.

The Necessity to Develop Chinese ESG Evaluation Systems

Although global ESG rating firms and credit rating firms have developed various ESG evaluation systems, due to the application of different data resources, data analysis methodologies, and ESG rating modeling, ESG ratings from different rating firms are not at all comparable. Lack of universal ESG ratings significantly limits the reliability and utilization of existing ESG scores. Moreover, investors prefer more qualitative ESG analysis rather than quantitative rating scores. As a result, major institutional investors establish internal ESG teams for their own analysis.

Since ESG ratings are determined by each country's standards, a bias exists, which negatively impacts ESG scores of companies from emerging markets due to the nature of those countries' economies. In particular, industrial sectors have the lowest ESG scores, as most of them operate in developing countries. Emerging markets countries also face challenges with underdeveloped regulatory frameworks, a shortage of expertise on ESG reporting and integration, and a lack of systematic readiness for ESG adoption.

As China's economy continues to grow rapidly, Chinese companies are trying to catch up with their competitors from more economically advanced countries regarding ESG performance and ESG rating scores. Increasing numbers of Chinese companies are committed to improving their ESG performance to attract investors, reduce capital costs, and stay competitive, since developing a Chinese ESG evaluation system based on China's local market situation will become essential for companies to receive fair ESG scores compared to their competitors in more developed countries.

The Context for China's ESG Evaluation System Development

Chinese rating firms and leading ESG firms worldwide continue to optimize mechanical processes like data collection, information disclosure, and integration of global ESG and corporate governance standards as they seek a comprehensive ESG evaluation system. At the same time, it is necessary to consider four unique Chinese factors – legal environment, culture, shareholder structure, and governmental relationships during this process, as those four factors have had a profound impact on Chinese companies' corporate governance practice. Those factors will also play a part in how ESG implementation is integrated into Chinese companies. Though measuring the four elements could be challenging, doing so will strengthen the ESG evaluation system.

China's Legal Environment

A country's legal environment has a major influence on its corporate governance practice. This is an important factor to consider when evaluating the overall governance practice standards of companies in a particular country. In a country with a weak legal system, companies must apply extra effort to maintain sound corporate governance to offset the negative impact of the legal system. Along those lines, the S&P 360-Degree scoring methodology developed in 2004 suggested a country governance review as part of the corporate governance scoring framework.[9]

In China, the lack of enforcement of laws and regulations is a weakness which stems in part from the ongoing development of China's legal system, and from a lack of practical details regarding existing regulations. Misinterpretation of regulations and numerous gray areas of enforcement are all too common. Factoring China's legal environment in ESG evaluation can also help identify the weaknesses of the existing legal system and facilitate future regulation development.

China's Cultural Influence

Chinese culture inevitably and profoundly influences Chinese companies' corporate governance. Many of those cultural elements contribute to Chinese companies' successes to some degree, but some of those elements cause blind spots in their corporate culture and operation.

China's Confucian philosophy, inherent paternalism, and relationship-based nominal board culture are good examples of elements that exert treble influences on corporate governance. Ancient Confucian philosophy advocates etiquette and justice, which is helpful when establishing corporate governance rules for an organization, but it also emphasizes compromise and tolerance, which makes it harder to establish checks and balances in an organization, as many employees including senior managers will refuse to tell the truth simply to avoid conflicts. Paternalism values and maintains long-term relationships with customers and suppliers and rewards and looks after loyal employees, but paternalistic companies are normally controlled by an insider group with opaque decision-making processes. A relationship-based board can be very supportive at a company's early stage by unifying board directors and executive teams, but a nominal board (as opposed to one composed of experts) tends to perform few corporate governance functions and meetings and decisions are simply formalities, which nourishes opportunities for mismanagement or fraud and becomes an obstacle when trying to attract investors. Integrating these cultural elements into ESG evaluation systems require further research and study on cultural roots and potential solutions. But ESG evaluation systems without these cultural factors will fail to accurately measure Chinese companies' corporate governance.

Chinese Companies' Controlling Shareholder Structure

According to MSCI's Chinese corporate governance report in 2017, 81.9% of Chinese companies have a controlling shareholder structure, including SOEs and founder firms. The percentage was reduced to 79% in MSCI's 2019 research, which shows a trend of Chinese companies' shares opening to global investors, although at a slow pace. A controlling shareholder structure is not necessarily indicative of poor corporate governance, but from an ESG evaluation standpoint, it is essential to examine whether the board acts in the interests of all shareholders. Alibaba serves as a good example of how a founder controlling firm engages investors with transparent succession planning as part of its corporate governance practice. On the other hand, Luckin Coffee founders' abuse of the controlling power led to the company's crash and unnerved the market.

Founder controlled firms also face succession plan obstacles as founders reach retirement age, and it is natural in Chinese culture for one generation to pass the business to the next. However, some founders' children lack the interest or ability to take over the business from their parents. Those willing to take over normally execute the founder's core values, although younger generations are exposed to Western education and are less emotionally attached to the business. Therefore, whether a company's succession plan is to prioritize long-term business sustainability with the possibility of cultivating outside talent, or to remain a founder controlled structure by bequeathing the business to the next generation, companies are sure to inherit a very particular set of challenges and opportunities.

More research is necessary to understand the impact of founder firms with a controlling shareholder structure on corporate governance and ESG.

Chinese Companies' Relationship with the Chinese Government

One of the most frequent questions asked regarding Chinese companies is: "Are Chinese companies (non-SOEs) controlled by the Party?" The relationship between the two has been an enduring mystery to many Westerners. Alibaba's Jack Ma used to characterize the relationship between his company and the government as "being in love with the Party, but not marrying them".[10] Having strong ties with the government is obviously risky, especially to the extent it allows external influence on board decisions, but a good relationship can also mean companies have access to domestic resources and government support for long-term growth, which ultimately benefits all shareholders. When we emphasize stakeholder interest and CSR from a corporate purpose standpoint, the relationship between Chinese companies and the government might be viewed differently.

Ultimately, it is more fruitful to examine areas where board decisions could be influenced by government, and whether those decisions will help businesses maximize value creation and optimize all stakeholders' interests, than to object to the relationship entirely. Further research on measurement factors and methodologies is needed.

Non-government Advocate Organizations

In addition to the Chinese government's ESG regulations and reporting guidance (see Appendix 1), industrial organizations have been pushing China's ESG reform by leading ESG research, recognition, and corporate engagement.

The Asset Management Association of China (AMAC) was established in July 2012 with 147 members from the fund management and distribution industries. As a self-regulatory organization formed to enhance and supervise compliance, fiduciary duties, social responsibilities, sustainability, and healthy growth of the fund management industry, AMAC published a "Research Report on ESG Evaluation System of China's Listed Companies" in November 2018, which opened a new chapter in China's ESG investment practice. In May 2020, AMAC published a "2019 Research Report on ESG Evaluation System of China's Listed Companies" with updates regarding China's ESG evaluation development and challenges.

The China Alliance of Social Value Investment (CASVI) was founded in May 2016 with a mission to develop a quantitative assessment system of social value. Initiated by You Change China Entrepreneur Foundation, with 60 institutional members and a broad network across many sectors, CASVI is the first licensed international non-profit organization promoting social value investment in China. CASVI published "Discovering 'SV 99' in China" reports in 2017 and 2018 to compare SV 99 (social value of the top 99 companies) and CSI 300 (top 300 stocks on the SSE and the SZSE) on various social and environmental indicators and economic contribution indicators.

China ESG Leaders Association (CESGLA) was founded in August 2019 with 30 founding organizations led by Sina. CESGLA's founding firms are publicly traded companies like Ping An, Haier, COSCO Shipping, Bank of Communication, and Fosun Pharma. One of the association's goals is to standardize ESG report framework, ESG education, ESG information disclosure, and ESG evaluation.

ESG has slowly obtained recognition from different industries in China, as evidenced by the timeline of those organizations' founding and the nature of their different missions. The fact that publicly traded companies have realized the value of ESG and started to engage in ESG improvements in order to stay competitive in the global market indicates that an ESG revolution in China is coming.

In addition to the "China model" of economic and corporate governance development, Chinese companies' ESG performance trend and the emergence of ESG evaluation system research in China further prove the demand of diversified ESG integration and measurement models in the emerging market countries, and the need for a global ESG framework as guidance for each country's ESG regulation development. Although aligning with international standards is critical, given the differences in social, environmental, and economic conditions, establishing suitable models under a unified global framework should be the direction of the global ESG movement. China's ESG movement also set up examples and provided valuable data for the research and further development of emerging market countries' ESG models, which have already been initiated by international organizations such as OECD and IFC. Those institutions are comparing and analyzing ESG performance data and measurement standards from both advanced and emerging markets countries and are trying to establish a common standard for ESG integration, practices, and evaluation for publicly listed companies, private-owned companies, and SOEs in emerging markets countries, according to Professor Lourdes Casanova.[11]

ESG Revolution in China

China's highly ambitious plan to reduce the country's carbon dioxide emissions by at least 65% by 2030[12] and achieve carbon neutrality output by 2060 will require a rapid transformation of the economy. In September 2020, President Xi Jinping announced the government's intention to attain a zero-carbon emissions goal by 2060 as part of China's 14th Five-Year Plan. In September 2021, President Xi announced that China will no longer finance coal power projects abroad. By 2025, an expectation of a decrease in fossil fuel energy consumption of 13.5% and carbon emissions reduction of 18% is anticipated.[13] Thereafter, the government intends to increase the amount of renewable energy sources in its energy supply mix from 15% in 2018 to 85% by 2050 to achieve the 2060 carbon-neutral goal. Kicking off 2021, China has made some progress in numerous areas to demonstrate its commitment to the UN's Sustainability Development Goals (SDG) initiative.

ESG Regulation Reforms

New Green Bond Regulations Aligning with International Standards

In March 2021, the "Notice on Clarifying Relevant Mechanisms of Carbon Neutrality Bonds" was issued by the National Association of Financial Market Institutional Investors to guide and ensure that the use of carbon neutrality bonds' proceeds is only for green projects. In April 2021, the *Green Bond Endorsed Projects Catalogue (2021 Edition)* was jointly issued by PBOC,[14] National Development and Reform Commission, and CSRC, proposing three advancements: to clarify eligible projects (excluding coal and other fossil fuels projects), to unify a set of consistent standards in China, and to integrate an international "Do No Significant Harm" principle. At the time this chapter is being written, China and the EU agreed to reach common classification standards of green projects by the end of this year.[15] The common standards will enable European investors to have easy access to Chinese green bonds.

New ESG Reporting Guidelines

In June 2021, the CSRS released new ESG reporting guidelines that mandate environmental factors (e.g., pollution and waste management) disclosure, and encourage social factors (e.g., poverty alleviation and rural revitalization) disclosure for China-listed companies. The new ESG report guidelines stipulate ESG reporting as a requirement for most listing companies (the previous CSRS ESG reporting guidelines issued in 2018 only required environmental factors disclosure for heavy polluters), and social information reporting to be included in companies' annual reports beginning in 2021.

Most Chinese regulation reforms were lagging, lacked or have been without practical guidance, or were deficiently aligned with international standards. This time, regulators took a different approach to the green bond and ESG reporting regulation reform in 2021. The new Notice and Catalogue (discussed above) were issued at the beginning of the year before significant amounts of green bonds were issued. Both provided timely guidance and practical clarification for funds usage to avoid misunderstanding and were integrated with international principles while unifying domestic standards to ensure the alignment between China's regulations and international standards. The new ESG reporting guidelines were issued before companies filed their semi-annual reports to ensure the reporting requirements would be reflected in 2021 reports. In addition, issuing ESG reporting guidelines in June 2021 allowed China to maintain the same pace as many advanced countries.

The improvements of both regulation reforms in the first half of 2021 are proof of the Chinese government's new strategy for future regulation reforms.

Transforming to Green Finance

Promoting Green Finance Movements

In March 2021, the China Development Bank, China's top policy bank, issued its first carbon neutrality bonds supported by Shanghai Clearing House, one of several securities depositories in the country. The three-year bonds with a total value of RMB20 billion ($310 million) were offered to global investors.[16] The funds raised by the sales of CDB's green bonds will be utilized for green projects that are designed to reduce carbon emissions. Given the largesse of China's financial market, the bond sales were expected to significantly impact carbon emission reduction goals. The China International Capital Corporation (CICC), the underwriter of this green bond, is a leading player in the country's green financial market. This year, CICC underwrote China's first transition bond[17] with the Bank of China's Hong Kong branch; in 2017, the first real estate green bond with Longfor Chongqing Enterprise Development; and in 2016, the first financial green bond with Shanghai Pudong Development Bank.

Also in March 2021, State Grid International Leasing Company Ltd. issued asset-backed commercial paper, China's first innovative asset securities product designed to facilitate carbon neutrality. The RMB1.75 billion ($270 million) raised by the ABCP supports clean energy leasing projects in wind power, hydropower, and photovoltaic power. The fact that this asset-backed commercial paper was issued and managed by various Chinese trust companies, including State Grid-backed Yingda International Trust Co. Ltd and the Bank of China, indicates the leading roles that lenders are taking to encourage a nationwide green finance movement and to hopefully compel additional Chinese financial institutions to participate and support climate change initiatives.

Collaborating with International Climate Bonds Organizations

In March 2021, the Shanghai Office of the Climate Bonds Initiative (CBI)[18] was launched in Shanghai Lujiazui Financial City that confirmed Shanghai's role as the green financial center to promote green bonds, green standards, and green transition finance. In June 2021, CBI issued *Green Infrastructure Investment Opportunities, The Guangdong-Hong Kong-Macao Greater Bay Area 2021 Report* to promote the green infrastructure investment opportunities in the Greater Bay Area (GBA) and help raise funds for those infrastructure projects.

Taking a new strategy on green bond regulation reform, actively promoting diversified green finance programs, collaborating with international organizations, setting up common standards with the EU (who has been leading the green finance initiative over the past few decades), strongly indicates China's commitment to higher standards to provide green financing, as well as displaying the country's intention to become an active player in the global green finance initiative.

Carbon Emission Control

In March 2021, the chairman of the Global Energy Interconnection Development and Cooperation Organization published an article to discuss and propose solutions to achieve China's 2030 carbon dioxide emissions and 2060 carbon neutrality goals. The solutions include four focus points for emissions reduction and the means to accelerate the increase of non-fossil energy consumption. More importantly, the article calls for collaborative efforts between government, corporations, and non-profits to facilitate and advance the transition to a green economy.

National Carbon Trading Market

China has established eight regional pilot exchanges for carbon trading since 2013 and launched a national carbon trading market in Shanghai in July 2021 with the first ten companies signing deals on the first trading date of July 16, 2021. The national carbon trading market began with 2,225 companies joining as the first group. The national carbon trading market is overseen by the Shanghai United Asset and Equity Exchange and the Shanghai Environment and Energy Exchange. According to a South China Morning Post news article of June 23, 2021, the Shanghai Environment and Energy Exchange's national carbon emissions trading platform will operate like the SSE and SZSE, with the same trading hours, daily trading limits, and a 10% point trading price cap.[19] All transactions conducted in the eight regional pilot exchanges will eventually be taken over by the Shanghai Environment and Energy Exchange. The main purposes of the carbon emission trading platform are to enable carbon credit trading and establish similar financial instruments such as those in the US and European Union to help China achieve its carbon neutrality goal by 2060. China's national carbon trading market will expand to cover eight industries, a few of which are cement, electrolytic aluminum, steel, and chemicals, and this should occur within the next five years.

Renewable Energy Spot Trading Platform

In June 2021, Guangdong province launched renewable energy trading with four renewable energy generators and seven retailers who signed contracts during the first day of trading. The fact those four generators were making higher profits from the contracts than traditional power generators will motivate energy generators' conversion to renewable energy and facilitate the country's energy transformation in the long term.

Although the carbon price on the newly launched Shanghai national carbon trading market at the time this book being written is 52.78 yuan ($8.14 USD) per ton, which is notably less than other market prices, (the EU market is $49.78 per ton and the price in California is $17.94 per ton),[20] establishing a national carbon trading market is a significant milestone for the global climate change movement, given the fact that China is the world's largest emitter of greenhouse gases. In addition, the active progress of China's ESG initiatives focusing on the current climate emergency and energy transformation indicates that China may capitalize on a strategic opportunity in climate leadership, and the continuing momentum of the ESG revolution will help China catch up with ESG-leading countries. What, then, are the drivers of China's ESG movements that have been accelerating those initiatives?

Takeaways

- **International rating firms (e.g., MSCI)** and China's ESG rating scores expose Chinese companies' ESG performances to the global capital market, which will motivate lawmakers, financial institutions, and Chinese companies to encourage continual ESG improvement. China's autonomous ESG rating systems are still in their infancy, will grow quickly, and continuously develop to align with international standards.
- **A comprehensive Chinese ESG evaluation system** requires the capacity to integrate China's legal environment, cultural influence, and companies' controlling structures in their relationships with the Chinese government.
- **China's ESG regulation reform took a different approach** by aligning with international standards from the beginning, while issuing new regulations ahead of time to guide business practices and avoid confusion. These are positive signs of the Chinese government's determination to build a high-quality regulation system.
- **Green finance transformation and carbon emission control** play important roles in China's ESG revolution.

Notes

1   Robert G. Eccles and Svetlana Klimenko, "The Investor Revolution", May to June 2019, Magazine. https://hbr.org/2019/05/the-investor-revolution
2   PRI Signatory Update, January to March 2022. www.unpri.org/download?ac=16278
3   "The ESG Journey: Lessons from the Boardroom and C-Suite", KMPG, 2018. https://boardleadership.kpmg.us/relevant-topics/articles/2019/the-esg-journey-lessons-from-the-boardroom-and-c-suite.html
4   Variable interest entity (VIE) structure is a unique business structure in which investors do not have direct ownership but have controlling interest in the entity through special contracts (Greguras, 2020).
5   Zhenhua Xie, "China's Historical Evolution of Environmental Protection Along with the Forty Years' Reform and Opening-Up," Elsevier, Volume 1, January 2020. www.sciencedirect.com/science/article/pii/S2666498419300018
6   Peter C. Pang, "China: China's Evolving Environmental Protection Laws", Mondaq, June 18, 2020. www.mondaq.com/china/clean-air-pollution/955486/china39s-evolving-environmental-protection-laws
7   Syn Tao Green Finance report, "ESG Evaluation for SSE 50 Index Constituent Stocks on Epidemic Control," SynTao Green Finance, February, 2020, June 28, 2021. www.arx.cfa/-/media/regional/arx/post-pdf/2020/03/20/esg-evaluation-for-sse-50-index-constituent-stocks-on-epidemic-control.ashx?la=en&hash=6ED6474F4CC3C2F26683D34AF86F0BFA24BA796B

8   Ninjing Liu, "Ping An, CEIS Launch China-Specific ESG Rating System," Seneca ESG, December, 2020, June 28, 2021. www.senecaesg.com/blog/ping-an-ceis-lau nch-china-specific-esg-rating-system/

9   Standard and Poor's report, "Standard & Poor's Corporate Governance Scores and Evaluations: Criteria, Methodology and Definitions," Standard & Poor's Governance Services, McGraw-Hill Companies Inc., January, 2004. https://pdf4pro.com/cdn/ standard-amp-poor-s-corporate-governance-scores-2e0f9.pdf

10 Shujie Leng, "'Be in Love with Them, but Don't Marry Them': How Jack Ma Partnered with Local Government to Make E-Commerce Giant Alibaba, and Hangzhou, a Success," October, 2014, June 28, 2021. https://foreignpolicy.com/ 2014/10/31/be-in-love-with-them-but-dont-marry-them/

11 Interview with Professor Lourdes Casanova on Boardroom&Beyond podcast in May 2021. https://boardroomandbeyond.com/chinese-multinationals-roles-in-the- worldwide-esg-revolution-a-conversation-with-professor-lourdes-casanova/

12 "China's Former Grid Chief Sees Emissions Peaking Early in 2028," Caixin, 2021, May 12, 2021. www.caixinglobal.com/2021-03-23/chinas-former-grid-chief-sees- emissions-peaking-early-in-2028-101678773.html?originReferrer=ESGnewsletter

13 Jiang Simin, "CGTN: Leading with Action: China in the Fight for Carbon-Neutral Future," Business Wire, April, 2021, June 25, 2021. www.businesswire.com/news/ home/20210416005435/en/CGTN-Leading-With-Action-China-in-the-Fight-for- Carbon-Neutral-Future

14 Climate Bonds Initiative press release, "Notice on Issuing the Green Bond Endorsed Projects Catalogue," Climate Bonds Initiative, (2021 Edition), April, 2021, June 25, 2021. www.climatebonds.net/files/files/the-Green-Bond-Endorsed-Project-Catalo gue-2021-Edition-110521.pdf

15 Wang Liwei and Luo Meihan, "China, EU Set to Agree on Green Finance Definitions by Year-End, Official Says," Caixin, June, 2021, June 28, 2021. www.caixinglobal. com/2021-06-28/china-eu-set-to-agree-green-finance-definitions-by-year-end-offici als-say-101732940.html

16 CISION staff article, "CICC Underwrites the First Financial Green Bond Issued by China Development Bank," CISION, March, 2021, June 25, 2021. www.prnewsw ire.com/news-releases/cicc-underwrites-the-first-financial-green-bond-issued-by- china-development-bank-301250744.html

17 A transition bond is a new financial tool to fund the climate change initiatives and energy transition.

18 Climate Bonds Initiative (CBI) is a not-for-profit international organization launched in 2012. By providing annual studies on the evolution of the green bonds market and standards and guidance on green bonds, CBI advocates climate change consider- ations through financial institutions' investing and lending activities.

19 Enoch Yiu, "China's Carbon Neutral Goal: Shanghai's New National Carbon Emissions Trading Platform Unveils Trading Rules, Sets Stage for Launch," South China Morning Post, June, 2021, June 28, 2021. www.scmp.com/business/article/ 3138367/chinas-carbon-neutral-goal-shanghais-new-national-carbon-emissions- trading

20 Caicai Du, Xuewan Chan, Qinqin Peng, and Ziyi Tang, "In Depth: China's Launch of World's Largest Carbon Market Has a Sputtering Start", August 5, 2021. www. caixinglobal.com/2021-08-05/in-depth-chinas-hasty-launch-of-worlds-largest-car bon-market-results-in-sputtering-start-101751641.html

Chapter 5

Driving ESG Revolution from China to the World

In this chapter, I review

- Major Drivers of China's ESG Revolution
  Policymakers and regulators
  Shareholders
  Chinese corporations

- Challenges and Opportunities of China's ESG Revolution
  Reposition in global value chain
  Opportunities for US–China collaboration
  "Greenwashing" awareness

- Contribution to the Global ESG Movement

The years 2020–2021 were destined to be an extraordinary period for many people, the world, and China. As the ESG movement gained more traction, the concept became the predominant focus of the "movers and shakers" of the global business community then, and China, which began the ESG revolution journey as the world's second-largest economy and one of the most dynamic, decided to "take up the mantle" toward becoming the world's ESG leader. The country's leaders pledged to no longer be a follower.

In 2021, the Chinese government boosted China's ESG revolution by kicking off the year with several inaugurated regulation reforms, launching its national carbon trading markets in the middle of the year, and making a climate commitment toward plans for 2060 carbon neutrality prior to the 2021 United Nations Climate Change Conference (COP26) that occurred at the end of the year.

In their book, *Innovation from Emerging Markets: From Copycats to Leaders*, Professor Lourdes Casanova and Professor Anne Miroux explain how Chinese companies leverage China's market capacity and supply-chain system to expand in the global market and influence host countries' economies. With China's

DOI: 10.4324/9781003302919-8

determination on its ESG revolution and climate commitment, how will China and Chinese companies utilize their capital and supply-chain power to drive the ESG revolution from China to the world? Let us first review the most influential stakeholders which drive China's ESG revolution.

Major Drivers of China's ESG Revolution

The ESG revolution is a long-term journey for the globe as well as China. The COVID-19 pandemic, social and political protests, and environmental disasters have highlighted the roles that businesses can and should play in society and pushed ESG discussions to a boiling point, thus launching the beginning of that endeavor.

Policymakers and Regulators

Chinese lawmakers and regulators have been the biggest drivers for the ESG movement over the past several decades and will continue their essential roles in prodding China's ESG revolution. The CSRS issued new ESG reporting guidelines in June 2021, which mandate disclosure of environmental factors and encourage social factor disclosure for listed companies in Shanghai and Shenzhen stock exchange markets (A-shares[1]). In addition to the new ESG regulations, Chinese companies are required to provide ESG compliance reports by all the Chinese stock markets (including Hong Kong, Shanghai, and Shenzhen), all of which are, incidentally, members of the UN Sustainable Stock Exchanges Initiative.

HKEX has been actively driving the ESG reporting initiative since 2012 and released its first ESG reporting guidance that year. The HKEX has updated its guidance a few times since then, with the most recently updated guidance in July 2020 (see Appendix 1). ESG reporting became mandatory for listed companies on the HKEX beginning in 2015, which mandates detailed investment-related information disclosure on climate-related risks and a board of directors' involvement of ESG adoption as part of a company's business strategy. In addition, the HKEX provides educational tools (e.g., ESG-reporting E-training was launched in 2020) and materials such as "How to Prepare an ESG Report," (a step-by-step guide to ESG reporting), "Leadership Role and Accountability in ESG," (a guide for board and directors), and "Making Inroads into Good Corporate Governance and ESG Management" to help companies improve their ESG reporting quality. In addition, the HKEX recently launched Sustainable and Green Exchange, an online platform addressing ESG reporting data availability, accessibility, and transparency issues. The Sustainable and Green Exchange also provides visibility for companies regarding how their financial products meet sustainable standards, provides investors information for their decisions, and provides all stakeholders with related information regarding green finance.[2]

In mainland China, the Shenzhen and Shanghai Exchanges issued ESG reporting guidance data in 2006 and 2008, respectively, and since 2018, the CSRS has required companies that are industrial polluters to be listed with the government's Ministry of Environment and Ecology to disclose details of their pollution amounts and pollution control measures. Furthermore, the SSE's Science and Technology Innovation Board (STAR) requires companies to report their efforts to fulfill their corporate social responsibilities. According to data from SynTao Green Finance, as of June 2020, 86% of CSI300 A-share companies have issued ESG reports, very close to the 90% reporting rate among S&P 500 companies.

Domestic Asset Owners, Asset Management Firms, and Investors

Given the fast growth of ESG investors over the past decades, most large international asset management firms have their own ESG teams that analyze portfolio companies' disclosure and collect information on industry-specific ESG issues and companies' ESG risk management. China's anticipated positive GDP growth in the coming decades statistically indicates that these international asset management firms will steadily increase their standing in Chinese A-share companies over time. However, global investors' collective ownership of A-share companies is relatively low. Consequentially, their influence on China's A-share companies' ESG reporting compliance and performance will remain limited in the short term.

Conversely, China-based asset owners and asset management firms have rapidly adopted ESG themes in recent years. At the time this chapter is being written, 5 asset owners and 89 asset management firms in Hong Kong and mainland China have become PRI signatories, which represents 3% of total asset owners and investment managers globally who have signed the PRI. Chinese domestic asset owners and asset management firms will play important roles in China's ESG revolution in the coming decades.

The following case study of Ping An will help us understand how the China-based asset management firm integrated ESG as part of its business strategy.

Case Study 5.1   Ping An Insurance Group ESG Adoption – Leverage the Power of Capital to Encourage ESG Adoption[3]

Ping An Group (with over 30 subsidiary companies) is China's leading asset management firm listed on the Shanghai and Hong Kong stock markets. At the end of 2020, Ping An launched the XinHua CN-ESG

System, which currently provides quarterly ESG scores for 3,900 A-share companies.

Ping An's ESG efforts started two decades ago. The company has completed the first two stages of building its corporate governance and management system according to international standards. It has fulfilled corporate social responsibilities such as non-profit education, public donations, poverty assistance, and disaster relief. Ping An considers itself within the third stage of ESG adoption with clearer ESG requirements from domestic and international regulators. To integrate ESG as part of its business strategy, Ping An has taken the following steps:

Phase One: Identify four main drivers of Ping An's ESG effort

- *To align and balance different stakeholders' interests*
- *To maintain long-term sustainable goals and long-term value creation of the business*
- *To remain within high-standard corporate governance*
- *To comply with regulatory requirements and meet the growing demand from asset owners regarding ESG integration*

Phase Two: Establish ESG strategy execution plans externally

- *Committed to support the Chinese government's strategy to achieve carbon neutrality and to fulfill China's commitment under the Paris Agreement*
- *Launched the XinHua CN-ESG System to establish technology-enabled ESG evaluation tools to help other Chinese companies with their ESG performance analysis and improvement*
- *Launched a group-wide "Green Finance" project to become a pioneer in the field, and to lead the nationwide green finance movement*

Internally

- *To modify its organizational structure to enable regular communication between the board and different levels of ESG committees and senior management teams regarding its ESG strategy integration status*
- *To establish an operational policy and procedure system to support ESG reporting and ESG practices review in different levels of the group*
- *To utilize cutting-edge technologies to simplify its ESG-related procedures and improve ESG-reporting efficiency.*

Phase Three: Integrating ESG into an investment decision process

- *Establish Ping An's Responsible Investment Policy around key principles: ESG integration, active ownership, theme-oriented investment, and prudence and information transparency*
- *Set up requirements for subsidiary companies' investment procedures and asset class attributions*
- *Establish ESG-oriented risk management and asset allocation*
- *Establish AI-empowered tools to apply key principles criteria into an ESG evaluation system*

While many companies still view ESG integration as regulatory compliance, Ping An took a proactive approach to embrace ESG as part of its business strategy. In addition, Ping An's AI-empowered ESG system focuses on helping other Chinese companies improve their ESG improvement and ESG reporting, which enabled Ping An to become a pioneer and leader in global ESG digitalization. ESG adoption helped strengthen Ping An's overall competitiveness and enhanced its global brand reputation. Moreover, ESG integration will further assist Ping An with better risk management and investment performance. By supporting the government's ESG strategy and helping other Chinese companies improve their ESG performance, Ping An will continue to create and influence a sustainable business and investment environment in both China and global contexts.

In addition to domestic asset owners and asset management firms, Chinese public pensions and sovereign wealth funds are likely to stimulate domestic ESG assets due to both their significant AUM size and their top-down decision-making structures. The Hong Kong Monetary Authority has signed the PRI as the first public sector asset owner in China. In mainland China, the government-backed pension program, together with the National Council of Social Security Fund, represents about 80% of mainland China's pension assets. The National Council of Social Security Fund issued its first-ever responsible investing mandate in September 2020, which may be a sign of the ESG trend in Chinese public pension and sovereign wealth funds, but this trend needs to be further monitored.

Moreover, the expanding number of China's middle class and their increasing wealth will drive the growth of professionally managed funds with ESG-themed investments. With younger generations worldwide increasing their focuses on corporate purpose and environmental and social issues, similar younger Chinese middle class' purchasing power will promote ESG products and eventually push ESG-themed investments also.

Chinese Corporations

As we discussed in Chapter 1, SOEs have been playing important roles in the China's economic reform and growth. According to statistical data in 2020, a total of 1,150 SOEs were listed on the SSE and SZSE, representing 30% of 3,800 listed companies in those two exchanges, and 300 SOEs were listed on the HKEX exchange accounting for 15% of 2,000 companies. Most SOEs are in energy, minerals, infrastructure, utilities, and financial services sectors resulting in a considerably large amount of capital, so they consequently have been the most significant allies of China's environmental, social welfare, and long-term strategies and will continue to fervently advocate for other Chinese companies to strive to improve their own ESG reporting and performance standards.

In addition to SOEs, some leading Chinese companies have also initiated ESG integration into their business strategy process. Xiaomi Corporation is a good example.

Case Study 5.2   Xiaomi ESG Integration – The Power of Supply Chain to Integrate ESG into Core Business[4]

Xiaomi Corporation, headquartered in Beijing, China, was founded in April 2010 by Lei Jun and six co-founders, and has been listed on the HKEX since 2018. The company employs 18,000 workers and has success-fully expanded its business throughout China, Southern Asia, Southeast Asia, and Europe.

As one of China's leading multinational electronics companies, Xiaomi's main products are smartphones and home appliances. Since the first quarter of 2018, Xiaomi has been ranked the fourth-largest smart-phone manufacturer, following prominent global brands Samsung, Apple, and Huawei. According to a global smartphone quarterly market data report, Xiaomi succeeded Huawei to become the third-largest manufac-turer in the fourth quarter of 2020. Xiaomi has also produced a large variety of home appliances in recent years.

In 2014, the company was ranked the most successful technology startup with a valuation of over $46 billion, and by 2019, Xiaomi was ranked 468th as the youngest company on Fortune's Global 500 list. In 2021, they announced its investment in a new electric vehicle project for the near future.

Considering Xiaomi's success as one of the fastest growing technology companies of the previous decade, what is its position in today's world-wide ESG movement? Let us glance at the company's perspective, current strategy, and future plans:

Phase One: Establish the company's ESG approach in three stages

- *Foundation – ensure the business entity and its operational compliance at all levels*
- *Fulfill social responsibility as a good corporate citizen*
- *Create social value and brand value via ESG integration*

Phase Two: Identify the most significant ESG-related risks facing major stakeholders

- *Large number of stakeholders including network suppliers and users*
- *ESG engagement with suppliers to mitigate supply-chain risks and protect brand reputation*
- *Focus on data security and user information privacy and commit to meet privacy requirements*

Phase Three: Establish procedures to address ESG-related issues in manufacturing and the online environment

- *Ensure regulatory compliance as a minimum requirement*
- *Set up supplier social responsibility agreements to specify ESG requirements (including business ethics, environmental and labor rights) and establish an annual audit system*
- *Establish an ESG risk management procedure including monitoring and an online education mechanism*
- *Establish an information security control system throughout the entire supply chain and conduct strict privacy compliance assessments with an internal professional team*
- *Establish "whistle-blowing" channels with a 24/7 reporting platform open to all stakeholders*
- *Build an ESG-themed environment by providing supply-chain financing, and drive ESG adoption for small- and middle-sized companies.*

Since companies around the world are searching for and exploring ESG integration solutions, a KPMG 2018 ESG research report advised that businesses need to identify ESG factors that most significantly impact risks and opportunities, build roadmaps to determine productive strategies, and communicate key ESG risks that stakeholders may encounter as important elements for corporate ESG integration. Xiaomi's ESG approach demonstrates how that thriving company embraces ESG as part of its business strategy, as the KPMG report suggested.

Xiaomi's phase one approach simply repeated the founder's value creation approach: begin with the little things (a practical foundation) then focus on building the social and brand values instead of starting by aiming for perfection (an erudite maxim), a two-pronged philosophy that has driven Xiaomi's success from the beginning.

Xiaomi's phases two and three strategies were the highlights of the technology company's ESG adoption as significant parts of its growth strategy and execution plan. Given the broad range of ESG factors, all industries and companies are exposed to assorted ESG risks, and individuals' ESG interpretations may also differ. The company emphasized the most important ESG factors and risks to stakeholders and built an ESG-themed environment to protect and influence them that focused on applying these factors in its daily operations. While bringing innovation into new areas, Xiaomi's ESG approach might not yet be perfect but may inspire other companies while continuing to improve theirs over time.

Moreover, Xiaomi's approach to drive ESG integration in its supply chain demonstrated the company's ability to amplify supply chain influence with purchasing power, similar to the Western companies that introduced CSR compliance to Chinese companies in the 1990s. Xiaomi's approach exemplified Chinese companies' initiative at enhancing their lead roles within the international business community to promote ESG evolution.

According to Professor Andrew Kakabadse, global business communities need to think about how to determine meaningful engagement on ESG with critical stakeholders as an important part of their ESG agenda. Xiaomi's ESG strategy echoes the professor's perspective and demonstrates to the world how a company identifies and addresses ESG-related risks and integrates ESG into day-to-day operating procedures. In addition, Xiaomi placed on its agenda a desire to influence the under-addressed small- and mid-sized companies, which represent a significant percentage of every economy. Xiaomi not only set up good examples for other companies in China and other countries but also explored innovative approaches to facilitate an ESG ecosystem.

Challenges and Opportunities in China's ESG Revolution

Same as companies from every country across the world today, the lack of talent resources and funding resources are the biggest challenges for Chinese companies' ESG adoption. ESG experts are short in various functions and sectors throughout each organization. On the other hand, ESG implementation is costly in both short- and long terms: short-term cost occurs when hiring ESG professionals, setting up ESG key performance indicators, and establishing ESG reporting systems; long-term costs include infrastructure investments across energy, industrial, transport, and building sectors, and new emission technology development. According to Tsinghua University's Institute of Climate Change and Sustainable Development data, China will need an estimated RMb170 trillion ($26 trillion) to achieve its 2060 carbon-neutral goal.

Moving Up the Value Chain

It took China over 30 years to become "The Factory of the World" with over 50% of total global manufacturing output. Apple's global supply-chain system in China that allowed iPhone's worldwide success is the best testimonial to China's comprehensive supply-chain system, its sophisticated and skilled workers, and affordable and scalable engineering resources. However, let us not forgot that China's export-oriented manufacturing started two decades before the era of iPhones, and the manufacturers have been rapidly moving up the value chain, shifting from mass production of cheap, low-skilled required, labor-intensive products (e.g., textiles), to high-value, more sophisticated goods.

China's industrial shift has created a skilled and higher paid workforce in China, which significantly has enhanced Chinese workers' household income and average education levels. The process has also triggered global supply-chain relocation with lower skilled and low-paid jobs moving from China to other Asian countries (such as Vietnam, Indonesia, and India) starting in the middle 2010s. The relocation was accelerated by COVID-19, while the region's supply-chain system will continuously rely on China's supporting network in the coming decades.

Global supply-chain relocation from China to other countries will generate positive social impact on everyone. The receiving countries will gain more job opportunities, manufacturers, and exports, while China will be able to achieve its new development goals of a high-quality economy and greater consumer market. In the meanwhile, global consumers will be able to enjoy less expensive products, and the global business community will have less supply-chain disruption risks due to over-dependence on one country.

In addition to social impact, moving up the value chain will stir up technology innovation, productivity improvement, and cost reduction. The momentum will then lead to regulation reform, business model optimization, and less energy consumption, which will drive China's ESG movements. The "Made in China 2025" strategy introduced in 2015 highlights the Chinese government's plan to address the country's manufacturing cost pressures from labor cost increases, and the social pressure with the upcoming shrinking workforce and growing aging population.

Moreover, according to research regarding currency internationalization, staying in downstream of the global value chain was one of the top reasons that prevented the Japanese currency's global use, although Japan led the Asian economy for four decades. Taking lessons learned from Japan, Chinese manufacturers moving up the global value chain will aim to accelerate China's RMB internationalization too.

However, China and Chinese companies must deal with challenges during the industry transformation, such as potential unemployment issues due to labor-intensive production relocation to other countries, workforce skillset transformation, and technology advancement needed to support the transformation. In addition to the trend of shifting some labor-intensive manufacturers from the coastal region to inland regions over the past few years that helped absorb a certain number of extra labor resources, technology upgrades have also occurred in most industry sectors. As a result, China's rural vitalization strategy, which was proposed in 2017 containing significant details in China's 14th Five-Year Plan, has been critical for the country's continued industry transformation.

Collaboration with the US to Lead the Worldwide ESG Movement

Since the 2018 trade war, the US–China relationship has entered a challenging period. Factors including human rights and China's territorial claims[5] have further complicated the relationship, so an "icebreaking moment" is needed to establish collaboration between the countries to seek a new balance. Will the current climate emergency and worldwide ESG revolution be the opportunities to "break the ice?" Let us review some initiatives and progress below.

Leading Global Efforts on Climate Crisis and Carbon Pricing Framework

The initiative of the US and China to collaborate on climate change and energy started in the middle of 2020, leading to the US–China Joint Statement on Addressing the Climate Crisis, a milestone declaratory event issued on April 17, 2021, after meetings between the two countries' officials in Shanghai.[6] The joint statement is the framework of both countries' intentions to promote and implement the Paris Agreement through a partnership. Although details of the collaboration require further discussions and negotiations, the intention regarding climate change intervention stresses the urgency of the dilemma and the need for the world's two largest carbon polluters to curb emissions. The joint statement could possibly be the turning point in the global effort to combat climate change.

This August, the IPCC (Intergovernmental Panel on Climate Change) issued its 2021 climate report based on the past eight years of climate science advancements with over 14,000 studies being cited that statistically compare global warming increments to varied annual mean temperature changes.[7] This report helps explain the consequences of global warming and addresses concerns that global warming's impact on rising sea levels and broad-range wildfires are not only non-reversible but will also likely worsen at speeds much faster than originally believed. Scientists project that global warming will cause an increase of more than one-and-a-half degrees Celsius by the early 2030s. The report concludes that while climate change is part of modern life, the situation will not improve unless human influences are constrained and stress the need to limit their impact by immediate cuts in greenhouse gas emissions. Calls for policymakers to enact meaningful domestic policy reforms with emphasis on international collaboration to prevent the acceleration of worsening climate conditions are also warranted. As the world's two biggest carbon emitters, the US and China produce almost half of the fossil fuel fumes that heat the planet, so it is safe to state conclusively that US–China collaboration is the key to battle climate change.

In an earlier section of this chapter, I mentioned China's proactive approach to green transformation and carbon emission control to meet the country's aggressive commitment to its carbon neutrality goal by 2060. Although China's approach to carbon emission control is not enough to benchmark international standards, the Chinese government is making progress to remain content with its 2060 commitment. Daily trading volume has been increasing in China's newly established national carbon trading market in Shanghai. Carbon price differences across the globe will establish a universal framework to allow carbon trading on the international market. The US and China collaboration on climate change will accelerate a global carbon pricing framework too.

Conversely, recent discussions regarding the negative impact of political involvement on climate change efforts and climate negotiations between the US and China obviously require that overcoming those disagreements is the initial step for both countries to jointly collaborate and lead the global effort regarding the climate crisis. Likewise, China must conquer its own hurdle by connecting the country's carbon trading market to the international market and embrace global standards.

Demands for US–China Collaboration to Establish Global ESG Standards

In addition to climate crisis urgency, the rise of the global ESG movement has accelerated due to COVID-19. Meanwhile, the increase of ESG-themed investments and a new phenomenon known as "greenwashing" have created needed demands for a global framework for ESG implementation, disclosure, and evaluation since current prevailing ESG standards, each having different focuses, causing unavoidable confusion and complexity[8] toward ESG adoption and reporting. Zooming into the three major ESG reporting frameworks today[9]: SASB provides sector-specific guidance on ESG factors covering 77 industries and has been adopted by over 1,000 companies from the US, Canada, UK, and other countries[10]; TCFD offers general and sector-specific guidance but is limited to climate-related topics[11]and has been incorporated into the mandatory reporting requirements in the EU, UK, and Hong Kong; GRI focuses more on labor and human rights topics. Rectifying this scenario is the basis for the US and China to establish an effective collaborative relationship to standardize a global framework.

Neither the US nor China has led the global ESG movement or been the pioneers of global carbon emission control/carbon trade market establishment over the past few decades. However, domestic ESG and climate-related policy changes in both countries will reshape the global landscape in both fields, given the collective economic size and influence of these two countries and their increasing interdependency. While China has been proactively promoting its ESG movement as discussed in the early part of this chapter, US regulators also made significant progress in 2021 on climate change-related reporting requirements, ESG reporting metrics, and green finance transformation.[12] Therefore, when both countries compete in the ESG movement to catch up with international standards, this new competitive synergy will be essential to formulate both countries' ESG policy reforms, which will then lead to an efficacious global framework on ESG standards and carbon-trading pricing.

As I mentioned previously there is no "one-size-fits-all" solution for global ESG adoption and measurement due to different economic, social, and geographic environments globally, it is essential that cohesive efforts be made on ESG improvement and a reduction of human impact on climate change; hence, the demand for a global framework as guidance for each country's policy development is warranted. Moreover, the increasing influence of China and the success of the "China model" indicate the different paths China and other emerging market countries that have been taken have been successful and will be continued for their economic development and ESG implementation. The "China model" may not be applicable to all emerging market countries, but it reveals factors that need to be considered and possibly integrated into their economic models and ESG standards, despite many of them being different or even contradictory to Western models. For a global framework to work effectively, identifying the intersecting methods of various models used by advanced and emerging market countries is essential.

Given the Chinese and American influence and representation in emerging markets and advanced markets, respectively, collaboration between the US and China will not only accelerate the global ESG movement but also contribute to research and exploration of the interactions of other countries' ESG policies and "mine for synergy" to cross these paths.

Other Global Risks Demand Collaboration between the US and China

Regulation framework globalization is not a new concept in the business world, since all US multinational companies have been required to comply with various antitrust, anti-corruption, and anti-bribery enforcements for their overseas operations. The 2012 GlaxoSmithKline whistleblower lawsuit is a perfect example that corruption is a global risk for multinationals that requires a global regulatory framework. Although the urgency of global anti-corruption cannot compare with climate change, the economic and moral damage to the victims and the society are immeasurable. When China's anti-corruption reform started in 2018 and relevant research regarding the potential effectiveness of how anti-corruption procedures could lead to transnational law agreements between the US and China on multinationals' corporate governance practice,[13] consideration should be given to anti-corruption as another area for the US and China to collaborate.

At this point, I think it's important to understand that with today's multi-dimensional development, the context of ESG has evolved globally, and the demand for global collaboration on ESG adoption is rising. Will the world-wide movement of climate change mitigation and ESG integration be opportunities for the US and China to collaborate? It's time for global superpowers to put aside their national interests and the competition for global supremacy and openly share empathy with and sympathy for each other and effectively collaborate to combat all global crises. While seemingly elusive, doing so defines mutual winning.

"Greenwashing" in the Chinese Context

"Greenwashing" is a side effect of the global ESG movement. Therefore, the reasons why greenwashing has occurred are commonly understood as: first, a lack of a unified framework and measurement systems for ESG performance. Although increasing numbers of regulations are requesting ESG disclosure, companies are setting up different formats of ESG reporting and focusing on information disclosure that favors the business. Therefore, it's not easy to evaluate the effectiveness of a company's ESG performance reporting and to validate the accuracy of their ESG reporting; second, a lack of specification for ESG disclosure and the requirements for third-party validation. With a growing number of companies disclosing ESG-related information, the accuracy and reliability of the ESG data has raised unavoidable questions; third, an eagerness to impress investors. ESG was mainly driven by the demand of investors starting from the launching of the ESG as a measurement system in the early 2000s. When primary motivation of ESG disclosure is to attract investors, it's reasonable for companies to try to report whatever information is welcomed by their investors.

Greenwashing activities in the global context share three common afflictions: first, increasing risk on ESG-theme investments. Poor-quality ESG reporting does not reflect companies' ESG performance, which will most likely expose investors to unexpected investment risk once the real ESG performance is revealed; second, shaking investors' confidence and trust. The ultimate goal of the global ESG movement is to establish an ecosystem, within which the poor ESG performers have difficulty surviving. As one of the most influential groups in the establishment of this ecosystem, investors' confidence and beliefs will impact the development progress; third, damaging companies' long-term value. Simple ESG labeling turned out costing more for companies while also incurring reputation damage. Let us take HSBC as an example in the following short case study.

Case Study 5.3   What Has Greenwashing Cost HSBC?[14]

In October 2022, HSBC's ads that were posted at bus stations across London and Bristol right before COP26 were banned by the UK advertising watchdog, Advertising Standards Authority (ASA). The bank ads were critiqued for highlighting the significant amount of USD ($1 trillion) HSBC had invested in climate-friendly initiatives, while failing to acknowledge the bank's own contribution to emissions. ASA also pointed out that HSBC's ads were misleading due to omitting material information regarding the bank's continuous investment in companies with notable levels of carbon emission. ASA requested HSBC provide adequate information regarding the bank's contribution to carbon dioxide and greenhouse gas emissions. ASA's rulings and claims were welcomed by different groups of stakeholders. Given these demands, what did the HSBC ads look like?

According to a Lexology article, HSBC's ads stated, "aiming to provide up to $1 trillion USD in financing and investment globally to help our clients' transition to net zero", and "helping to plant two million trees which will lock on 1.25 million tonnes of carbon over their lifetime".[15]

As a result, HSBC has become the greenwashing example in the financial sector since late 2022, resulting in incalculable costs to the bank toward recovering from the negative publicity impact in the global media.

China and Chinese companies have similar experiences in terms of greenwashing as their counterparties in the rest of the world, except in two aspects.

First, the early stages of China's ESG sustainability-related regulation, disclosure, and measurement systems. In many developed countries, the history of companies' voluntary ESG disclosure and reporting are traced back to the 1990s, when carbon accounting framework research emerged, while the launching of the Carbon Disclosure Project (CDP) in 2002 was widely accepted by Western companies as part of their ESG reporting and rating systems. Despite China's young economy and newly implemented ESG concepts as part of the global ESG movement, an increasing number of Chinese companies are now participating in the global ESG rating system, and the development of Chinese ESG evaluation systems has made an impressive achievement. To be fair, China's ESG evaluation system nearly started from scratch in the past few years despite having no CDP equivalent version.

Second, the conflict between China's fast-growing ESG-theme investment in the past few years and the slow development of the ESG ecosystem. The size of China's domestic market and population exacerbated the number of individuals and organizations involved in the ESG movement, as well as amplified the negative impact of greenwashing. The existence of a knowledge gap and resulting confusion have quickly turned into greenwashing by market trends and media influences. ESG evolution in China has led to an increasing demand for highly paid ESG experts, which has stimulated a growing number of ESG education organizations that have not received appropriate qualification scrutiny.[16] China's fast ESG evolution is also nourishing opportunities for misusing ESG evaluations offered by third-party ESG consultant and international rating firms. Such was the case of Sunny Optical Technology (Group) Co., which received an issuance of sustainability-linked bonds in February 2023, when the ESG rating information offered by various consulting and rating firms did not support each other.[17]

China's ESG evolution is part of the global ESG movement. Therefore, one side effect of its process is no different than that of the rest of the world, as has the rising awareness of greenwashing among Chinese stakeholders.[18] It will take time for the country's regulation system to mature, as well as for companies and investors to fine-tune their ESG implementation approaches and reporting systems toward substantial ESG adoption, so that simple ESG labeling can be avoided. At the same time, I hope that by pointing out the immaturity of China's regulation system and the country's economic environment, this discussion will help build the awareness of greenwashing in China, while also emphasizing the importance of scrutiny and investigation before any business and investment decisions are considered.

China's Contribution to the Global ESG Movement

China has been the world's second-largest economy for ten years since the global ESG movement accelerated in 2020. The unexpected COVID-19 pandemic, Black Lives Matter movement, exacerbated natural disasters, and climate deterioration have all had a deleterious effect on the global economy. To become a global leader, the country needs to contribute to the global community, support, and help other nations. The Chinese government has strategically taken actions and commitments on the journey of moving the ESG revolution from China to the world, with two notable examples below.

Promoting Global Green Energy Transformation

In July 2021, the Industrial and Commercial Bank of China Bank Ltd. (ICBC) withdrew from a 2,800-megawatt Sengwa coal project in northern Zimbabwe,[19] even though ICBC had signed a formal notice of interest in 2020. ICBC's withdrawal from the Sengwa coal project marked the first time a Chinese bank proactively walked away from a coal-power project, broadcasting a significant message regarding Chinese overseas prospects and energy-financing projects. ICBC's withdrawal also left the Zimbabwe coal project in limbo, at least for now. With Western and South African banks under increasing pressure not to fund projects that contribute to climate change, funding from a Chinese bank was the final hope.

As the largest funding provider for overseas coal power plants, China had plans of building more than 40 gigawatt-generating coal power plants in Asian developing countries. The China Development Bank and the Export-Import Bank of China had funded over $50 billion in coal projects across Asia over the past two decades. ICBC's withdrawal indicates the shift in China's overseas energy strategy, which echoes the ongoing energy transformation on the African continent initiated by the 2020 cancelation of a coal-fired plant in Kenya.

In September 2021, Chinese President Xi made a public announcement[20] that China will not build any new coal power projects abroad. The announcement further signals China's commitment to green and low-carbon energy and the nation's initiative to influence and lead global energy transformation. Both leaders of the US and China, the world's major energy project financiers, are working toward a joint leadership role in global energy transformation as collaborators to combat climate change. In the meanwhile, China's decision to eliminate overseas coal-fired energy investment accelerated the dialogue for climate collaboration before the upcoming UN climate talks in Egypt in November 2021.

During the same speech, President Xi also addressed China's initiative to provide support to developing countries in energy transformation. While also aiming to achieve its 2060 carbon neutrality goals, China's green transformation agenda will add to its strategy the intention to support developing countries build green and low-carbon energy projects in their own countries for a zero-emissions future.

COP26 Commitment

The late 2021 COP26 climate summit in Glasgow was the world's biggest climate change conference since the 2015 Paris Agreement. Around 200 countries were asked to submit their detailed plans for attaining emission reduction by 2030.

In October 2021, a few days before COP26, China released its plan to peak the country's CO_2 emissions prior to 2030 and achieve carbon neutrality before 2060.

China's September 2021 decision to stop building coal-fired power plants abroad and its new climate commitment in October 2021 was highly praised by international climate research organizations. A report from World Resources Institute stated that

> bold climate action by China could generate savings of $530 billion in fuel, operations, and maintenance costs over thirty years. Ambitious climate action would also save China nearly 1.9 million lives and generate roughly $1 trillion in net economic and social benefits in 2050.[21]

In addition to China's climate commitment, perhaps the most significant achievement realized at the COP26 summit was the agreement between China and the US to collaborate and boost climate policy adoption in future decades.[22] As the world's two largest economies and two biggest CO_2 emitters, both countries' joint climate actions will have a significant influence on worldwide emission control toward slowing the world's climate deterioration.

Takeaways

- To achieve China's aggressive carbon neutrality goals while the nation transforms into a green economy, **Chinese lawmakers will be the biggest drivers of its ESG revolution**, while other stakeholders in the country will actively participate.
- **The ESG movement will improve China's international position**, as well as help China ascend the value chain and change the business mindsets of Chinese companies' leaders. Some Chinese companies' ESG strategies will demonstrate their lead roles in the ESG movement, serving as best practices for the rest of the world, while also paving the way for those companies' further growth in the global market. As a consequence, greenwashing has appeared in China as a side effect of ESG evolution.
- **The demand for a global ESG framework raises the necessity and urgency of US–China collaboration,** which will serve as an important first step toward global collaboration to fight various global crises. The partnership requires the leaders of both nations to consider placing national needs secondary to global obligations.
- **Leveraging the power of capital and supply chain, China and Chinese companies** open a new era of their ESG leading position around the globe.

Notes

1   A-Shares are yuan-denominated stocks of China-based companies listed on Shanghai and Shenzhen Stock Exchanges.

2 World Economic Forum press release "A Leapfrog Moment for China in ESG Reporting," World Economic Forum, 2021, May 12, 2021. www.weforum.org/repo rts/a-leapfrog-moment-for-china-in-esg-reporting

3 World Economic Forum press release "A Leapfrog Moment for China in ESG Reporting", Pages 14–15, World Economic Forum, 2021, May 12, 2021. www.wefo rum.org/reports/a-leapfrog-moment-for-china-in-esg-reporting

4 World Economic Forum press release "A Leapfrog Moment for China in ESG Reporting", Pages 19–20, World Economic Forum, 2021, May 12, 2021. www.wefo rum.org/reports/a-leapfrog-moment-for-china-in-esg-reporting

5 The Associated Press, "US China Agree to Cooperate On Climate Crisis With Urgency", April 18, 2021. www.npr.org/2021/04/18/988493971/u-s-china-agree-to-cooperate-on-climate-crisis-with-urgency

6 "US–China Joint Statement Addressing the Climate Crisis", April 17, 2021. www. state.gov/u-s-china-joint-statement-addressing-the-climate-crisis/

7 Assessment Report, "Climate Change 2021, The Physical Science Basis", IPCC, Pages 22–24, August 7, 2021, August 15, 2021. www.ipcc.ch/report/ar6/wg1/

8 "SASB Standards & Other ESG Framework", SASB website, www.sasb.org/about/ sasb-and-other-esg-frameworks/

9 Catherine Clarkin, Melissa Sawyer, and Joshua L. Levin, "The Rise of Standardized ESG Disclosure Frameworks in the United States", Harvard Law School Forum on Corporate Governance, June 22, 2020. https://corpgov.law.harvard.edu/2020/06/22/ the-rise-of-standardized-esg-disclosure-frameworks-in-the-united-states/

10 Value Reporting Foundation report, "SASB Standards," Financial Reporting Lab. www.frc.org.uk/getattachment/0079d012-0730-4357-b6bc-22f2ddb66606/FRC-LAB-SASB-Snapshot-2021.pdf

11 Task Force on Climate-Related Financial Disclosures, "Recommendations of the Task Force on Climate-related Financial Disclosures", June 2017, August 27, 2021. https://assets.bbhub.io/company/sites/60/2020/10/FINAL-2017-TCFD-Report-11052018.pdf

12 Lyndsey Zhang, "ESG Revolution in the US," Governance, Issue 321, May 2021. www.governance.co.uk/journals/

13 Matthew S. Erie, "Anticorruption as Transnational Law: The Foreign Corrupt Practices Act, PRC Law, and Party Rules in China," *American Journal of Comparative Law* (forthcoming), May 19, 2017, https://ssrn.com/abstract=2971092 [https://perma.cc/ U4JF-F5XA] (discussing how the overlapping systems of anti-corruption in the US and China form a transnational law compliance system).

14 Betsy Reed, October 2022, "Watchdog Bans HSBC Climate Ads in Fresh Flow to Bank's Green Credentials", www.theguardian.com/business/2022/oct/19/watchdog-bans-hsbc-ads-green-cop26-climate-crisis

15 Lexology, January 2023, "ASA's Ban on HSBC's 'greenwashing' Adverts Indicative of Increasing Regulatory Scrutiny", www.lexology.com/library/detail.aspx?g=695d6 6ac-de09-4977-92d8-aafcb392a7fc

16 Manghua Wang and Junwen Zhang, February 2023 "年薪百万背景不限，机构集体恶补ESG". https://mp.weixin.qq.com/s/hadsZd2ZaVNX2GNkA-ij5g

17 Weixin, February 2023, Manghua Wang and Junwen Zhang, February 2023 "绿侦探第一案： "漂绿"者的画像", https://mp.weixin.qq.com/s/pvyVsLSRXI9bx69 DHP2V0g

18 Enlighten, July 2021, "伪ESG中的 "漂绿"行为是什么？" www.shqiray.com/cn/ news/e-esg-zhong-de-biao-lu-hang-wei-shi-shen-ma.html

19 Caixin Global, "Biggest China Bank Abandons $3 Billion Zimbabwe Coal Plant", July 01, 2021, Caixin Global. www.caixinglobal.com/2021-07-01/biggest-china-bank-abandons-3-billion-zimbabwe-coal-plant-101734432.html
20 Xuejiao Cai, "Xi Says China Will Not Build New Coal-fired Power Plants Abroad", Caixin Global, September 22, 2021. www.caixinglobal.com/2021-09-22/xi-says-china-will-not-build-new-coal-fired-power-plants-abroad-101776340.html
21 World Resources Institute, "Statement: China Releases New Climate Commitment Ahead of COP26", October 28, 2021. www.wri.org/news/statement-china-releases-new-climate-commitment-ahead-cop26
22 BBC News, "COP26: China and US Agree to Boost Climate Co-Operation," BBC News, November 11, 2021. www.bbc.com/news/science-environment-59238869

Reshaping Social and Regulatory Systems

Chapter 6

Building a High-Quality Social System

In this chapter, I review

- China's 14th Five-Year Plan (FYP)
  Highlights of China's 14th FYP
  The impacts on China's ESG landscape

- China's Social Credit System (SoCS)
  SoCS' punishments and rewards systems
  SoCS' impacts to China's ESG revolution

- Trends to Watch
  Flexible working
  Education system reform
  Social entrepreneurship

China's social credit system (SoCS) was first brought to my attention in the fall of 2019, when I was told that a college friend, Jason (not his real name), was placed on the Chinese government's travel restrictions blacklist. Jason owned a microloan business in China in the early 2010s and filed for bankruptcy a few years ago due to a loan default. Upon closing the business, he has been working for a small consulting firm. However, being on the blacklist has restricted him from traveling by air or high-speed train and staying in expensive hotel rooms (relegating him to "regular trains" or bus use and staying in "cheap" hotel rooms only). Those travel restrictions have made it difficult for Jason to travel long distances for business trips or conferences.

The new SoCS reminds me of the differences between China's prior credit check process and the process in the US. While the personal credit score system in the US and other advanced countries has been widely used for mortgage, job applications, and other important social and business references, in China, a stamped recommendation letter containing an applicant's salary amount

DOI: 10.4324/9781003302919-10

provided by an employer was required to attest to an individual's credit worthiness for a mortgage application. I then became curious about the pending updates to the new credit system in China, as well as any possible alterations to the existing travel restrictions.

Having now learned about the new credit system, sympathy is extended to my friend Jason. My research of China's new SoCS has enlightened and now convinced me that the new system will serve an important role in changing individual and businesses' behaviors; implementing it will accelerate the establishment of a trustworthy society and help improve the regulatory standards of China's business landscape and Chinese companies' corporate governance development and ESG adoption.

China has changed so rapidly since I initially left! As I write this book, changes are occurring so quickly that companies are designing initiatives to improve their corporate governance practice and become and remain in compliance with newly released regulations. The new-generation Chinese companies and the younger generation Chinese entrepreneurs are leading the trend of businesses' contribution to societal improvement and employees' work-life balance, both of which are in alignment with their peers in advanced countries. Moreover, the issuance of China's 14th Five-Year Plan (FYP) has marked the beginning of China's economic transformation from a moderately prosperous society into a modern socialist country.

This chapter starts by reviewing China's current FYP that sets up the government's goal of high-quality economic development over the next five years. The chapter then discusses the sensitive nature of SoCS, and the trending societal changes in China.

China's 14th Five-Year Plan (FYP)

China's FYPs are a series of social and economic frameworks that have been issued by the Chinese government since 1953, focusing on tasks and goals to be accomplished within each five-year timeframe. The objectives and policies covered by FYPs include economy, population, environment, public service, and the quality of each citizen's life. Since the P.R. China's establishment in 1949, the Chinese Communist Party, which has developed and directed all plans to present, has partaken in important functions by establishing economic strategies, growth targets, and various reform initiatives.

In the early period of China's social and economic development, an FYP was the "planning" established by the central government to provide detailed development guidelines for all provinces. The initial concept of a planned economy subsequently evolved into a socialist market economy. Then in 2006, when the 11th FYP was enacted, the government labeled forthcoming plans as "guidelines" that describe the means for local governments to establish their own individualized development strategies and policies without the encumbrance of complying with a centralized plan. As time progressed, FYPs also became the "thermometer" for the rest of the world to observe the Chinese government's social and economic development process and progress during each successive FYP.

Highlights of China's 14th FYP

Unlike previous FYPs, China's 14th FYP (2021–2025), which was released at the end of 2020, is the first plan that does not set a specific GDP growth target. Instead, the new plan addresses other economic indicators such as the unemployment rate, energy consumption, and carbon dioxide emissions, all aimed at improving people's lives and environmental protection with a shifting focus toward the *quality* of economic development. Also, for the first time, the new FYP comprises perspicuous proposals for national security development and capability, food production, energy and financial security, an assessment of current global conditions, and evident challenges facing China's domestic economic recovery and international growth, all of which indicate the improvement and maturity of China's economic and social environments.

Moreover, the new FYP sets economic targets concentrating on "energy intensity", "low-carbon intensity", and technology self-reliance, and provides recommendations to achieve these targets from different aspects with the following highlights:

Social development, the top priority of the new FYP, sets the tone from the top as the ultimate development goal of all subsequent sectors, including financial, asset management, consumer and retail, manufacturing, automobiles, healthcare and life sciences, and technology.

Technology is a significant and separate sector in the FYP, as well as the centerpiece of all industry sectors with its mission of "steadfastly pursuing innovation-driven development to comprehensively shape new development advantages". Key trends in the technology sector include the development of cutting-edge technology, a business-leading innovation model, an advancement in basic research, technological innovation systems, and innovative talent development.

Financial sector focuses on optimization of policy-based financing. China will continuously open its financial sector toward further reform of state-owned commercial banks and sustainability development of other financial service providers. Moreover, the banking sector will continuously promote pilot testing for e-CNY and China's central bank digital currency.

Asset management and insurance (intuitional asset owner) focuses on promoting the opening of capital markets, RMB internationalization, green finance, and digitalization transformation, while developing and promoting financial products that diversify household wealth allocation.

Consumer market, with the rise of indigenous Chinese brands, has become the cornerstone of China's economy that is being transformed into a consumer-driven economy. Within the next five years, a surge in consumer and retail markets is expected to stimulate consumption in all sectors.

Energy transformation focuses on developing renewable energy, smart energy, contributions to the establishment of a national carbon market, and promotion of a green and low-carbon economy.

Aiming to stir and guide the entire country's economic transformation, the FYP contains an ambitious and broad range of activities in various social and economic venues. Moreover, China's 14th FYP explicitly points out its three key features as the "new development dimensions" that help define goals and objectives. These three dimensions will, with purpose, inevitably foster China's ESG movement.

The Three Developmental Dimensions of the 14th FYP

Three new dimensions have been recommended in the 14th FYP to guide the nation's development in the next five years[1]:

The development stage – transition from a high-speed development model to a high-quality model. China's consistently formidable GDP growth rate over the past 20 years (averaging 8.7% per year according to World Bank 2001–2020 data[2]) has enabled the country to become the second-largest economy in the world. Given global economic and political uncertainties, not setting a specific GDP growth target allows the Chinese government and companies to focus on economic recovery from the COVID-19 pandemic as well as review and refine its strategic response to domestic and international challenges and risks.

The development philosophy – innovation, coordination, environmental protection, openness, and sharing. The new philosophy is consistent with targets established in the new FYP, such as accelerating technology independence, digital transformation, intelligent manufacturing, promoting a green economy and renewable energy methods, and strengthening comprehensive supply-chain networks.

The development strategy – "dual circulation" led by "internal circulation" (aka, the domestic market) with "external circulation" (aka, the global market), each reinforcing the other. China's large domestic market has been the impetus of the Chinese economy's rapid growth over the past several decades, so the "dual circulation" strategy will help expedite its domestic economic recovery and growth, which will ultimately boost the global economy by the purchasing power acquired from the ever-expanding amount of consumer goods marketed in China. In addition, a strengthened domestic market will enhance Chinese companies' competitive advantage globally.

According to Professor Lourdes Casanova, the two elements that most applicably warrant the success of Chinese multinationals are: *China's fast-growing economy and domestic market*, both that allow multinationals to cultivate the domestic market first before "going global", thus making their domestic markets "base camps" for their continuous international growth; and the *Chinese government's support and guidance* that advocates nationalism when needed, allowing Chinese companies to be more resilient during a crisis.

How Will the 14th FYP Reshape China's ESG Landscape[3]?

Since ESG has been at the top of the global business communities' priority list and China's ESG evolution has made significant progress during the past few years, how will the three key features of China's 14th FYP facilitate the country's ESG progress?

E – Environmental

Improving performance on "E" factors is an especially important feature of the high-quality development model that runs concurrently with China's 2060 carbon-neutral goal. The 14th FYP integrates indicators related to energy consumption and carbon dioxide emissions and makes environmental protection one of its main themes and an integral part of its new development philosophy. In addition, the plan's recommended new development philosophy is characterized by innovative environmental protection to encourage and support green finance, renewable energy vehicles, and investments in renewable energy projects. Making environmental protection a part of the development philosophy, combined with the dual circulation strategy, will prompt the discovery and refinement of alternative domestic resources to help improve "E" factors and further China's energy transformation, attract direct foreign capital in related business sectors, and eventually help raise environmental protection standards and influence good business practices to benefit the global ecosystem.

S – Social

Shifting from high-speed to high-quality models will allow the Chinese government and companies to increase their focus on improving people's livelihoods and social well-being. The 14th FYP's philosophy and dual circulation strategy will encourage technology development in healthcare and life science and also promote social responsibility considerations while companies pursue value branding and the advancement of their supply-chain networks. Eventually, the Chinese business community will experience a collective mindset change toward "S" factor improvements.

G – Governance

A high-quality economic model indicates a higher standard regulatory system and good corporate governance practices. Shifting from high-speed to high-quality models will allow Chinese regulators to focus on improving regulatory system standards and close the gap between Chinese regulations and those of advanced countries, resulting in opportunities for Chinese companies to refine and sharpen governance models and improve their corporate governance practices. With regulatory challenges due to a surge in digital and sustainable economy transformations, the new development philosophy and dual circulation strategy will help encourage and improve collaboration with different sources domestically and internationally.

The three key features of China's 14th FYP indicate the country's economic growth is moving into a mature stage. After chasing rapid growth over the past few decades, the Chinese government realizes social and economic priorities have dramatically shifted; now needed are improvement in institutional guidance quality for economic growth, citizens' improved living standards, and strategic relationships with other countries to enhance a healthy and sustainable global economy. The new dimensions and objectives initiated in the 14th FYP support China's commitments to carbon emissions peaking by 2030 and carbon neutrality by 2060 to align with the global ESG movement.[4]

China's Social Credit System (SoCS)

China's SoCS was launched in 2014 and originally planned for nationwide implementation by the end of 2020. The system's structure is built to comprise a credit score ranking system of all Chinese citizens and businesses, desiring to eventually establish a society based on mutual trust, where compliance with regulations provides rewards. Ideally, China's SoCS will function as equally as those operating in most advanced countries. Although full implementation of the system was delayed due to various reasons (including COVID-19's impact in 2020), significant progress has been made in pilot cities that have enacted a trial period.

In 2020, the COVID-19 pandemic tested the efficiency of SoCS that proved its role as a highly flexible platform that enables new policy priorities, although the initiatives and different stages of SoCS infrastructures across regions and administrative levels in China were still being set in place. Chinese government agencies were concurrently and without hindrance issuing sets of COVID-19 and virtually similar pandemic-related regulations, thanks to SoCS infrastructure components. SoCS' resiliency and efficiency made 2020 a cornerstone year to prepare for the next step in China's SoCS development. Pivoting from an IT construction phase to the installation of key data-supported frameworks and mechanisms will fulfill SoCS' digitization process to perfectly align with the 14th FYP's new development goal of technology independence.

Therefore, it is important to understand that China's SoCS as a national credit system is designed to function as a mechanism to encourage and force organizations and individuals toward behavioral changes for the good of the society, and as a platform to support the enhancement of China's regulation reform that is anticipated to evolve quickly and become mandatory soon. It's also necessary to point out that legitimate concerns exist regarding SoCS, as it may serve as a platform for the government to impose control on almost all aspects of its citizens' lives. At the time this book is being written, some exaggerated controls invoked by the Chinese government during the COVID-19 lockdown may certainly accelerate those concerns. However, the pandemic will be over sooner or later-hopefully sooner – as will the pandemic-related procedures also!

The Traditional Version of China's Social Credit System

A SoCS is not new in China. Being born and raised there, I am familiar with two terms, *Huko* and *Dang'an*, that have existed since the 1950s and, in my opinion, have been serving as China's SoCS in traditional hard copy versions.

Huko is the official government registration of household members. Every Chinese household must have one Huko booklet that lists all the household members who have historically lived at a residence. Huko is required to be updated with stamps by local government authorities and all citizens must register their Huko with local government authorities when moving to another city due to education or job changes. Huko was used as a citizen's official identification before China began issuing citizen ID cards in 1984. Today, a citizen's ID card is used for travel and hotel registration, similar to Americans who use their US driver's license. However, Huko can also serve as the substitute for the citizen ID card when needed.

Dang'an is the official government record of a Chinese citizen's education and employment history and is noted if/when a Chinese citizen changes jobs or schools. Any rewards or penalties incurred during an education and/or employment, as well as any legal consequence from criminal or civil law cases, will be recorded on an individual's Dang'an.

China's SoCS is an advanced and modern system with combined functions of the traditional Huko and Dang'an. Today's technology, with a broad range of information obtained from big data systems, enables SoCS to dynamically monitor and record an individual's social activities and behaviors. Meanwhile, the SoCS has already been extended to include businesses and has been referred to as China's Corporate Social Credit System (CSCS) in recent reports by some policy consulting firms.

Punishments and Rewards of China's SoCS

Gathered from a research report on *China's CSCS* published in November 2020 by the strategy and Chinese policy consulting firm Trivium China, I sensed a strong degree of alarm and a profound lack of privacy regarding CSCS from Westerners who are accustomed to their well-established legal system containing the social contract code, but, more importantly, the serious amounts of respect and demand they have for privacy. The CSCS mandate applies to all companies registered in China, which has inadvertently led to a widely held concern of Westerners who regard the impact on foreign companies' operations in China – including the confidentiality of those companies' personnel information such as compensation data-as a violation of their privacy.

Perhaps the following violation consequences[5] incurred by poor social credit performers are the main reasons why China's SoCS and CSCS are facing such strong resistance from the West:

- Travel bans: Individuals on a blacklist are prohibited from traveling by airplane or high-speed train and may not reserve rooms at expensive hotels. A citizen in violation remains on a blacklist for two to five years.
- School bans: Children whose parents have poor social credit scores are restricted from attending certain universities or schools.
- Public shaming: The government maintains a publicized list of individuals and businesses who have poor social credit scores.
- Privacy: The government monitors as much of a citizen's daily actions as possible. Individuals can lose credit points due to walking a dog without putting it on a leash, smoking in a non-smoking area, or cheating in online video games.
- Joint liability: Engaging with companies with poor social credit scores can reduce the score of an individual or business.

While restricted punishment was established for poor performers, the purpose of China's SoCS is to reward good performers. In 2021, social credit rewards for businesses contributed to COVID-19 containment, while penalties were imposed on companies that took advantage or violated restrictions during the pandemic. Due to the availability of social credit data, Chinese citizens and businesses are able to access a simplified loan-granting process and expedited access to funding, both geared to help high-score individuals and businesses who have been seriously affected by the COVID-19 pandemic.

In addition, individuals who help take care of disabled people or non-relative elderly people, or who donate to college funds to support poor students, will receive positive credits and be rewarded with special discounts for better hotel rooms or other benefits.

Considering Western standards, the violation consequences of SoCS may sound extreme as far as a citizen's freedom and privacy are concerned, and the joint liability for companies may also appear to be unfair. However, for a country with nearly 19% of the world's population and 18% of global GDP, what can be more effective than those punitive and rewarding measures to quickly draw people's attention and force behavioral changes?

China's SoCS Impact on ESG Revolution

Although "G" is the last factor in the term ESG, I believe it should be the forerunner and the *core* of ESG integration. "G" ("Governance") defines an organization's culture, standards of behavior, and attitudes toward innovation and failure. When considering SoCS's impact on a business' performance and the results of that relationship to society, "G" is the primary element of the three. For this reason, I will address how SoCS accelerates China's ESG movement in reverse order.

Facilitate Regulatory Enforcement – "G"

In the same year that the Chinese government launched the SoCS in 2014, President Xi Jinping declared its top priority was to establish a "comprehensive law-based governance" system. Enhancing the enforcement mechanism of existing laws and regulations has been on SoCS's agenda since its beginning. The new roadmap for the "construction of a 'rule of law society until 2025'" issued by the Party's Central Committee in January 2021 further highlights SoCS's role in supporting China's regulatory system development over the next five years. Regulatory enforcement will surely help improve China's corporate governance standards, Chinese companies' corporate governance development, and also facilitate the country's ESG evolution.

Establish a Trustworthy Economic Society – "S"

As silly as the negative comments of poor SoCS score performers could sound about consequences they've experienced, China's SoCS scoring system will help foreign businesses find faithful business partners in China by publishing a poor performers list. Public shaming a borrower and joint liability will also stimulate internal and supply-chain audits to eliminate bad partners, force individuals and business to avoid adverse behaviors, and eventually establish a more trustworthy society for people's livelihoods and for businesses.

Enhance Environmental Protection – "E"

Businesses' environmental protection compliance is a significant criterion to evaluate a company's SoCS scores, which will definitely elicit "E" responses from the business community. However, let us not forget that compliance is just a *basic* requirement of a high-quality economy. The business behavior changes and business purpose changes led by other initiatives of the SoCS will help upgrade environmental protection standards to a higher level, along with China's regulators' effort to establish a higher standard regulation system.

From a business' operational viewpoint, the implementation of SoCS is in line with China's ESG evolution, which will accelerate a company's ESG improvement in many aspects. With its mechanism to reinforce behavior changes, China's SoCS will stimulate the development of China's ESG landscape and help to establish a fair and competitive market with information transparency, which will benefit both Chinese and foreign businesses and investors.

China's SoCS implementation is facing many domestic challenges at the moment, such as a unified definition of "credit", an accumulation of thousands of documents from regional sources, and lack of a standardized evaluation system. The central government is taking steps to tackle those challenges with an upcoming social credit law and many other approaches, with a clear determination and commitment to building a streamlined and digitally integrated SoCS.

Although from Western standards the approach of China's SoCS might sound extreme, and considering most political and economic systems in Western society that we are familiar with, are we satisfied should they continue functioning status quo? Probably not. We are simply just either used to them or never had an opportunity to voice an opinion when those systems were implemented. Since China's SoCS is new and contains peculiar mechanisms of which they and most countries are not familiar, we may rush to judgment based on habit, similar to a preconceived notion of a new Enterprise Resource Planning (EPR) system criticized by many who may be forced to change their behavior to allow that protocol to work properly. Understandably, each and every one of us values a good EPR system that performs a magnificent job on behalf of a company's internal control and financial reporting operations.

In another word, while we from the West expect Chinese multinationals to respect our well-established regulations when they conduct business in the West, Westerners should reciprocally do the same when doing business in China, especially when matters of trust and compliance are concerned. The purpose of SoCS is to enforce behavior change and to establish a faithful society, which will ultimately benefit both foreign and Chinese domestic businesses and individuals. Some will argue that SoCS is a tool for the government to impose control on almost all aspects of its citizens' lives. To what extent will the Chinese government recognize and consider the public concerns regarding intrusive data collection, data protection, and invasion of privacy? We will have to find out in the coming years. In the end, it is about understanding and respect.

Trends to Watch

Led by new dimensions outlined in China's 14th FYP and the progress of SoCS, improving people's livelihoods and building a trustworthy social system will both be front and center in the next phase of China's corporate governance development. The following are trends gaining popularity.

Flexible Working in China

China's "996" working culture refers to the work schedule of 9:00 a.m. to 9:00 p.m., six days a week (72 hours per week). "996" has been adopted by giant Chinese technology companies such as Alibaba and JD.com in the past decades,[6] which quietly violates Chinese labor laws. The "996" working culture has received public criticism in recent years with an anti-996 campaign that took place in 2019.

The nearly two-year economic disruption caused by the pandemic almost turned remote working worldwide into a new norm. In the US, big technology companies such as Amazon, Google, and Apple have adopted a hybrid work model, allowing employees to work from home for certain days of their choice. The hybrid model is favored by over 70% of participants according to a Microsoft survey across 31 markets. In China, the government has advocated on behalf of its citizens' livelihoods in accordance with the 14th FYP that was released at the end of 2020, solidly echoing the global social equality movement. The "work from anywhere" working culture has gained popularity in China due to the pandemic.

To respond to China's development strategy as well as the global social equality movement, a few Chinese companies took the lead in ending the "996" working Culture[7]: first, ByteDance (Tiktok's parent company) is the first tech company in China who officially ended the "996" working culture. In November 2021, it released a new company policy that officially mandates that employees in China only work from 10:00 a.m. to 7:00 p.m. on workdays. Any overtime during the workday, weekends, and holidays needs to be pre-approved; second, the Chinese online travel giant, Trip.com Group Ltd, implemented the hybrid model trial in 2021 for over 1,600 employees. The model received strong support from participants with positive feedback for employee satisfaction and job efficiency. Trip.com will soon make the hybrid model available across the company's 33,000 employees. More companies in China are requesting shorter working hours or offering the hybrid model to their employees, including the video-sharing mobile app, Kuaishou Technology.

Despite Chinese authorities' enhancement of law enforcement measures since 2020 to shatter some companies' "too big to fall" myth mantra, ensuring labor rights for tech workers and gig workers has become obstinately abundant in the Chinese media ecosystem, declaring the "996" work culture is no longer acceptable or tolerated by the public or regulators any longer In addition to relaxing the requirements of working hours, advocating for "work from anywhere" and cancelation of the "996" work culture will significantly reduce commute time for employees, improve their livelihoods by spending more time with their families, and help reduce carbon emission as an added bonus by reducing car usage. In addition, the trend of flexible working hours for employees indicates the rise of the new business mindset of young Chinese entrepreneurs.

Change the Education System

In the middle of July 2021, the Chinese government issued a new "Double Reduction" education policy that limits private tutoring services and prohibits foreign investment in Chinese private education companies. The policy targets China's abnormal education phenomenon, which made after-school tutoring a necessity as part of primary and middle school education and led to excessive competition in school admissions. The abnormal education system has caused extreme inequality in the education system. The new policy aims to reduce the total amount of the time commitment caused by homework and reduce the financial burden of off-campus or after-school training programs. New rules prohibit after-school tutoring courses during weekends and national holidays involving curriculum subjects for elementary and middle school students.

Key developments with the new policy include[8]: first, eliminate private for-profit off-campus and after-school training that duplicates the subject-based courses (e.g., Chinese literature, history, geography, foreign language, biology, and chemistry) offered in compulsory school. Existing private training institutions with subject-based courses are required to transfer to non-profit organizations; second, tighten the review and approval process of non-subject-based training institutions (e.g., sports, art, music). Different standards in each area are to be defined; third, scrutinize the training material of off-campus training institutions to prevent unapproved curricula and foreign content. A new filing and supervision system will be established for this task; fourth, prohibit foreign capital in subject-based training institutions.

The purpose of the new policy is to improve the quality of school education, standardize off-campus training, relieve students from excessive study burden so they have more time for hobbies and sports activities, and relieve parents from financial burden and the anxiety of school admissions, all of which intend to improve the quality of life for Chinese families.

Overseas-listed private education service companies were hit badly by the new Double Reduction policy, resulting in an 80%–90% stock price drop during the year 2021. For example, the revenue earning of New Oriental and Technology Group (NYSE: EDU), an English-language learning company that has dominated the industry for decades, was down 86%. Its competitor, TAL Education Group (NYSE: TAL), has seen its stock price drop by 93%.[9] Many smaller after-school training service companies have been forced to change their business models.

Chinese culture respects good education and the competition of school administration, so children's school schedules and expenses are the centers of most Chinese families' day-to-day routine, holiday schedules, and financial resource allocation. The Double Reduction policy will certainly stir essential changes in China's education system, Chinese families' education planning for their kids, and the quality and lifestyles of Chinese families. Moreover, concurring with other regulation development as responses to cybersecurity concerns, the new policy will clearly bring fundamental changes to the Chinese regulatory system in the education sector. We can optimistically anticipate further guidelines issued by both central and local governments on this subject.

The Rise of Social Entrepreneurship in China

When China was hit by the Omicron virus wave in the spring of 2022, I had an opportunity to speak with a young entrepreneur, Charlie (not his real name), co-founder of a quickly growing tech startup company in Beijing. When asked about his understanding of ESG, Charlie told me that as a non-environmentally sensitive startup, his company did not set aside a budget for philanthropic activities but always tried to use energy-efficient products whenever a situation arose. Charlie added, "With today's pandemic crisis, being about to keep the business running and pay my three-hundred fifty employees on time is the most significant ESG for me" and learned that all the co-founders and executive managers have voluntarily taken significant pay-cut since the pandemic outbreak, while his company paid all employees their full salaries, "Most of our employees rely on paychecks to pay mortgages and raise their families. We will do our best to ensure their family can survive the pandemic crisis". I was deeply moved by Charlie's genuine comments.

In concluding our conversation, Charlie mentioned his admiration for an inspiring figure in China's young entrepreneur community, Yiming Zhang, the founder of ByteDance, who announced his retirement in May 2021.[10] Following is a pertinent case study:

There are different opinions regarding Zhang's resignation. Some think his resignation is a strategic move to allow Liang to navigate the rising tide of Chinese regulations targeting tech giants, while others believe ByteDance's

Case Study 6.1   ByteDance Founder CEO Yiming Zhang's Resignation

ByteDance Ltd., a Chinese multinational internet technology company, was founded by Yiming Zhang in 2012. The company is registered in the Cayman Islands and headquartered in Beijing.

Yiming Zhang, who was named one of Time magazine's 100 Most Influential People of 2019, received his education from Nankai University in China, majoring in microelectronics and software engineering. Before starting his first company in 2009, he worked for Microsoft and Kuxun, a Chinese travel website.

Unlike other Chinese tech giants who are focused on domestic market growth, ByteDance which is 40% owned by US venture capital firms has concentrated on expanding into the global market. Interestingly, Zhang's management style of ByteDance is modeled on Google's management style.

As a result of Zhang's vision and leadership, ByteDance had several successful products in addition to TikTok including the news application (app) "Toutiao" that attracted tens of millions of followers daily (Toutiao's platform contained a missing person alert that helped find 13,116 missing persons as of 2020); an AI research lab led by a former executive from Microsoft Research Asia; an online education app "Gogokid" that connects children with native English-speaking tutors; and a ride-hailing application "Didi Chuxing".

Over the past few years, ByteDance has faced serious scrutiny on three occasions by the Chinese government: in 2018 by Chinese regulators for improper content of its news app "Neihan Duanzi"; in 2019 by US regulators due to TikTok's violation of children's online privacy protection; and in 2020 by Chinese regulators due to its collaborative tool "Feishu's" potential circumventing of internet censorship attempts.

TikTok and "Douyin" (the latter is the former's Chinese version) have been popular since 2017, while the former was caught in diplomatic tussling between the US and China in 2020. ByteDance announced its new division "BytePlus" in April 2021 with the intention of selling TikTok.

ByteDance's platform supports 800 million daily active users and over 1 billion accumulated users across all content platforms. In 2018, ByteDance became the world's most valuable startup with a valuation of $75 billion, surpassing Uber, and in April 2021 announced its IPO plan was valued at $185 billion.

> *On May 20, 2021, 38-year-old Yiming Zhang, an AI coding genius, announced his resignation as CEO will occur by the end of the year to better focus on the company's long-term strategy as well as provide public service to the country. Zhang named his college roommate, current HR head of ByteDance, Rubo Liang, to be his successor.*

planned IPO will significantly increase Zhang's wealth and draw considerable media attention; therefore, Zhang's resignation is to avoid potential troubles being a wealthy entrepreneur within the current social climate.

In all the Chinese companies that I have studied, Yiming Zhang's leadership style centered on "social entrepreneurship", acknowledging that retreating from leadership and installing a competent executive would soon benefit the company. Yiming Zhang represents the new generation of Chinese entrepreneurs, who grew up in an advanced technology era, sharing the same senses of purpose and social mission as those from advanced countries.

These new-generation entrepreneurs will reshape Chinese companies entirely in contrast to older generation Chinese companies. The latter were either established controlled structures and heavily relied on their founders' charisma and personal commitment, or deeply influenced by traditional family business mindsets and struggled with leadership transfer to their children or other family members who are not competent to take the leading roles. Given a certain time, these young entrepreneurs and their companies will certainly influence Chinese companies' business purposes, corporate cultures, corporate governance development, and ESG adoption.

Therefore, I would like to use Zhang's words to conclude this chapter:

> With our business growing well, it is time to think about how we cannot simply scale, but make innovative, meaningful, long-term progress towards our mission to "Inspire Creativity, Enrich life".
>
> (Zhang Yiming [A Letter from Yiming on May 19, 2021, from ByteDance's website])

Takeaways

- **China's 14th FYP sets up new dimensions to transfer the country's development strategies from high speed to high quality**. It is the first plan that does not set a specific GDP growth target but instead focuses on the improvement of people's livelihoods, encourages business innovation and technology development, continuous ESG improvement, and emphasizes the utilization of the dual circulation concept that domestic growth leads to global market growth.

- **SoCS's punishments and rewards mechanism** seems extreme by Western standards but *will likely be the most effective system for rapid behavioral and mindset changes* to establish a trustworthy society that benefits both Chinese and foreign businesses.
- **The trend toward continuous improvement in China's social systems**, combining ongoing ESG integration into business practice within the international and domestic markets, and a comprehensive business mindset change led by young entrepreneurs.

Notes

1 KPMG report, "The 14th Five-Year Plan: Sector Impact Outlook," KPMG, 2021, May 16, 2021, https://assets.kpmg/content/dam/kpmg/cn/pdf/en/2021/01/14th-five-year-plan-industry-impact-outlook.pdf

2 The World Bank, https://data.worldbank.org/indicator/NY.GDP.MKTP.KD.ZG?locations=CN

3 KPMG report, "The 14th Five-Year Plan: Sector Impact Outlook," KPMG, 2021, May 16, 2021, https://assets.kpmg/content/dam/kpmg/cn/pdf/en/2021/01/14th-five-year-plan-industry-impact-outlook.pdf

4 Jinghan Xu and Lauren Zelin, "China's 14th Five-Year Plan Sets Foundation for Climate Action, But Important Details Are Still Needed," World Resources Institute, May 22, 2021, June 30, 2021, www.wri.org.news.statement-chinas-14th-five-year-plan-sets-foundation-climate-action-important-details-are-still-needed

5 Drew Donnelly, "An Introduction to the China Social Credit System," New Horizons, April 15, 2021, https://nhglobalpartners.com/china-social-credit-system-explained/

6 Zheping Huang, "TikTok Owner ByteDance Mandates Shorter Working Hours", Bloomberg, November 1, 2021, www.bloomberg.com/news/articles/2021-11-01/tiktok-owner-limits-workday-to-nine-hours-in-blow-to-996-culture

7 Leslie Wang, "Burning Out", CKGSB, April 18, 2022, https://english.ckgsb.edu.cn/knowledges/burning-out/

8 JDSUPRA, "China Release 'Double Reduction' Policy in Education Sector," JDSUPPA, August 24, 2021, www.jdsupra.com/legalnews/china-releases-double-reduction-policy-1019987/

9 Elliott Zaagman, "The Casualties of China's Education Crackdown", Techcrunch, September 22, 2021, https://techcrunch.com/2021/09/22/the-casualties-of-chinas-education-crackdown/

10 Zhang Yiming, "A Letter from Yiming," ByteDance official website, May, 2021, June 1, 2021 www.bytedance.com/en/news/60a526af053cc102d640c061

Chapter 7

Building a High-Quality Regulatory System

In this chapter, I review

- China's commitment to a Higher Standard Regulation System
  Intellectual property (IP) protection
  Antitrust law enforcement
  Minority shareholder interest protection
  Newly launched Beijing Stock Exchange

- The Upcoming New Regulation Reforms with Legal Enforcement
  Data security and personal information protection
  Board directors' fiduciary duty and legal responsibility
  Credit rating system reform and anti-corruption enforcement

Like many other emerging market countries, China has a very restrictive regulatory system, while the problems have always been the absence of practical guidance and a lack of an enforcement mechanism. Since China is now a world-leading economy with many pundits predicting that it will surpass the US and become the largest in the coming years, many have questioned if China is still considered an emerging markets country. Where are the lines drawn between advanced and emerging markets? How can China become a real leader in the global economy?

Businesses are obligated to serve their home countries' economic and social development and are required to comply with those countries' regulations and laws. Therefore, the interconnection between a nation's wealth distribution, percentage of middle-class, social stability, and political culture, all impact the expectation and relationship between government and business. As a result, the cohesive level of these elements indicates the developmental level of a country's economy, social, and political systems.[1]

DOI: 10.4324/9781003302919-11

Having a high-quality regulatory system is one of the top criteria for a country to be considered a global economic leader. The Chinese government has been on a mission to accomplish that goal. This chapter will review a few notable recent and upcoming reforms and enforcement in the Chinese regulatory system, some of which concurs with the improvements of China's legal system.

China's Commitment to a Higher Standard Regulation System

China has realized that the traditionally lagging regulatory system does not fit its ambition in the global economy, and establishing a high-standard regulation system and closing the standards gap between itself and other advanced countries must become priorities. Therefore, regulation standards improvement is a vital part of China's 14th FYP's new development strategy of transitioning from a high-speed development model to a high-quality model, while the SoCS's agenda consists of enhancing the enforcement mechanism of existing laws and regulations. The sense of urgency has led the government to initiate regulatory reforms containing more guidance, monitoring, measurement, and enforcement mechanisms.

Intellectual Property (IP) Protection

Intellectual property (IP) rights protection is an especially important topic in China's corporate governance development and one of the top concerns of Western companies, primarily those from the US doing business in China. IP protection is a common problem in most emerging markets countries due to lacking innovation ability and IP protection regulations there, and China's enlarging economy and rapid growth pace have exaggerated this problem. The IP topics should be initiated from the top as part of business ethics and morals and executed as basic business practice of regulatory compliance. Otherwise, violations of IP rights will continue to cause tragic consequences for Chinese companies, as we have witnessed with the notable banning of Huawei from the US market.

At the same time, Chinese tech companies' fast growth has catapulted the country from a technology importer to an innovator over the past decade. China's proliferating economic global value and its plan to transfer the country's economic development strategy from high-speed to high-quality style, in addition to various innovative improvements, have innervated a powerful engine for the country's industrial and economic transformation. A mindset change has been occurring in the country that is reflected by an increasing number of IP applications granted to Chinese companies as a result of regulatory reforms.

The following highlight remarkable changes in China's IP landscape since the landmark year of 2019.

China Became the Top IP Filer in 2019

China bypassed the US in 2019 with a total of 58,990 IP applications filed with the World Intellectual Property Organization (WIPO),[2] versus a total of 57,840 IP applications by the US. In addition to China, the number of other participating Asian countries also soared over the past few years that resulted in total Asia-based IP applications to be over half of the total worldwide number, according to WIPO information. The 2019 surge of IP filers from China and other Asian countries indicates a trend toward an innovation shift in Asian emerging markets in the coming years. The number of IP applicants from China (68,720) topped the WIPO list again in 2020 (the number in the US was 59,230).[3] Of particular interest and worth mentioning, 2005 was a historic year for China, when it first entered the WIPO IP application top ten list with only 3,020 IP applications, when the US, who was first, had 48,482 filings. The contrast between China's fast growth and the US's stable but slow growth in numbers over the past 15 years echoes the trend of China's technology growth and industry transformation from low-value, high labor-intensive industries to high-value, mid-range products manufacturing.

Establishment of New IP Court of Appeals at the National Level in 2019

In January 2019, the new IP Court of Appeals was formally introduced, subservient only to the Supreme People's Court (China's equivalent to the US Supreme Court) with highly experienced IP judges appointed. Since the establishment of the IP Court of Appeals, several cases have been adjudicated by the Supreme People's Court, including Michael Jordan's trademark case against the Chinese company Qiaodan Sports, who has used the "Qiaodan" company name to identify its products brand and other commercial applications, in addition to approximately 200 trademarks closely related to Jordan's name, image, and likeness. Jordan's trademark case was filed in 2012 and finally resolved in 2020 in Jordan's favor after the establishment of the IP Court of Appeals.

China's Patent Law Amendment Enacted in 2021

On June 1, 2021, the fourth amendment to China's Patent Law became effective,[4] many years after the previous amendment that took effect in 2008. The amended patent law adjusted its enforcement mechanism by significantly increasing the maximum amount of punitive damages inflicted on a petitioner; extending the patent protection term from 10 to 15 years; joining the Hague Agreement[5] on industrial design patent practice and allowing partial design patents; and granting pharmaceutical patent holders extended terms with additional tools for protection. Although there is still room for further improvement in China's new patent law, the new amendment made significant improvements in patent rights protection to align with international patent practice, and allow for the spurring of pharmaceutical and biotech development in China. The fourth amendment also includes a broad anti-monopoly provision to align with Chinese regulators' anti-monopoly law provisions, which will be discussed below.

Antitrust Law Enforcement

Immediately after the Chinese government suspended Ant Group's IPO, the State Administration for Market Regulation issued a draft of *Guidelines for Anti-Monopoly in the Platform Economy* on November 10, 2020,[6] and placed Chinese tech giants under a microscope. The following April, Alibaba was fined a record-high RMB 18.2 billion ($2.8 billion) by Chinese regulators, and more than 20 Chinese tech giants made public pledges to comply with China's antitrust laws. Other than preventing monopolistic activity, protecting a fair and competitive market, and promoting equality and inclusion in the business environment, China's antitrust law enforcement will likely lead to regulatory reform in the following areas:

Consumer Data Collaboration and Protection

Chinese tech companies have collected a large volume of consumers' data containing a wealth of information, including individual behavior. Alibaba has established its own credit system that has been used to collaborate with the SoCS to establish a unified credit scoring system. Obviously, the government's access to a tech company's database has become a security consideration of other countries where local consumers' information has been collected by those companies. The lamentable Huawei and TikTok scenarios have proven the legitimate concerns regarding the challenges for those companies' international growth. On the other hand, enhancing antitrust law enforcement to prevent those tech giants from growing uncontrolled will also protect consumers' data collected by them. With the dual circulation new development strategy initiated by China's 14th FYP, future regulation reform should support Chinese companies' growth strategy in both domestic and international markets and protect consumers' interests in both markets.

M&A Transactions Involving VIE Structures under Antitrust Review

After lawmakers' most recent attempt to fix VIE structure loopholes in the 2015 Foreign Investment Law draft, regulators have been staying silent regarding VIE structure issues until the new antitrust law guidelines clearly addressing those mergers and acquisitions (M&A) transactions involving a VIE structure are subjected to antitrust review.[7] Although the antitrust review of M&A transactions is not directly targeting the legal status of a VIE structure, the government's review will tighten VIE structure utilization. This approach could be duplicated in other regulatory reforms to indirectly eliminate a VIE structure as a side effect of improving regulations in other areas.

New Legal Framework with Severe Penalties for Violations

Enforcement of the new antitrust law primarily targets Chinese tech giants and sends a strong warning signal of the government's intention to exert state power over companies who violate the law. The message is congruous with the 14th FYP to transform the economy from high-speed to high-quality models, particularly for companies that were accustomed to maneuvering in legal gray areas. Those companies will now face severe consequences and punishment for any violation.

The law is likely to awaken all tech giants and may possibly damage China's economy and investors' interest and faith for the time being. However, in the long-term, a well-regulated economic environment is essential, especially as China's economy transitions to the digital era, and plays a greater role in the global economy. Enforcement of the new antitrust law clearly indicates Chinese regulators are committed to a higher standard of regulations that will sustain and strengthen Chinese companies and the country's entire economy.

Minority Shareholders Interest Protection

Compared to investors from advanced countries such as the US and UK, Chinese investors are much less sophisticated. Given the short history of China's stock market, limited ownership of institutional investments in Chinese companies, and China's nascent corporate governance code, shareholder engagement and minority shareholders' interest protection concepts are new to Chinese investors. A 2020 amendment to China's securities law added a representative action provision that provides a path for shareholders' class-action suits.[8] As this book is being written, the new law's validity was tested when the first minority shareholder interest protection lawsuit was litigated in favor of 315 minority shareholders, becoming an important milestone in Chinese stock market history. Adding drama with symbolism, the defendant in this case was the first publicly traded company in modern China's history. Below is the case study:

Case Study 7.1   Feilo Acoustics Co., Ltd. Minority Shareholders Interest Protection

Feilo Acoustics Co., Ltd. (FEILO) is P.R. China's first joint-stock listed company. The company was approved by the People's Bank of China to issue shares to the public in 1984.[9] The company's shares were listed and traded from the Trust Business Department of the China Industrial and Commercial Bank of China in 1986 and transferred to the SSE in 1990 after its reopening.

FEILO is one of the oldest Chinese brands of sound reinforcement equipment, electro-acoustic components (speakers), ballroom lighting, and other related products. Over its nearly 40-year history, FEILO has extended its product offerings to software, multimedia communications, intelligence systems, etc. The company has restructured many times due to the fast change in the Chinese consumer market.

In July 2019, CSRC issued an Investigation Notice to FEILO due to suspected information disclosure violations. In November, the Shanghai Regulatory Bureau of the CSRC issued an administrative penalty decision based on two findings: FEILO's failure to meet projected revenue recognition requirements; and incorrect 2017 mid-year and third-quarter financial reports that indicated a false revenue forecast and an inflated profit.

In August 2020, several FEILO investors filed a lawsuit claiming that the information from FEILO's financial reports caused significant investment losses and demanded compensation of RMB146 million ($23 million) from the company. The Shanghai financial/civil court determined the scope of the shareholders' rights, issued a "notice of rights registration", and, according to "Guidance on Represented Litigation" rules, of the 315 plaintiffs (most of whom were retail investors), only 5 of them could act as class-action representatives.

On May 11, 2021, the court ordered FEILO to compensate the plaintiffs a total amount of RMB123 million ($19 million), averaging RMB390,000 ($61,000) per plaintiff.[10] That case was the first judicial practice of ordinary represented litigation since the Chinese Supreme Court issued its "Guidance on Several Issues of Represented Litigation in Securities Disputes" manual on March 24, 2020.

The outcome of the FEILO case provides a replicable sample for the further promotion of China's class action lawsuit system and has become a symbolic milestone of the country's regulatory reform – the establishment of a fair, efficient, and effective legal protection system for small and medium investors. As a result of the FEILO case, Chinese society will benefit from:

- An increased understanding of retail and minority shareholder rights
- Investors deepening trust in the Chinese legal system
- The establishment of a representative litigation mechanism in Chinese regulation reform
- Chinese regulators' commitment to establish a higher standard legal system

The FEILO case was not only the first but also a momentous event in China's representative litigation trend that shows minority shareholders are able to protect their interests within the legal system. However, shareholder engagement, which is a significant part of today's ESG movement, has a broader scope than shareholders' interest protection. To establish a shareholder engagement mechanism in Chinese markets demands a more comprehensive regulatory system and corporate governance code, trusted and experienced proxy agency firms, and significant share structure changes in Chinese companies to allow a higher percentage of institutional investors. Those elements will take time but change will happen quickly with the government's participation. For now, it is prudent to be patient.

Launching Beijing Stock Exchange with a Registration-Based IPO Process

In November 2021, the opening of the Beijing Stock Exchange marked mainland China's third main financial center, after the Shanghai and Shenzhen stock markets. The Beijing Stock Exchange was built on the former new third board[11] in Beijing. The new exchange aims to build a multilayered capital market to enhance financing systems for SMEs or startups with high growth potential and advanced technology, which is in line with President Xi Jinping's common prosperity policy of reducing wealth gaps across the country. A total of 81 stocks were traded on Beijing Stock Exchange on the first trading day, including 10 pre-approved newly listed stocks and 71 stocks transformed from the New Third Board. Stock price of the 10 newly listed companies surged during the day and triggered temporary trading halts, while performances for the other 71 stocks were mixed.

The Beijing Stock Exchange employs the same registration-based IPO mechanism as those of Shenzhen's ChiNext and Shanghai's STAR Market, which paves the way for listed companies on Beijing's exchange to migrate to ChiNext or STAR Market once qualified. ChiNext and STAR Market launched in 2009 and 2019, respectively, and aimed to attract innovative and fast-growth companies. Consequently, the overlap between the Beijing exchange and the others is insignificant, as the three exchanges were established to target companies of different sizes and areas within industrial value chains. In addition, the requirements for individual investors to participate in Beijing's exchange are identical to STAR Market's.

Despite the Chinese government's aggressive tightening of regulation and law enforcement of the Chinese financial market and deliberate targeting of giant Chinese companies while also restricting Chinese companies from seeking overseas listings, the opening of the Beijing Stock Exchange is a positive sign of the government's intention to consistently enact regulation reform while simultaneously open its financial market to the rest of the world. Moreover, the opening of the Beijing exchange with a registration-based IPO mechanism, multilayered capital markets, and direct channels to other main financial centers not only enables capital accessibility for SMEs but also indicates the nation's financial market development has entered a new phase with compatible and comprehensive financing structures, which is the foundation of establishing a higher standard financial regulation system.

Although the registration-based IPO system has been promoted by Chinese regulators since 2013, the system was first adopted by Shanghai's STAR Market in the middle of 2019. Compared with the old approval-based IPO system, the new registration-based IPO aims to make the approval process more transparent and market-oriented. At the moment, there's no clear sign of further reforms in Chinese stock exchange markets for the wide adoption of registration-based IPOs. In the long-term, and in order to compete with other stock exchange markets, a registration-based IPO will be the direction when all actors (including regulators, investors, and issuing companies) are increasingly ready for the new system in terms of the maturation level of the institutional system, stock exchange market, investor sophistication, and the quality of Chinese companies' governance system.

The Trend of Regulation Reform Along with Legal Enforcement

In addition to those economic regulation reforms, some legal policy tightening will inevitably influence and impact financial markets. In this section, I would like to point out a few upcoming financial regulation reforms related to legal policy enforcement.

Upcoming Regulation Reform Due to a Newly Established Data Security and Personal Information Protection Legal Framework

Perhaps the July 2021 tragedy of Didi Global Inc., the Chinese version of Uber, compares to Ant Group's IPO's suspension in November 2020 (case study 3.3). After going public in NYSE on June 30, 2021, immediately prior to the newly proposed cybersecurity review rules implemented by the Cyberspace Administration of China (CAC) that July, Didi was subject to review two days after its IPO and was banned from engaging with new users in China, while the company's data app was removed from Chinese app stores. Since the cybersecurity review mixed regulation compliance with a legal framework (as the rules were based on China's National Security Law), the cybersecurity law and the measures on cybersecurity review[12] concern Didi's operational collection, use, and management of customers' personal information. Meanwhile, and in addition to Didi, other mobile companies in China are also under scrutiny. The new cybersecurity review requirement forces many Chinese companies to pause their overseas IPO plans.

China's Cybersecurity Law became effective on June 1, 2017, and addresses the safety protocol of personal information handling and cross-border data transfer.[13] China's Data Security Law, which was drafted in April 2021, was published on June 10, 2021, and became effective on September 1, 2021. That law broadens its scope to include data location and utilization but, more importantly, emphasizes data security law violations.[14] Also, the Personal Information Protection Law, published in August 2020, took effect on November 1, 2021,[15] and requires operational changes in certain businesses regarding security and privacy compliance – especially in IT infrastructure design – and privacy and surveillance considerations similar to the EU's General Data Protection Regulations. All three laws will become the first extensive data security and personal information protection legal framework in China.

Didi is the first company to come under security review utilizing the new legal framework. At the time this book is being written, Didi's stock price is only half of its trading price on the first day of its IPO. Didi is cooperating with the Chinese government to resolve its controversial IPO issuance, but the solution has not yet been achieved.[16] On the other hand, to remain compliant with the upcoming new regulations and legal framework while pursuing their overseas IPOs, many companies have started to look for solutions, a notable example being the Canadian coffee brand Tim Horton, who proposed on August 24, 2021, to incorporate a new independent entity in China and partner with a state-backed entity in China to safeguard its customer data. It's too early to tell if Tim Horton's proposed concept will lead to a solution for future Chinese companies' overseas IPOs. Regardless of how the upcoming regulation change contributes to Chinese companies' domestic and international business operations and corporate governance structure and practice, it's likely safe to predict that positive outcomes will be realized.

Upcoming Corporate Governance Regulatory Reform Due to Board Directors' Legal Responsibilities Enforcement

In previous chapters, I reviewed the existence of the patriarchal culture and nominal board feature that impaired the independence and objectivity of

Chinese company boards. Although listed companies are required to have at least one-third of board members as independent directors, the independent directors are not typically involved in important decision-making functions due to lack of competency, or lack of trust since they are considered outsiders. The Chinese regulators restrict university professors from taking independent director positions as part of the country's anti-corruption reforms, [17] but many outside directors are still academic professors or influential celebrities. Relying on companies to improve board directors' qualifications to offer independent opinions and their participation in decision-making will be challenging because of the prevailing controlling structure in Chinese companies. Conversely, should consideration be given to the allegation that independent directors' fiduciary duties and responsibilities may be compromised due to false prestige while they serve as board directors on Chinese companies'? Specifically, do they understand their personal liability and risk exposure as "showcase" directors? Those outside directors are paid an annual salary of RMB80,000 to RMB100,000, and many of them serve on several companies' boards but do not participate in decision-making privileges despite being given voting power. Unfortunately, lessons are learned the hard way. In late November 2021, a wave of Chinese A-share companies' outside directors' resignations occurred after a ruling from a Guangzhou court in the middle of the month. Below is the case study of this ruling.

Case Study 7.2   Kangmei Directors' Personal Liability vs. a Company's Financial Fraud[18]

Kangmei Pharmaceutical Co. is one of China's biggest publicly traded drugmakers. The company was founded in 1997 by Xingtian Ma and became a listed company on the SSE via an IPO in March 2001. Although the company has claimed to be undergoing share-trading reform, its insufficient corporate governance mechanisms and internal controls were not questioned until the discovery of a financial scandal in 2019. It is worth mentioning that four of the five independent directors were university professors, and another was a certified accountant with an accounting firm,[19] despite Chinese regulators' restriction of academic professors serving as independent board directors.

In 2019, Kangmei was discovered for RMB89 billion ($14 billion) financial fraud between 2016 and 2018 with an overstated cash position of $4.3 billion using false bank deposit slips and forged transaction records. The company also manipulated the stock price by transferring company funds to related parties to create fake trading transactions of its stock.

In 2000, the company's loss reached RMB27.7 billion ($4.3 billion), five times the loss in 2019 RMB4.7 billion ($735,000).

> *In April 2021, Kangmei's creditor filed a lawsuit seeking bankruptcy and restructuring of the company.*
>
> *In November 2021, the Guangzhou court (a city-level court) ruled the directors, executives, and external auditors of Kangmei compensate 55,037 investors for their losses totaling RMB2.5 billion ($391 million) caused by the financial fraud. The five independent directors were each liable for an amount between RMB123 million ($19 million) and RMB246 million ($38 million). Kangmei's former chairman and founder, Xingtian Ma, was sentenced to 12 years in prison and fined RMB1.2 million ($188,300). In January 2022, Ma's appeal was rejected by the Guangdong Higher People's Court.*
>
> *Ma and other executives illegally raised huge amounts of funds by manipulating Kangmei's stock price and trading volume from 2015 to 2018. In addition to planning and directing the financial fraud, Ma paid a total of $1.1 million to bribe a number of government officials from 2005 to 2012 in exchange for various benefits to the company.*
>
> *At least five government officials involved with Ma's bribery case were removed from their positions and punished, including the former Party secretary of Guangzhou, and the former chief of the investor protection bureau at CSRS.*
>
> *In December 2021, Kangmei was rescued by a local SOE from the pharmaceutical industry.*

After the first class-action lawsuit ordering FEILO to compensate minority shareholders for the company's financial fraud, Kangmei's case marked the first ruling in China that ordered independent directors and executives to compensate investors. The remarkable amounts of individual fines ordered by the court set up an alarm to remind board directors about their fiduciary duties and liabilities and indicated the Chinese government's determination of zero tolerance for market misconduct and the need for the upcoming enforcement of directors' legal responsibility against companies' regulatory violations.

Kangmei's case triggered a wave of outside board director resignations from publicly listed companies in mainland China. Moreover, Kangmei's case will stir profound thinking, discussions, and questions among individuals serving as outside directors regarding Chinese companies' governance systems regarding directors' qualifications, compensation, competence, and protection. The lack of board mechanisms that ensure necessary company information is being communicated to directors prevents board directors from performing monitoring roles. Moreover, the negligence creates personal risks for those directors since they are legally liable for the consequences of misconduct or regulatory violations. In addition, the Directors and Officers Liability (D&O insurance) policy that is recommended in the West is not widely accepted in Chinese companies yet. Until the Kangmei case, many Chinese companies did not disclose whether or not their companies' insurance policies included D&O coverage. Kangmei case will certainly put D&O insurance coverage into the consideration of Chinese listed companies and policymakers. Although there are debates in the global market regarding the pros and cons of D&O coverage, hopefully, the topic will soon be addressed in China with regulatory guidance or recommendation.

Although there is no public information at the moment regarding China's corporate governance regulations reforms with more practical guidance to reflect the issues revealed by Kangmei case, the necessity of regulatory improvement is convincing.

Upcoming Credit Rating System Reform Along with Anti-Corruption Policy Enforcement

Corruption is a social problem caused mainly by a country's governmental structure, political system, and quality of its institutions. While growing as an emerging markets country, anti-corruption has been a topic on every Chinese government's agenda in order to ensure the Party's political power in the government. With China's goal for a higher standard regulation system, the overlap of the government's recent financial regulation reform and anti-corruption movement is explicit.

In August 2021, Chinese regulators suspended all credit rating requirements for interbank market bond issuers after discovering a series of scandals and defaults of bonds that had high credit ratings. Those scandals and defaults were directly related to instances of severe corruption, which revealed deep-rooted credit rating system loopholes that included inflated ratings.[20] Several top Chinese rating agencies were banned from offering false high credit ratings for new interbank bonds due to their involvement with selected scandals, including China Chengxin International Credit Rating Co. Ltd, the biggest credit agency in China with 42% market share. Chengxin is a joint venture with Moody's Investor Service (Moody's Investor Service owns 30% shares of the joint venture). Chengxin was involved in a bond default by state-owned Yongcheng Coal and Electricity Holding Group Co. Ltd.

The following case study of Yongcheng Coal and Electricity Holding Group Co. Ltd. will highlight the relationship between the necessity for reform of the bond market's legal framework, credit rating system, and anti-corruption enactment.

Case Study 7.3   Yongcheng Coal and Electricity Holding Group Bond Default Revealed Financial and Legal Problems

On November 10, 2020, Yongcheng Coal and Electricity Holding Group Co. Ltd., a state-owned company in central China and a subsidiary of Henan Energy and Chemical Industry Group Co., Ltd., defaulted on an RMB 1 billion ($152 million) corporate bond. After the default, China's top financial officials announced the government's zero tolerance policy of bond market misconduct and suspended new debt issuance totaling RMB15.5 billion ($2.4 billion) of over 20 Chinese companies, marking the beginning of bond market regulation reform.

Below are highlights of a series of bond defaults and problems that led to the reform[21]:

From January to October 2020, five additional Chinese SOEs failed to pay, including Tsinghua Unigroup, a high-profile state technology group, and Huachen Automotive Group, an SOE in Liaoning province. Yongcheng and Huachen previously received AAA credit ratings from China's top credit rating agencies. Their defaults raised red flags for the credit rating sector.

***The Yongcheng default was later found to be connected to the corruption of Henan Energy and Chemical Industry Group's two former chairmen, one of whom was sentenced to life in prison in 2016.**[22]*

Before 2010, Yongcheng Coal and Electricity Holding Group was the most profitable unit of Henan Energy, the largest state-owned company by asset volume in Henan Province, central China.

In 2010, Henan Energy invested RMB10 billion in five ethylene glycol projects totaling 1 million tons of annual capacity, and RMB6.3 billion in another ethylene glycol project in Guizhou province. At that time, the coal-based ethylene glycol production cost was 16% less than oil-to-ethylene glycol, which made Henan Energy's investment very promising due to low coal prices and decent-sized coal reserves. However, because of various reasons, the five projects did not start production until 2015, and the Guizhou project did not start production until 2018, when ethylene glycol's selling price significantly dropped as those projects started production. The details of those projects' investments were questionable.

In addition, Henan Energy made other investments in a joint venture company in the chemical sector through a series of capital reorganizations and equity investments and signed various related-party procurement agreements, which made the "black hole" quite complicated ... until Yongcheng's default in November 2020.

In November 2020, China's interbank bond market's self-regulatory body, the National Association of Financial Market Institutional Investors (NAFMII), launched an investigation into the Yongcheng rating scandal. The interbank bond market accounted for 86% of China's outstanding onshore bonds at the end of 2020.

In December 2020, China Chengxin International Credit Rating Co. Ltd., the rating agency of Yongcheng, was banned from performing new interbank bond rating business for three months as a result of NAFMII's investigation. Other financial intermediaries related to Yongcheng's default were also disciplined by regulators, including Haitong Securities Co. Ltd.[23]

In March 2021, the Securities Association of China (SAC) reported its concerns of credit rating agencies' lack of quality control, e.g., supporting evidence. Of the 23 defaulting issuers in 2020, those rating agencies did not reflect any negative adjustments six months prior to the defaults of 14 issuers, and no negative adjustments were made in one month of nine issuer defaults.[24] SAC's findings echo NAFMII's investigation findings. At that point, China's credit rating sector's inflated ratings and failure to reflect risks were confirmed.

In addition to the bonds' defaults, the Chinese real estate "gray rhino" that has been transforming the Chinese economic structure in the past decades is further pushing the need for credit system reform. The systemic risk of the Chinese real estate sector started with Evergrande Group's debt defaults in 2020. Below is the outline of the Evergrande debt crisis:

Case Study 7.4   Brief Overview of Evergrande Group Debt Crisis Situation[25]

Evergrande Group (formerly known as the Hengda Group) was founded by Kayan Hui in 1996 in Guangzhou, China. Evergrande Group's businesses include wealth management, electric car manufacturing, food and drink sectors, and sports clubs (Evergrande Group is the owner of Guangzhou Hengda, one of the biggest soccer teams in China). Mr. Hui was once the richest person in Asia with a personal fortune of RMB10 billion ($1.6 billion). As of December 2021, Evergrande Real Estate owned over 1,300 projects in more than 280 cities across China.

In 2020, Evergrande became one of China's biggest companies, with over $300 billion in debt. When Chinese regulators tightened financing *policies for real estate developers that year, Evergrande defaulted on interest payments. With over $300 billion in debt and hundreds of unfinished projects, Evergrande's liquidity crisis shook China's real estate industry and global bond market.*

Evergrande's "too big to fail" dilemma revealed potential systemic problems, if Evergrande had collapsed, including: First, many homeowners paid their deposit while the construction of their buildings were not started. Those homeowners will not be able to recover the deposit nor receive their new home; Second, firms engaged with Evergrande for businesses, including construction and design service providers and material suppliers, are at risk of significant financial loss, including bankruptcy; Third, banks and other lenders may be forced to lend less to others, which will affect the financial system; Fourth, global investors will lose confidence and an appetite for Chinese companies.

Therefore, carefully handling the Evergrande debt crisis is essential for the stabilization of China's financial and bond markets. In May 2022, Evergrande received the bondholder's approval to extend payments by six months. When the extension was granted, Evergrande had 13 outstanding bonds with a total balance of RMB55.85 billion ($8.38 billion).

The significant amount and a potentially serious chain reaction of Evergrande Group's debt crisis could have turned the company into "China's Lehman Brothers" if the problem was not handled carefully. Evergrande's debt default has shocked Chinese bank sectors and led to stock price plunges for all property-developing companies. Although Chinese regulators are no longer willing to tolerate "too big to fall" monopolistic behavior, smoothly and carefully handling situations like Evergrande debt, strategically balancing financial market stability, and reducing property-sector leverage in the economy are unsolved challenges for the Chinese government at the moment. And the necessity for Chinese credit rating system reform is being further pushed to the forefront.

Upon overhauling the credit rating industry, Chinese regulators are proposing more reforms that aim toward a more market-oriented credit rating system where investors pay for credit ratings to facilitate rational decisions by the investors based on creditworthiness analysis made with consideration of the investors' interest and risks. A market-oriented system will also encourage competition among participants and improve credit rating quality. In the short term, the credit rating system reform might shrink the credit rating sector, but the long-term effect will help build a high-quality credit rating system and enhance investors' confidence.

The Chinese government's disciplinary approach to its credit rating system aims to establish a more market-oriented system where investors instead of issuers would pay for credit ratings reports. Although establishing such a new credit rating industry might take time, the direction is clear for the time being. Of the many problems revealed by the Yongcheng and Evergrande default cases, I would like to highlight two significant trends: the unavoidable connection between corruption and financial market scandals; and the necessity to improve regulation system and legal framework simultaneously. Therefore, upcoming regulation reforms in China's financial markets and legal enhancement mechanisms in related areas will go "hand-in-hand".

Takeaways

- **China's recent regulation reforms in intellectual property protection, antitrust law enforcement, and minority shareholders' interest protection** are closing the gaps between China and advanced countries in the compliance and enforcement areas of these regulations.
- **The trend of simultaneous reforms in financial regulations and legal frameworks** are effectively improving China's institutional system.

Notes

1   Andrew Kakabadse and Nada Kakabadse, *The Geopolitics of Governance – The Impact of Contrasting Philosophies*, Page 88, , Palgrave, 2001. https://searchworks.stanford.edu/view/4672494
2   The World Intellectual Property Organization (WIPO) is a specialized United Nations agency consisting of 193 member countries. The WIPO was founded in 1967 and is headquartered in Switzerland. WIPO's main functions are to promote worldwide IP protection and offer IP administration services according to treaties signed by member countries.
3   WIPO staff article, "Innovation Perseveres: International Patent Filings via WIPO Continues to Grow in 2020 Despite COVID-19 Pandemic," WIPO, March, 2021, May 16, 2021. www.wipo.int/pressroom/en/articles/2021/article_0002.html
4   Stephen Yang, "China: Review of the 4th Amendments of China's Patent Law," Mondaq, January, 2021, July 19, 2021. www.mondaq.com/china/patent/1000092/review-of-the-4th-amendment-of-china39s-patent-law-
5   The Hague Agreement is an international industrial design protection system administered by the WIPO and covers 92 countries. The Hague system protects the lifecycles of industrial design via a mechanism of protection for renewal applications.
6   Sofia Baruzzi, "China Releases Anti-Monopoly Guidelines for Its Platform Economy," China Briefing, 2020, May 20, 2021. www.china-briefing.com/news/china-releases-anti-monopoly-guidelines-for-its-platform-economy/
7   Karry Lai, "Prime: China's New Anti-Monopoly Rules for Tech Companies," IFLR, 2021, May 20, 2021. www.iflr.com/article/b1r3bt1z7g1771/primer-chinas-new-anti-monopoly-rules-for-tech-companies
8   Qi'ang Chen and Victor Yang, "China Launches Class-Action Lawsuit System for Its 167 Million Securities Investors," *Clyde and Co.*, August 13, 2020. www.clydeco.com/en/insights/2020/08/china-launches-class-action-lawsuit-system-for-its

9   "Shanghai Feilo Acoustics Co., Ltd., Baidu (n.d.)," (translated), May 16, 2021, June 1, 2021. https://baike.baidu.com/item/上海飞乐音响股份有限公司/10185026?fr= aladdin#1

10 "Feilo Audio: Regain the Sorrows of the Past," (translated), China Economic Net, May, 2021, May 16, 2021. http://finance.ce.cn/stock/gsgdbd/202105/15/t20210515_ 36560072.shtml

11 China launched the new third board (the National Equities Exchange and Quotations) in 2013 to facilitate financing for China's non-listed firms. The new third board allows firms to exchange equity and raise funds. As if May 2022, over 6,000 companies was listed on China's new third board. https://english.www.gov.cn/news/topn ews/202205/04/content_WS627262d9c6d02e533532a3b8.html

12 Zhijing Yu, Vicky Liu, and Yan Luo, "China Initiates Cybersecurity Review of Didi Chuxing and Three Other Chinese Mobile Applications", Covington, July 6, 2021. www.insideprivacy.com/international/china/china-initiates-cybersecurity-review-of-didi-chuxing-and-three-other-chinese-mobile-applications/

13 Leo Zhao and Lulu Xia, "China's Cybersecurity Law: An Introduction for Foreign Businesspeople", China Briefing, March 1, 2018. https://bit.ly/3jiG8rD

14 Thomas Zhang, "China Releases Data Security Law: Some Expert Observations and Comments", China Briefing, June 23, 2021. https://bit.ly/3gAqAy2

15 Thomas Zhang, "Personal Information Protection Law in China: Technical Considerations for Companies", China Briefing, August 23, 2021. https://bit.ly/ 3ynDgOF

16 John Liu, Dong Cao, and Ben Scent, "Xi's Data Clampdown Spurs Novel Solution from Tim Hortons China", Bloomberg, August 24, 2021, August 25, 2021. www. bloomberg.com/news/articles/2021-08-24/xi-s-data-clampdown-spurs-novel-solut ion-from-tim-hortons-china

17 Fortune, "A Chinese Court Fined Five Independent Directors Hundreds of Millions of Dollars. Now China's Board Members are Quitting", November 22, 2021. https:// fortune.com/2021/11/22/china-kangmei-pharmaceuticals-fine-independent-corpor ate-board-directors-quit/

18 Wang Juanjuan and Denise Jia, "Kangmei's Former Chief Gets 12 Years in Final Verdict", January 11, 2022, Caixin Global. www.caixinglobal.com/2022-01-11/ kangmeis-former-chief-gets-12-years-in-final-verdict-101828412.html

19 Wu Yujian, Wang Juanjuan, and Denise Jia, "Kangmei Verdict Spurs Wave of Independent Directors to Quit", November 20, 2021. www.caixinglobal.com/2021-11- 20/kangmei-verdict-spurs-wave-of-independent-directors-to-quit-101807640.html

20 Zhang Yuzhe and Guo Yingzhe, "PBOC Suspends Mandatory Ratings for Interbank Market Bond Issuers", August 12, 2021, Caixin Global. www.caixinglobal.com/ 2021-08-12/pboc-suspends-mandatory-ratings-for-interbank-market-bond-issuers- 101754516.html. Iris Hong, "China Punishes 11 Companies Linked to Yongcheng Coal Default," Asia Financial, January 19, 2021. www.asiafinancial.com/china-punishes-11-companies-linked-to-yongcheng-coal-default

21 Tom Mitchell and Sun Yu, "String of Defaults Tests Safety Net for Chinese Bonds," Financial Times, November 23, 2020. www.ft.com/content/e842dceb-d97c-42f7- bc3a-347c864d6e46

22 Yu Ning and Denise Jia, "In Depth: How Ethylene Glycol Led to the Yongcheng Coal Default," Nikkei, December 17, 2020. https://asia.nikkei.com/Spotlight/Caixin/ In-depth-How-ethylene-glycol-led-to-the-Yongcheng-Coal-default

23 Peng Qinpin and Han Wei, "Yongcheng Coal Default Leaves Rating Agency Banned From Ratings for Three Months", Caixin Global, December 30, 2020. www.caixi nglobal.com/2020-12-30/china-chengxin-hit-with-business-ban-in-yongcheng-coal-default-101644657.html

24 Reuters Staff, "Chinese Industry Association Flags Rating Agency Shortcomings," Reuters, March 10, 2021. www.reuters.com/article/us-china-ratings-sac/chinese-industry-association-flags-rating-agency-shortcomings-idUSKBN2B309K
25 BBC, "Evergrande: China property Giant Misses Debt Deadline", December 9, 2021. www.bbc.com/news/business-58579833. Chen Bo and Denise Jia, "Evergrande Unit Discovers $2.1 Billion in Cash Was Seized by Banks", March 23, 2022. www.caixinglobal.com/2022-03-23/evergrande-unit-discovers-21-billion-in-cash-was-seized-by-banks-101859658.html. Chen Bo and Denise Jia, "Evergrande Dodges Onshore Default with Six-Month Debt Extension", March 7, 2022, www.caixinglobal.com/2022-05-07/evergrande-dodges-onshore-default-with-six-month-debt-extension-101881486.html

Part IV

The Key Geopolitical Elements of Chinese Corporate Governance

Chapter 8

Regional Agreements and Partnerships

In this chapter, I review

* Regional Comprehensive Economic Partnership (RCEP)
  RCEP distinguish from previous regional trade agreement
  China's opportunities and challenges in RCEP
  Geopolitical impacts

* China's Belt and Road Initiative (BRI)
  Positive impacts of China's BRI
  Future development

* China–Africa Collaboration
  Achievements and challenges
  Major problems
  The future of China–Africa collaboration

China's continuous GDP growth in the post-pandemic era enabled the country to prepare for the next stage of its economic growth and global position. However, perpetually complicated globalization has created an intricate interdependence among many countries across the globe, so no country can consistently grow if the remaining of the world are struggling. Helping those countries who suffered deeply during the pandemic and contributing to rebuilding the regional and international ecosystem, while seeking its own opportunities, have inevitably become China's task and mission for the coming years.

On the other hand, the increasing tension between China and the US due to their relationship change from strategic partners to competitors is currently impacted by the accelerating pace of the ESG movement that has expanded to the rest of the world. As a result, a multitude of divergent reactions, including concerns from Western and emerging countries regarding Chinese companies' business practices and ESG performance, have been voiced. Those are

DOI: 10.4324/9781003302919-13

vociferous demands for improvement! The tension has also forced China and other major countries to reconsider their global strategies and roles in the contemporary international business climate.

Although the global business landscape in the post-pandemic era offers more opportunities and challenges for China and Chinese companies, for the purpose of this book, I will focus on reviewing three regional agreements and partnerships. As China is the dominant country of these three regional agreements, addressing those opportunities and challenges and their resulting effects on the country's corporate governance development and ESG movements is of utmost relevance. As pointed out by Professor Andrew Kakabadse and Nada Kakabadse in their co-authored book, *The Geopolitics of Governance – The Impact of Contrasting Philosophies*, the essential links between corporate governance structure, political and geopolitical concerns, and international relations[1] result in the formation and development of cross-country trade agreements. Therefore, these trade agreements unavoidably contain complicated geopolitical and diplomatic considerations and impact, which adds complexity to the partnerships among member countries and peripheral parties. The three regional agreements below are not exceptional. Therefore, I think it's necessary to list the highlights of those geopolitical and other international factors, although the purpose of this book is not to further analyze nor offer suggestions.

Forming productive partnerships with other emerging market countries and neighboring countries has been China's long-term strategy, most notably involving the recent Regional Comprehensive Economic Partnership (RCEP), China's Belt and Road Initiative (BRI) launched in 2013, and the Forum on China–Africa Cooperation (FOCAC) that was initiated 20 years ago. Signing RCEP agreements that had been in the negotiating and ratifying phases since 2012 seems like a natural move for China and other member countries of the region, due to the assistance needed for some member countries to recover from the pandemic, and China's desire to strengthen its influence in the region as well as to advance its internationalization strategies. However, China and Chinese companies have struggled because of the increasing criticisms regarding project quality and other ESG problems involving the BRI project and other African projects. In addition to various financial and operational challenges encountered during BRI projects due to the COVID-19 disruption, a number of economic and political problems were revealed by the China–Africa collaboration projects, including some that were completed and delivered to host countries.

How can China continue the BRI and its collaborative relationships with African countries? What can Chinese companies do differently in RCEP agreements with lessons learned from both BRI and China–Africa projects? How will China handle the geopolitical challenges and build constructive relationships with various stakeholders within the global landscape? First, let us start by understanding RCEP and the elements that distinguishes that new agreement from others.

What We Should Know about RCEP

Historically, international and regional economic agreements and partnership frameworks have been led by advanced countries, and most of the finished products resulting from those trade agreements have been shipped to advanced countries' markets due to their consumption demand and ability, and emerging market countries' lack of efficient and effective trade rules and tariffs systems. That dilemma applied to most Asian trade agreements in the past, including the Comprehensive and Progressive Agreement for Trans-Pacific Partnership (CPTPP), effective in December 2018, and its predecessor, the Trans-Pacific Partnership (TPP) that took effect in February 2016. Because of CPTPP's structure with advanced countries taking lead roles, that Asia-Pacific regional trade agreement has not continued due to advanced countries' dissatisfaction with agreement outcomes (e.g., the US withdrawal from TPP and a tariff disagreement between Canada and major Asia-Pacific counties). If the effectiveness of a regional trade agreement is dominated by advanced countries who are not part of the region, what does a regional trade agreement really mean to the region? Who are the ultimate beneficiaries from a regional agreement?

The answers to those questions may be a few of the motivating factors found in the initial RCEP framework that was first launched during the Association of Southeast Asian Nations (ASEAN) summit in Cambodia in 2012. The RCEP was signed in November 2020 and contained four major differences from prior Asia-Pacific regional trade agreements: The RCPE is ASEAN-centric and significantly influenced by China, an emerging markets country, and is the first trade agreement among China, Japan, and South Korea only that is exclusively designed for Asian interests to focus on economic cooperation.

What Makes RCEP Different from Previous Regional Trade Agreements

Since the worldwide business community is still engaged in post-pandemic economic recovery, what roles will the RCEP play in Asian and global economies? How will China help member countries simultaneously recover from the pandemic and accelerate ESG adoption? What opportunities will the RCEP create for China? Let us review the following highlights of the RCEP to seek answers.

The World's Largest Trade Bloc

According to World Bank's 2019 GDP data, RCEP member countries' total GDP is $25.84 trillion (28% of the global trade total) compared to $24.37 trillion of the US–Mexico–Canada North American Free Trade Agreement (NAFTA) and $18.85 trillion of the EU Economic Area.[2] As of 2020, RCEP's 15-member countries represent 30% of the world's GDP and population and its GDP percentage is expected to grow to 50% by 2030 according to an HSBC report. Since all member countries are from the Asia-Pacific region with complete cohesion anticipated by January 2022, the RCEP will create a regional supply-chain ecosystem, introduce and encourage financial investment, and imbue intellectual property (IP) protection rules to promote free trade in Asia.

RCEP Member Countries' Diversity

Compared to previous Asian trade agreements, RCEP members are much more diverse in many aspects, including population sizes, wealth levels, geography (inland and archipelago countries), services and products trading, and types of imports and exports. Having smaller sized countries (e.g., Laos) and others with unstable political environments (e.g., Myanmar and Thailand) will create more complications and less ambition for the RCEP. However, member countries' diversity will also make RCEP more influential for the region's sustainable economic development, peoples' livelihood improvement, regulatory practices, social responsibility, environmental protection, and perhaps political stability.

ASEAN-Centric

The ASEAN-centric framework[3] is essential for RCEP's success – especially during post-COVID-19 recovery – and for structural transformation in the region for these main reasons: First, ASEAN's half-century history (including its predecessor, the Association of Southeast Asia (ASA) that began in 1961) has already gained the trust from its ten member countries, revealing the cohesion that is very important in Asian culture, leading all of them to join the RCEP. Doing so will bring that organization's membership to 15 countries; second, an ASEAN-centric feature has established a fair and non-biased platform for RCEP that will enhance regional cooperation and ensure implementation of a rule-based trade and investment framework and other structural reforms for all member countries to benefit; third, and most importantly, the ASEAN-centric concept is a key element for RCEP to bring China, Japan, and South Korea into one trade agreement. Despite the historical disputes among those countries, collaboration under the RCEP framework may ease negotiations of the trilateral trade agreement that has stalled notwithstanding many years of mediation.[4] In addition, collaboration among them will provide significant financial contributions to East Asia's economic development.

China's Influential Role

China's important role in RCEP members' post-pandemic recovery is essential for RCEP member countries, especially those who are small and least developed. The COVID-19 crisis worsened the economic situation of many member countries such as Laos and Cambodia, both of whom have been struggling, while Thailand has had to close its borders and banned nonresident foreigners, and the Philippines' infection numbers continue to increase. Since the COVID-19 outbreak, most advanced countries in the world, including the US and UK, have struggled to reopen their domestic economies due to several waves of COVID-19 variances in 2020 and 2021. China's effective control of the COVID-19 crisis in 2020 positioned the country to be one of few countries with positive GDP growth in 2020 and strong GDP growth in 2021. China's stable economic growth, the increasing prosperity of its middle class, and consumers' purchasing power and consumption of imported goods and services will create many opportunities to help other member countries' economies recover once the RCEP becomes effective. In addition, due to global digital, technological, and green economy transformations, there is an urgent need for economic and structural support among RCEP member countries. With China's technology advantage in the region and its leading roles globally in digital and green transformation, those countries will benefit by partnering with China.

Intellectual Property (IP) Protection

IP rights is RCEP's most advanced improvement compared to any other Asian trade agreement. Unfortunately, many Asian countries are well known for their lack of commitment to IP rights protection. The size of China's economy and its fast growth pace amplified the IP violation issue in China over the past two decades. However, regional trade deals previously agreed upon neglected to acknowledge IP protection challenges and the seriousness of its application. Inserting IP rights in the RCEP indicates the regional partnership's intention to establish high-standard trade orders and a healthier ecosystem in the region. China started to take serious action on IP protection beginning in early 2019 with the establishment of a new IP Court of Appeals, new regulations on IP disputes, provisions in the 2019 Foreign Investment Law for IP transaction restrictions, and the most recent patent law amendment that occurred in June 2021. Due to an increasing number of IP ownership rights by Chinese companies and the proliferation of technology in China, Chinese IP protection regulations are needed not only to protect IP rights from advanced countries like the US, but also to protect Chinese companies' IP ownership rights. As discussed in an early chapter, technology independence is one of the most important focuses of China's 14th FYP. As a result, further regulatory and funding support for research and development will occur, and the fostering of IP ownership rights by Chinese companies will further change the mentality and understanding of IP protection in China. With China's dual circulation strategy proposed in the 14th FYP, its IP protection improvement will undoubtedly stir IP rights protection within its partner countries and other RCEP member countries.

Regional Collaboration Enhancement

The RCEP marks the first time an agreement has occurred between China, Japan, and South Korea,[5] three of the four largest economies in Asia. Will the RCEP help build economic cooperation among those countries to create positive energy for Asia-Pacific regional development? These is no certain answer at the moment. Signing the agreement is the first step and a positive sign of their intention to work together; however, substantial collaboration among them requires win-win strategies that need further discussions and exploration, while global economic development is dependent on their input to stimulate economic collaboration as well as repudiate historical problems between them.

Therefore the RCEP is a landmark trade agreement that offers not only tremendous opportunities but also surmountable challenges for China and the region.

Opportunities and Challenges for China through RCEP

Joining RCEP as the most influential country in the region marks a new chapter of China's growth journey in the global market as a leader. Despite high expectations from other RCEP member countries and their global partners, the unceasingly complicated geopolitical environment and many other uncertainties are raising challenges to China's own growing strategy through RCEP. What are the opportunities and challenges confronting China?

Enhance Regional Products and Services Exchanges and Capital Market Collaboration

China's comprehensive supply-chain ecosystem that is essential to the region's development. With the ongoing global supply-chain relocation from China to other Asian countries, China's support system will continuously serve and benefit global supply-chain development in other Asian countries toward the establishment of a regional supply-chain system. In addition to growing consumer demands from the Chinese market that will bring more manufacturers and export opportunities for member countries, China's perpetual technology development and growth requires a larger consumer market to absorb new products.

The RCEP will create more win-win partnerships between China and other Asian countries for products, services, and technology exchanges.

Due to the size of RCEP's member countries' collective GDP, successfully leading the RCEP can also help China enhance its influence on the region's capital market and ESG movement.

Strengthen China's Economic Influence and RMB's International Adoption

The Chinese currency's (RMB) international usage in both trade settlement and countries' foreign currency reserve has been far behind China's economic growth. (Details regarding RMB internationalization will be discussed in Chapter 9.) Despite the Chinese government's restricted currency control and the time needed for China to prove its stable economic growth are the major factors for the RMB's global utilization, establishing a solid currency zone is a prerequisite condition for China to promote its currency within the global market. The potential increase of trade and capital market transactions between China and other RCEP countries could generate broader utilization of the Chinese RMB. China's leading role and contribution to the region's economic recovery by promoting a subsequent increase in RMB usage, along with other RCEP's members' continued collective GDP growth, may determine if the RCEP will become a great opportunity for China to establish its economic zone and currency zone.

Accelerate Asian Countries' ESG Performance

ESG adoption is a big challenge for RCEP at the moment. The RCEP has received warranted criticism from advanced countries for its lack of labor rules, worker and human rights, and environmental protection. Due to the fact that many RCEP member countries have been underdeveloped and primarily focused on economic issues, the RCEP's 2012 creation was premature, relative to ESG adoption, which was not then considered. However, the worldwide ESG movement (in lieu of severe disasters from climate changes) now requires the world – including RCEP countries – to commit to ESG integration, even though most RCEP countries are presently fighting for economic recovery and economic growth simultaneously. With China's active ESG movement driven by the country's top asset management firms and corporations, there is considerable likelihood and also ample opportunities to initiate and influence RCEP member countries' ESG implementation via compliance requirements for investment projects created by asset management firms such as Ping An Group, or by supply-chain ESG integration strategies initiated by Chinese companies such as Xiaomi.

Improve Regional Regulation Infrastructure

China's continuous effort on improving its regulation system will also help improve the regulatory infrastructure of the region toward future corporate governance development, while also accelerate business mindsets and behavior changes for corporate governance betterment. China has been actively working on improving its regulatory environment in various regulatory areas such as IP protection and antitrust law enforcement as discussed in early chapters. Becoming the most influential member of RCEP and taking leading roles in the region's post-pandemic recovery and ESG movement indicate China's rising influence on the region's regulation system environment, which is one of the most significant elements of future governance development. Because of the integration among ASEAN countries' economies and their central roles in RCEP, China's significant influence within RCEP will most likely facilitate its role as a leading country for the region's regulatory standard framework, including ESG-related disclosure requirements and other legal frameworks such as IP protection and cybersecurity laws to meet the demands of the burgeoning trends in technology and digital economies.

In order to build a better corporate governance development infrastructure, Chinese companies have also established some new and advanced corporate governance models, such as succession planning (e.g., Pinduoduo founder's retirement), social entrepreneurship (e.g., ByteDance CEO's resignation from CEO roles to better focus on the company's social responsibility and long-term strategy), Government also enhanced the legal system's support of shareholder interest protection (e.g., Feilo Acoustics minority shareholder lawsuit). Those new corporate governance practice and mechamisms will influence business mindsets and behavior changes in Asian countries that have close cultural ties and business partnerships with regional partners.

Improve Chinese Companies' Overseas Corporate Governance Practices

Although the criticism of BRI and China–Africa collaboration projects today has been focused on "E"- and "S"-related issues, the fundamental reason of these issues is these Chinese companies' governance model of their overseas operations. Substantial improvement is needed in several aspects, including business mindset, corporate culture, respect host countries' cultures and business practices, local laws and regulations compliance, and transparency of business operations and decision-making process. While writing this book, I had a chance to speak with Selebalo Ntepe, the Deputy Chair of the Institute of Directors in Lesotho, an organization that supports the launching of the first set of the country's corporate governance code. Mr. Ntepe shared his opinions regarding Chinese multinationals operating in Lesotho. Carefully acknowledging that while his country is highly reliant on Chinese financing for various business projects, he believes cultural differences between China and African countries are not a hindrance. Mr. Ntepe is optimistic about China and Lesotho's future collaborations with mutual cultural respect and empathy between the two countries.

Since Chinese companies are trying to improve their corporate governance practices in overseas operations for future BRI and China–Africa projects, RCEP will provide a beneficial platform for them to lead the region's collaborative business efforts.

RCEP's Geopolitical Impact

The fact that RCEP was launched during the ASEAN summit illustrated ASEAN's diplomatic and geopolitical consideration in the early 2010s, which led to RCEP's geopolitical impact on the following below, although the global geopolitical landscape has changed dramatically over the past ten years.

Asia's Rise[6] and the Rise of the "Asian Century"

As the home of 60% of the world's population, Asia's continuous and progressive increase in economic contributions to the global economy over the past three to four decades (one-third of global GDP in 2000 is expecting to reach 50% by 2050[7]), an increasing number in the middle class, an emerging younger generation as the engine of its future workforce, and an anticipated increase in purchasing power over the next three to four decades are telltale signs of an ascending economic powerhouse. Asia's rise has increased the continent's importance to the US and China, as well as drawing recent attention to the "Asian Century", a concept initiated to indicate the twenty-first century will be dominated by Asian politics and culture, under the assumption of current global demographic and economic development trends, in comparison with the nineteenth century as Britain's imperial century, and the twentieth century as the American century. Therefore, establishing RCEP as an Asian-based trade agreement will further stimulate Asian economic growth with the potential to establish an Asian economic zone that will protect the region from an economic crisis caused by other regional economic zones. The result of this economic zone will accelerate global recognition of the "Asian Century".

Protect ASEAN Countries from the US–China Contest

The year 2016 was clearly an evidential turning point in the US–China relationship with China publicly recognized as an economic threat to the West, given various incidents that occurred that year, including the establishment of TPP in 2016, which evolved to CPTPP in 2018. Although tension has been building and exacerbated by the rapid growth of China's global and regional economic influence since 2010, Asia's rise has further amplified the significance of China's growth versus the US and made Asia the initial battleground of the US–China contest. Paradoxically, many viewed the establishment of TPP as serving a geopolitical purpose to reduce its members' dependence on Chinese trade and bring them closer to the US. Even though CPTPP is nearly moribund mainly due to the US' withdrawal from TPP (as discussed above), none of its Asian countries members has withdrawn from CPTPP. The continuous existence of CPTPP will be a counterbalance between the US' and China's influences in the region, but the US can return at any time and reactivate its participation in CPTPP. On the other hand, forming RCEP as an Asia-only trade agreement that helps to secure China's partnership in the region is crucial in the area's post-pandemic recovery period. In addition, using RCEP's neutral platform to bring China, Japan, and South Korea into one trade agreement will undeniably benefit Asia. If those three countries can discover any synergy for future direct collaboration, that will make RCEP more meaningful for the region's development, as most ASEAN countries, some of which are minimally developed, are relatively small and rely mainly on exports for economic development. The establishment of RECP contains ASEAN's diplomatic and geopolitical considerations, as well as an economic element of it.

RCEP's Geopolitical Impact on China[8]

RCEP provides a platform and opportunity for China to escalate its decree-setting role in the region as the largest economy. Due to its growing global influence, China's comprehensive supply-chain system will tighten the integration between China and other RCEP members, increase resilience in the region to attract external investment, and enhance its flexibility in the trade war with the US. The economic cohesion of RCEP will hasten the formation of the Asian economic zone, which together with China's dominant position in trade deals and infrastructure projects will accelerate the Chinese RMB's currency zone and RMB internationalization. As most RCEP members are also China's China BRI partner countries, China's efforts of enacting regulations and standards in BRI countries will make RCEP a booster for those counties to access BRI funds, and for China to achieve its planned BRI goals.

RCEP's Geopolitical Impact on Other Asian Countries

The formation of RCEP raises the urgency for the US to rejoin CPTPP, although that may not be the US' priority given its focus on economic recovery and other international affairs, such as the 2021 Afghanistan withdrawal, the 2022 Russian–Ukraine regional war, and the resulting economic and geopolitical dilemma. In addition, India's withdrawal from RCEP indicates that tension between that country and China will continue, which cannot be reconciled by the current RCEP framework.

Although economic cooperation is one of the key elements of RCEP, given the combined economic influences of member countries, RCEP's geopolitical impact is equally important to RCEP member countries, the region, and the world. It's also worth mentioning that most of the impact will be realized by collaboration under the RCEP framework, and the geopolitical impact on each party will continue evolving with the continuous change of global geo-development and the progress of RCEP.

Will member countries be able to benefit from RCEP as expected? Can China's economic growth potentials and quickly evolving ESG revolution boost RCEP member countries' economies and accelerate sustainability development in the region? Will RCEP become a catalyst for the Asian economy zone? Will RECP reshape the global geopolitical landscape[9]? Likewise with Japan and South Korea, will China be able to continue its unceasing momentum and develop successful collaboration with those two countries within the RCEP umbrella? Can China diplomatically manage the contemporary tension with Australia without causing harm to the amicability within the RCEP? The RCEP offers tremendous opportunities as well as challenges to all the actors and their stakeholders, including China!

Fortunately, the RCEP is not the first regional partnership led by China. By virtue of the experiences and lessons learned from the BRI and China–Africa projects over the past few decades, the Chinese government and companies should become more sophisticated with their handling of economic and political matters, and more conscious of the development of sustainable strategies and other social and economic impacts on host countries. Next, let us review China's experiences from the BRI and African projects.

Overview of China's BRI and Its Future Development

The BRI is a global infrastructure development strategy launched by the Chinese government in 2013, with the initiative to increase China's economic links to Southeast Asia, Central Asia, Russia, and Central and Eastern Europe. The BRI expanded to Latin American countries in 2017 and has grown quickly since then. In 2021, the BRI included 139 countries[10] (39 in Sub-Saharan Africa, 34 in Europe and Central Asia, 25 in East Asia and the Pacific, 18 in Latin America and Caribbean, 17 in the Middle East and North Africa, and 6 in South Asia). Those countries, including China, represent 63% of the world's population (the BRI covers 65 countries (including China), equivalent to 61.9% of the world's population, according to 2016 data).

Regardless of the debates regarding BRI's political intention and diplomatic ambitions, the multibillion-dollar BRI investment platform has positively impacted the economic status of the developing world. Most BRI projects are in the infrastructure, energy, and transportation sectors. According to 2018 data, the BRI initiated projects to build 203 bridges, 199 power plants, and 41 pipelines, and information from the China Global Television Network (CGTN) shows that China had signed 200 cooperation agreements with 138 countries and 30 international organizations using the BRI framework.[11]

Positive Economic and Social Impacts

BRI has drawn considerable attention over the past several years and various discussions have been triggered. For the purpose of this book, I will only highlight BRI's major impacts on partner countries, ESG concerns raised from those projects, and the challenges China is facing in the BRI's future.

Statistics data shows that the 82 overseas cooperation zones jointly built by China and countries under the BRI have created 300,000 local jobs and significantly contributed to local economic development and an improvement in peoples' livelihoods. Due to the increased dependence for external funding of African countries' infrastructure development of railways, roads, ports, and energy, BRI projects have become many African countries essential strategy for future economic development. Regardless of today's critics regarding China's motivation of those projects, the truth is that railways, bridges, pipelines, and power plants are needed for those countries and their people. Statistics show that at least 39 African countries have been covered by BRI, and an unofficial study estimated that China's investment in Africa through the BRI is around $5 billion per year. Selected BRI projects include telecommunications in Ethiopia, Sudan, and Ghana and railroad projects in Nigeria, Gabon, and Mauritania that have made tremendous improvements in local peoples' lives. Over time and as a result, China became the hope for people from some African countries. During my interview with Lynda Kahari, an experienced African banking executive who moved to Port Moresby, Papua New Guinea for a new position in 2020, Ms. Kahari shared her concerns regarding Port Moresby's outdated telecom infrastructure system that prevented her and many others from working at home during the pandemic. She also shared her experiences in Africa detailing how China built infrastructure systems to improve local people's lives, and on a personal note, the gracefulness extended to her aged mother in Africa who had received a vaccination supported by the Chinese government when the vaccine shortage was still a big issue for many developing countries.

However, despite the positive impacts created by BRI projects, an increasing number of questions have been raised over the past few years concurrent with the COVID-19 crisis and the escalation of ESG-related concerns of BRI projects.

Challenges for BRI's Future Development

China's BRI will undoubtedly continue with strategic adjustment due to the following key challenges that BRI projects are encountering.

Economic and Diplomatic Challenges

With the rise of debt forgiveness requests and potential loan defaults due to the COVID-19 crisis, some BRI projects have been delayed as many African countries' debts are from BRI-related projects. China has joined other G20 countries to agree to debt service payments suspension from 73 countries until the end of 2021. How will the Chinese government manage the collateral assets of those defaulting countries? Will China renegotiate new loan agreements with member countries and possibly risk or harm its reputation or resolve to help those countries? These questions require sophisticated consideration and diplomatic responses to address economic consequences.

ESG-Related Challenges from BRI Partner Countries

The worldwide ESG movement has stirred an energy transformation trend as well as ESG concerns in BRI partner countries. Several impasses exist so a few are worth mentioning: Egypt postponed a coal-fired power plant construction project funded by China; Bangladesh canceled a coal plant plan; and many African countries raised environmental questions of China's BRI project. In addition, pressure has been mounting from partner countries' unions regarding labor rights considerations and controversies regarding local labor law, and workforce equality has been recently intensifying in Central Asian countries Kazakhstan, Kyrgyzstan, Tajikistan, and Uzbekistan. The workforce-related issues of BRI projects on host countries' local communities and working people will be further examined by various local and international organizations. Since addressing and improving those socially related factors have become one of the priorities on the Chinese government's agenda, properly handling those questions with local organizations and governments may be challenging but could also lead to ideal opportunities for China to amplify its economic influence in partner countries through improving ESG performance of BRI projects. On the other hand, because of various environmental and social issues related to China's BRI projects and a lack of transparency during BRI projects' process, there may be potential for cancellation of unfavorable agreements. For example, Tanzania's new president requested the cancellation of a $10 billion port project, and Nigerian legislators voted to further review all loan agreements related to Chinese projects.

Competition from the Group of Seven Industrialized Countries (G7)[12]

During the most recent G7 summit that occurred in June 2021, a new infrastructure financing plan was agreed to by leaders of the G7 countries to counter China's BRI, in addition to offering higher quality support to help developing countries in Latin America, the Caribbean, Africa, and the Indo-Pacific region with a broader range of services for them to recover from the COVID-19 pandemic by using G7 models and standards. The demand for high-quality physical, digital, and health infrastructures will cost approximately $40 trillion through 2035, according to World Bank estimation. Currently, there is no timeframe or pertinent details regarding the funding sources of G7's proposal.

Nevertheless, competition is always good for developing countries and the global economy, regardless of whom, which model, and what standards will be applied for the infrastructure systems and other projects needed for the developing world for recovery and further development. Given the competition between G7 and China, the world should expect better quality support (including collaboration terms, project quality, and operation transparency) for developing countries. In addition, the competition from G7 will also stimulate Chinese companies' ESG integration in their overseas operations.

Different Opinions of BRI's Geo-Development Impacts

China's BRI has drawn worldwide attention over the past several years concerning the Chinese government's true purpose of BRI, given the fact that all megaprojects of BRI are financed by Chinese governmental and institutional loans. Many of those projects do not expect economic return and their corporate governance practices are questionable according to Western standards.[13] (According to statistical data, the Chinese government is expecting investment losses of 80% in Pakistan's BRI project, 50% in Myanmar's, and 30% in Central Asia's.) Research has produced various conclusions and findings, some of which are summarized below[14]:

- Lack of strict geographical boundaries in Chinese BRI projects allows fewer entry barriers for partner countries.
- The Chinese BRI has potential to transform the global geopolitical landscape.
- The Chinese BRI is a geo-economic or commercial project to stimulate cross-continental capital, commodities, labor, and resource flow via infrastructure construction to capture China's industrial overproduction.

• The Chinese BRI is the new "Silk Road" with infrastructure projects to reshape China's image in the world, "a geo-cultural construct" to symbolize its resumption of the ancient Silk Road that connected China to the rest of the world.

Different opinions from research convinced me that the investment size and planned duration of the BRI signify the Chinese government's intentions are complicated, and its true purpose is likely to evolve and be reevaluated over time. The BRI's geopolitical, economic, financial, technological, and strategic features will potentially grow China's influence and transform international relationships on a global scale. Therefore, the challenges of BRI's future development are complicated too. Although the BRI has generated a positive social and economic impact on partner countries, those infrastructure projects will continue to improve livelihoods and facilitate economic development.

However, while BRI was once welcomed by an increasing number of countries, its popularity has slowed down with the rise of various problems and challenges as discussed. In order to recapture some of the lost momenta and eventually achieve BRI's long-term goals, the Chinese government will unavoidably have to solve the current problems BRI projects are running into and deal with the geopolitical and geo-economic challenges and competition from other advanced countries. Moreover, Chinese companies need to improve BRI project performance according to international standards, as well as to help accelerate partner countries' ESG adoption through BRI projects' influences.

Considering the progression of the ESG movement over the past couple of years, the good news is that China and its financial institutions funding most BRI projects have prompted the need for more attention to be given to ESG consideration, which will result in safeguarding future BRI projects to build sustainable infrastructures in partner countries. Since the targeted completion of BRI will be in 2049, the process will likely lead to a new balance in various international relationships.

Key Points of China–Africa Collaboration

The China–Africa economic collaboration that started in the 1970s was marked by the 1,860 km Tazara Railway (from Tanzania to Zambia), a turnkey project financed and supported by China. Bilateral collaboration between China and Africa has been rapidly growing in recent decades based on African countries' economic development needs and China's well-known skills for building infrastructures. Infrastructure has been one of the most important China–Africa collaboration areas.

Impacts and Challenges

China–Africa collaboration has had a profound economic and social impact on African countries by providing job opportunities, education assistance, and economic growth. Since the first conference of the FOCAC held in Beijing in 2000, China's direct investment in African countries has skyrocketed more than 100-fold, and bilateral trade volume has grown 20-fold. According to a 2017 McKinsey survey of Chinese firms operating in Africa, 89% of employees of those Chinese firms are Africans (applying the percentage to over 10,000 Chinese-owned companies in Africa indicates several millions of Africans were hired by those companies at the time of the survey). In addition to Chinese direct investments in Africa that are mainly in infrastructure, resource-oriented mining, and agriculture sectors, the Chinese government has become one of the major scholarship aid providers for Africa over the past few years. A 2020 UNESCO Global Education Monitoring Report[15] shows that the Chinese government was the largest provider of that year with 12,000 scholarship opportunities for students in Sub-Saharan Africa, and China has increased its three-year scholarships for 2019–2022 to 50,000 (a 67% increase from 30,000 in the previous three-year period). Global scholarship aid (including those from China) created undergraduate, postgraduate, and secondary education opportunities that were otherwise not available for local students in Sub-Saharan African countries.

However, China–Africa collaboration is facing serious economic, political, and diplomat challenges including environmental and social issues similar to those of BRI projects. Due to the longer history of China–Africa collaboration compared to BRI projects, business practices and culture conflict issues revealed by China–African projects have become valuable learning opportunities for Chinese multinationals' global growth. The brief case study of Bui Dam Hydroelectricity Project in Ghana below highlights those challenges, including workforce management problems.

Case Study 8.1   SinoHydro-Ghana Bui Dam Hydroelectricity Project – Calling for Regulation Improvements for Multinational Companies' Home and Host Countries

Bui Dam is located in Bui National Park in Ghana. The dam started operations in 2013, generates 400MW of power, provides water for irrigation to nearly 30,000 hectares of land, improved the local fishing industry, and attracts tourists to the region. However, due to the fact that the dam's construction consumed a sizable land amount and caused resettlement of 1,216 people and various fish and animals in the region, the project has been facing challenges from environmentalists.

The Bui Dam has been a political, environmental, and local energy demand controversy for almost one century. The idea of building Bui Dam was initiated in 1925 when planning and discussions involving various experts and organizations from Great Britain and Australia occurred. The project construction started in the late 1970s with funding support from the World Bank but stalled due to local military coups until restarting in the early 1990s. There were many economic and ecology debates and discussions from the 1990s to the 2000s regarding the necessity of completing the construction of the dam until the project was resumed in 2002.[16]

In 2005, Ghana government authorities accepted a bid from SinoHydro (the project's construction contractor) with funding support from the China Import–Export Bank. The construction started in 2007 and the dam began operations in 2013. The total project cost was $790 million[17] *and loans through the Chinese Export–Import Bank totaled $562 million (71% of the total project cost). The size of the loan amount made the SinoHydro-Ghana Bui Dam Hydroelectricity (BUI) Project the largest Chinese investment in Ghana.*

However, the complicated workforce situation of the construction project made workforce management quite challenging. During the project's duration from 2007 to 2013, a total of 7,000 employees were reported as having worked on the project that consisted of multiple tiers (direct-hire and contracted workers, workers with different skill levels, and workers of both genders). The workforce comprised employees from several countries including China, Ghana, and Pakistan.

As a result, even after the project was completed. SinoHydro, a Chinese SOE hydropower engineering and construction multinational company, faced critics regarding labor-related matters due to various complications over the past several years. The dispute matters focused on

- *Lack of education opportunity and job security*
- *Unfair compensation due to lack of pay transparency*
- *Insufficient consideration on workforce safety and work-related injury compensation*
- *Management's poor relationships with trade unions including its mishandling of a 2008 workers' strike*
- *......*

Although the BUI project benefits both partner countries' economic and political needs in addition to an improvement in local peoples' livelihoods, its size and six-year duration (from 2007 to 2013) and the complications and challenges experienced during the project are probably incomprehensible. The BUI project has become study material for researchers regarding Chinese multinationals in Africa with key topics focusing on Chinese companies' compliance with local labor laws and their relationships with local labor unions, unfair competition, and the lack of environmental and local community considerations.

For the purpose of this book, let us focus on reviewing lessons that should be learned from the BUI project workforce-related issues and how those lessons can help improve Chinese companies' ESG performance.

Major Problems of Chinese Companies' Operations in Africa

Chinese multinational companies began functioning in the 1970s through the Africa–China partnership. Therefore, Chinese companies' operation in Africa not only serves as the best documentary of Chinese multinational companies' development over the past five decades but also reveals major problems of their overseas undertakings.

Lack of Transparency, Fair Competition, and ESG Compliance

As most Chinese multinationals' overseas projects in Africa are funded by Chinese financial institutions, the government's funding support provides those companies with better opportunities to win projects that are not funded by international financial institutions (such as the World Bank) or local governments. However, the supervision and auditing mechanisms with funding and operational processes are not comparable to projects funded by the World Bank or other international organizations. As a result, Chinese companies have less compliance responsibility requirements from Chinese financial institutions, contrary to international fund providers such as the World Bank which requires more restrictive compliance.

It is vitally important to understand that the BUI project was completed in 2013, when Chinese companies' overseas expansions were proliferating and most of those companies fixated on business development rather than corporate governance practice and ESG performance. Today, transparency and fair competition are important criteria for good corporate governance consideration and ESG integration, all of which require serious examination for Chinese multinationals' overseas operations not only in Africa, but also in all host countries.

The key to solving this problem lies with closing the gap between Chinese governance standards and international standards. Given China is on its ESG revolution path with regulation reform benchmarking international standards, Chinese financial institutions will implement strict funding requirements (such as those in the Ping An Insurance Group case study) for bidding, investing, and operational information disclosure to encourage and help Chinese multinationals' corporate governance development and ESG performance improvement.

Lack of Effort to Build Relationships with Local Communities

Most Chinese multinationals in Africa retain low profiles in host countries, similar to other parts of the world. Other than business-related activities,

Chinese companies traditionally do not get involved in local business affairs. The majority of employees with Chinese companies' African operation live in company-provided housing facilities that purposely isolate them from local communities mainly due to safety considerations and language barriers, according to a longtime friend who has been working for Chinese telecommunications, mining, and wood furniture manufacturing companies in Africa since the 1990s.

Lack of Equality, Inclusivity, and Labor Law Considerations

Chinese companies' unions are responsible for company events and certain employee benefits, both of which are unique features of Chinese companies' governance model. As a result, when Chinese multinationals operate in host countries, recognition of union independence and managing a beneficial relationship with a workplace's union becomes quite challenging for those Chinese companies. Chinese companies prefer to transfer employees from their headquarters to its overseas operations, which decreases job opportunities, especially management positions for the local workforce. In addition, many Chinese companies require longer working hours with or without providing compensation, and some overseas operations have reported hostile relationships between management and workplace unions.

Those situations have revealed the requirement to understand and respect local business practices and compliance with local regulations. As discussed in early chapters, multinationals' expansion strategies of imposing home country models to overseas operations that were employed by Western companies 40 years ago are obsolete for modern multinational operations, including those from China. While the success of the China model has been embraced by many Chinese companies, that does not imply that foisting the China model on Chinese companies' overseas subsidiaries will lead to the same success. Furthermore, without understanding local practices and regulations, unilaterally implementing or enforcing the China model may cause unnecessary conflicts with local organizations, local governments, and international standards. In addition, remaining compliant with host countries' regulations is one of the most important corporate governance functions for any organization. I trust that pointing out those issues and weaknesses will stir corporate governance improvement.

Party Influence and Government Intervention

Since most Chinese multinationals similar to SinoHydro in Africa are SOEs, party influence is always a major concern within those multinationals, as are executives' dual roles in those companies. A study[18] from Global Labor University summarized Chinese multinationals' successes in Africa based on five factors: cost advantage in overall project bidding; low-cost capital offered by Chinese state-owned financial institutions; use of inexpensive local labor;

access to cut-rate building materials; and political support from the Chinese government.

However, the Chinese government's support enhances Chinese companies' competition advantage in global market and facilitates these companies. Although party influence and government intervention are still the top concerns of Chinese companies' governance practice, perhaps what really matters are the anticipated impact to the disclosure transparency of information disclosure and decision-making process.

Lack of Regulations in Host Countries and Inspiration for Solutions

The research and studies of the SinoHydro-Ghana Bui Dam Project also revealed another element that contributes to those problems – the retardation of a regulatory system in host countries. It is normal for multinationals to lower business operation standards in countries with loose regulatory compliance requirement and enforcement mechanisms. Chinese multinationals are not the only ones with bad business behaviors and perfidious actions in developing countries. Multinationals from advanced countries share the same poor convention: For example, in 2020, the UK Supreme Court ruled against Shell Nigeria, Royal Dutch Shell's Nigerian subsidiary, involving an oil pollution lawsuit filed by Niger Delta communities who suffered from decades of pollution.[19] As a worldwide leading corporation, Shell did not prohibit its subsidiary in developing countries from ignoring local environmental matters and the impact on locals' livelihoods.

Of course, there are many other factors in host countries that also allowed those countries to become victims of multinationals' careless behavior, namely, government corruption, lack of professional personnel, and lack of educational resources. However, I believe that instead of blaming the poor for their poverty, the business world should focus on how parent companies and home countries of those multinationals can help improve business practices to avoid those problems.

I am convinced that the UK Supreme Court's ruling initiated one path in order to enforce multinationals' overseas operations: Multinationals will be held accountable for their overseas business activities and the consequential impact to host countries. To be fair, demands for improving home countries' regulation standards and an enforcement mechanism are essential to multinational behavior in host countries. ESG movement accelerated China's regulation reform to close the gap with international standards and stirred Chinese companies ESG integration in order to obtain an advanced position in the global ESG rating system. Therefore, ESG movement becomes an opportunity for Chinese multinationals to seriously reconsider their operation and compliance in host countries.

China–Africa Engagement in the New Era

The business operations and social impact criticism discussed above have led to some doubt regarding the China–Africa relationship, but this relationship overall has been promising due to the following reasons.

China's Unconditional Vaccine Supply during the COVID-19 Pandemic

Many African countries have been relying on a Chinese vaccine, and it's worth mentioning that many Chinese citizens over 65 years old have not yet received a vaccine in the early phase of the outbreak due to an insufficient vaccine supply in China, while many elderlies in South Africa, such as my interviewee, Lynda Kahari's mother had already received a Chinese vaccine. In addition to the Chinese government's vaccines, private companies such as the Alibaba Foundation donated untold numbers of medical equipment to almost all African countries.

Prospective Economic Collaboration

China's 14th FYP's strategy will create more trade, manufacturing, and development opportunities in African countries to stimulate digital transformation in Africa, provided effective collaboration and proper policy implementation occurs by those African countries' governments.[20] Some African countries are facing trade-off challenges due to the IMF's pressure to cut government spending for COVID-19 support, although part of the government spending was budgeted for infrastructure to benefit local citizens' livelihoods and economic development. Those African countries depend on Chinese lending to bridge the financial gap, although many issues that caused a recent reduction in Chinese loans need to be resolved in order to encourage Chinese lending for risk mitigation of those African projects, as well as for careful evaluation of debt sustainability with African countries.

Promising Diplomacy Development

Although there were some diplomatic claims in 2020 of mistreatment of Africans due to China's restricted control on COVID-19 testing and related procedures,[21] the diplomatic relationship between China and the continent has been promising. The 30-year tradition of the Chinese foreign minister's first trip of a new year is to visit Africa.[22] During a recent interview with an African Union Commissioner for Infrastructure and Energy conducted before an upcoming FOCAC forum, the commissioner expressed her desire to cooperate with China. That desire is designed to facilitate and increase the momentum and scope of cooperation toward Africa's infrastructural development and to proceed vis-à-vis African Union's agenda on energy sector development. The commissioner also expressed her gratitude for China's help, the assistance of which is the foundation of local economic development.[23]

Rebalancing Geopolitical Considerations in China–Africa Collaboration

Given the criticism of China's political ambitions in Africa and Chinese companies' behavior causing negative impact, it is also time for all parties to pause and reconsider certain topics of Africa's pressing interests:

- What are China's primary economic interests and political goals regarding its investments in Africa? Are those interests and goals causing any damage to the continent? Are those intentions different from other countries which are also investing in Africa?
- While China politically accelerated its global image and influences through the China–Africa collaboration, what did African countries benefit from collaborating with China?
- Will the China–Africa collaboration create any negative diplomatic and/or economic impact on other countries or regions? If so, are there any win-win solutions for China–Africa and other countries?

Most African countries were colonized for hundreds of years by numerous European countries, which made their geopolitical situation quite complicated (e.g., South Africa), and left them as victims of gold, natural resource, and wild animal plundering. With worldwide economic growth and demographic changes over the past several decades, Africa is viewed as the next global economic frontier by many Western investors due to their potential, young population, and soon-to-be innovative industry techniques. However, investing in Africa cannot just benefit investors' interests, but also needs to make sense for African countries to grow their economies. Given the undeveloped situation on the continent and the global pandemic crisis which impacts all countries, I believe the geo-development dimensions in Africa need to be reevaluated, and thereafter, a new balance will be established for future collaboration with Africa, including the China–Africa collaboration.

As with many other international agreements and partnership frameworks, the success of those three collaborative agreements dominated by China were not singularly guaranteed by the intention of the participants, but by the behavior of partners and members who work together with mutual respect that benefits them both and the other members. Conclusively, China and Chinese companies' success will be achieved by careful role planning with predetermined goals that are tied to the demands for China's regulation improvement and ESG adoption.

Improving China's regulatory environment will also help reshape corporate culture, which will positively influence business mindset of Chinese multinationals' leaders.

Of course, some critics China's motivation in those regional initiatives allege political ambition over humanitarian and economic support, which adds another challenging layer to the complexity of those accusations and an accurate portrayal of China's true motive. Regardless of the myriad of critiques, aiming to attain global superpower status, the Chinese government leaders have to answer an innocuous but challenging question: How will China handle this criticism and improve its diplomatic approach with its global partners in both economic and political dimensions? The answer to this question has the potential to positively persuade its adversaries.

Takeaways

- **RCEP was born as a result of a sophisticated evaluation of the Asian-Pacific region's need for economic growth, and to protect the region from conflicts caused by superpowers' geopolitical missions**. The development of RCEP will consolidate member countries' economies and also expedite the region's political development to effectively contend with external partners' geopolitical strategy changes. Actively influencing and leading RCEP will help China strengthen its global position in various areas including trade, RMB internationalization, and ESG and corporate governance developments.
- **Many of China's BRI projects were running into ESG-related concerns, regardless of progress made on improving member countries' infrastructures and their peoples' livelihoods**. Future development on BRI requires improvement in Chinese companies' governance practices, and furthering its collaboration with host countries' authorities to address concerns.
- **China–Africa collaboration projects have made positive economic and social impacts** on African countries, and future prospects are promising after overcoming challenges revealed by current BRI projects in Africa.
- **Global collaboration is the key to help improve multinationals' business practices** in host countries, while also help enhance those countries' regulation systems.

Notes

1 Andrew Kakabadse and Nada Kakabadse, *The Geopolitics of Governance – The Impact of Contrasting Philosophies*, Page 89, Palgrave MacMillan, 2001. https://searchworks.stanford.edu/view/4672494
2 Kate Whiting, "An Expert Explains: What Is RCEP, the World's Biggest Trade Deal?" World Economic Forum, May, 2021, May 21, 2021. www.weforum.org/agenda/2021/05/rcep-world-biggest-trade-deal/

3 Shandre Mugan Thangavelu, Shujiro Urata, and Dionisius A. Narjoko, "Impacts of the Regional Comprehensive Economic Partnership on ASEAN and ASEAN Least Developed Countries in Post-pandemic Recovery", ERIA, July 2021 issue. www.eria.org/uploads/media/policy-brief/Impact-of-RCEP-in-ASEAN-post-pandemic-recovery-new.pdf

4 Staff article, "Facing US Trade Uncertainty, China Seeks Closer Ties with Neighbours," Yahoo News, December 25, 2019. https://news.yahoo.com/facing-us-trade-uncertainty-china-seeks-closer-ties-075755330--finance.html

5 Peter A. Petri and Michael Plummer, "RCEP: A New Trade Agreement That Will Shape Global Economics and Politics", Brookings, November 16, 2020, August 24, 2021. www.brookings.edu/blog/order-from-chaos/2020/11/16/rcep-a-new-trade-agreement-that-will-shape-global-economics-and-politics/

6 Evan S. Medeiros (2019), "The Changing Fundamentals of US–China Relations," The Washington Quarterly, 42:3, 93–119, DOI: 10.1080/0163660X.2019.1666355

7 "Asia's Future Is Now", McKinsey, July 2019. www.mckinsey.com/~/media/mckinsey/featured%20insights/asia%20pacific/asias%20future%20is%20now/asias-future-is-now-final.pdf

8 Robert Ward, "RCEP Trade Deal: A Geopolitical Win for China", IISS, November 25, 2020, www.iiss.org/blogs/analysis/2020/11/rcep-trade-deal

9 Peter A. Petri and Michael Plummer, "RCEP: A New Trade Agreement That Will Shape Global Economics and Politics", Brookings, November 16, 2020. www.brookings.edu/blog/order-from-chaos/2020/11/16/rcep-a-new-trade-agreement-that-will-shape-global-economics-and-politics/

10 David Sacks, "Countries in China's Belt and Road Initiative: Who's in and Who's Out," Council on Foreign Relations, March, 2021, July 2, 2021. www.cfr.org/blog/countries-chinas-belt-and-road-initiative-whos-and-whos-out

11 Harri Taliga, "Belt and Road Initiative in Central Asia," ITUC, 2021, April 22, 2021. www.ituc-csi.org/IMG/pdf/belt_and_road_initiative_in_central_asia.pdf

12 Kyodo News staff article, "G7 to Launch Infrastructure Plan to Counter China's Belt and Road," The Jakarta Post, June, 2021, June 28, 2021. www.thejakartapost.com/news/2021/06/13/g7-to-launch-infrastructure-plan-to-counter-chinas-belt-and-road.html

13 Tami Groswald Ozery, "Illiberal Governance and the Rise of China's Public Firms: An Oxymoron or China's Greatest Triumph?" *University of Pennsylvania Journal International*, Pages 31–32, June 24, 2020. https://papers.ssrn.com/sol3/papers.cfm?abstract_id=3616513

14 Paul B. Richardson, "*Geopolitical Encounters and Entanglements Along the Belt and Road*", Wiley, April 12, 2021. https://onlinelibrary.wiley.com/doi/epdf/10.1111/gec3.12583

15 UNESCO staff report, "Global Education Monitoring Report 2020," UNESCO, 2020, July 17, 2021. https://resourcecentre.savethechildren.net/node/17803/pdf/373718eng.pdf

16 Project report, "Bui Dam Hydroelectricity Project, Ghana," Water Technology (n.d.), July 7, 2021. www.water-technology.net/projects/bui-dam-hydro-power-ghana/

17 Project report, "Bui Dam Hydroelectricity Project, Ghana," Water Technology (n.d.), July 7, 2021. www.water-technology.net/projects/bui-dam-hydro-power-ghana/

18 Glynne Williams, Steve Davies, Julius Lamptey, and Jonathan Tetteh, "Chinese Multinationals: Threat to, or Opportunity for, Trade Unions? – The Case of Sinohydro in Ghana", 2017. https://global-labour-university.org/fileadmin/GLU_Working_Papers/GLU_WP_No.46.pdf

19 Clare Connellan, et al. "Okpavi v Royal Dutch Shell Plc: UK Supreme Court Allows Nigerian Citizens' Environmental Damage Claim to Proceed Against UK Parent Company", White and Case, February 19, 2021, April 16, 2021. www.whitecase.com

20 Hannah Ryder, "Where Is the Africa–China Relationship Headed in 2021?", CSIS, February 17, 2021, August 24, 2021. www.csis.org/analysis/where-africa-china-relationship-headed-2021

21 Hangwei Li, "The Mistreatment of Africans in Guangzhou Is a Big Threat to China's Coronavirus Diplomacy", Quartz Africa, April 22, 2020, August 24, 2021. https://qz.com/africa/1842768/racism-to-africans-in-guangzhou-hurts-china-coronavirus-diplomacy/

22 Shannon Tiezzi, "China's Africa Diplomacy Starts 2021 on a High Note", The Diplomat, January 6, 2021, August 24, 2021. https://thediplomat.com/2021/01/chinas-africa-diplomacy-starts-2021-on-a-high-note/

23 "Interview: Upcoming FOCAC Meeting Comes at Critical Time to Spur Sino-Africa Ties: AU Official", Forum on China-Arica Cooperation Forum, August 4, 2021, August 28, 2021. www.focac.org/eng/zfzs_1/t1897113.htm

Chapter 9

RMB Internationalization

In this chapter, I review

- China's RMB Internationalization
  China's RMB internationalization programs
  Primary geopolitical influences since the 2010s

- Key Factors for the Future RMB Internationalization
  China's digital currency
  Sustainable finance
  Russian–Ukraine regional war
  The "Ballooning" US debt

RMB's internationalization initiative started in 2003 and 2004 when RMB's use for individuals was first established in Hong Kong and Macao, respectively. However, the progress of RMB internationalization is not comparable to China's economic growth in the past 20 years due to many domestic and international reasons.

Although China's GDP is projected to overtake the US in the coming years, the international adoption of RMB and dollar are far from comparable yet. As of May 2021, RMB accounted for only 4% of global trade transaction settlements, in contrast to 88% using US dollars, according to 2020 International Money Funds (IMF) data. Meanwhile, the share of RMB reserves held by central banks that year was 2%, while 59% used the US dollar. **Therefore, RMB internationalization is still a long journey!**

The US dollar has been the dominant global currency for decades, which has somewhat established a balance in the global monetary system. Divergent interests participated in that system until a 2018 study called for "a tripolar system centered on the dollar, euro, and renminbi to serve as a safety net for the global economy should the dollar regime collapse".[1] The severe global chain supply disruption caused by the 2022 regional war between Russia and

DOI: 10.4324/9781003302919-14

Ukraine re-emphasized the need for such a safety net. Moreover, RMB inter-nationalization has drawn greater attention when countries seek an alterna-tive currency for their necessary trade with Russia, since the Russian banking system has been sanctioned by the international finance system, which is dom-inated by the US.

This chapter reviews the progress, challenges, and key elements of RMB internationalization. The chapter also illustrates selected geopolitical influences on China's RMB internationalization because the inevitable impact of global geopolitical landscape changes plays remarkable roles in a county's currency policy and international adoption of that currency.

Having said this, please allow me to explain three important concepts, cur-rency internationalization, the role of an offshore currency market, and the US dollar's dominant global currency position, before we start this chapter.

Currency internationalization is the process of one country's currency being used for international trade, investment, and foreign currency reserve. Technically, currency internationalization should occur simultaneously with a country's growing economic influence. An organic method to grow a cur-rency's international use is through cross-border trading that consists of three steps: First, the dominant party (usually the buyer) has the leverage to request trade settlement with its home country's currency due to considerations of exchange rate risk, exchange cost, and convenience; second, in order to set the payment amount of a foreign currency settlement, countries would have to either hedge on an exchange market to set the exchange rate at the time of pay-ment, or reserve the foreign currency for payment on an agreed date; third, if the dominant party's home currency has established a stable value over time, countries may find the foreign currency reserve can not only help international trade settlement but also help prevent the local currency's value fluctuation. That country then will increase its reserve amount and then tie their currency to the reserved currency to stabilize their own currency's value and economy. Growing up in a southwest China province that shares a border with Myanmar, Laos, and Vietnam, I witnessed the first two steps of organic growth of RMB's use by those neighboring countries in the 1980s and 1990s.

However, a currency internationalization process is much more complicated since it involves a country's development strategies in many aspects, including monetary, financial, economic, and political policies.

What, then, is the role of an offshore currency market[2]? An offshore cur-rency market is an economic function to promote the global use of a country's currency. The most important aspect of an offshore currency market's develop-ment is to help separate a country's risks from its currency risks and improve the financial stability of its onshore currency market. Using the US dollar as an example, after the 9/11 terrorist attacks in September 2001, US central banks were able to maintain normal operations of US dollar securities held in European countries. That example not only shows how its offshore dollar market helped the US during the crisis but also demonstrates how it strengthened the US economy and its currency stability, which sustained the dollar as the dominant global currency over the past many decades. Over the following years, the US continued increasing its offshore versus onshore deposit ratio of 10.6% in 2004, 19.64% in 2007, and 25.5% in 2008, according to a 2010 Bank for International Settlements report. Hong Kong was the first and still is the largest offshore RMB center and will continue its role to accelerate RMB offshore market development for many years to come.

The US dollar's dominant global currency position can be easily explained due to its strong position in IMF's Special Drawing Rights (SDR) basket before and after RMB's joining. SDR basket currencies' assigned weights before the RMB joined were US dollar (41.9%), Euro (37.4%), Japanese Yen (9.4%), and British Pound (11.3%), the assigned weights after it joined in November 2015 were US dollar (41.73%), Euro (30.93%), RMB (10.92%), Japanese Yen (8.33%), and British Pound (8.09%). The most recent numbers (in 2022) were the US dollar (43.38%), Euro (29.31%), RMB (12.28%), Japanese Yen (7.59%), and British Pound (7.44%). The US dollar's dominant status has not changed, but other currencies have been forgoing their shares to the RMB, which gained significant momentum after the pandemic. Therefore, promoting RMB internationalization is a must-have strategy for China to enhance political and economic positions in the world despite anticipated resistance from the US and other advanced countries. In addition, those countries' domestic and global political environment changes due to various reasons could lead to the adjustment of China's RMB strategy, some of which will be addressed in this chapter.

Now, let us zoom into some highlights to understand China's RMB internationalization.

China's RMB Internationalization

The rapidly evolving and worldwide adoption of Chinese mobile payment platforms Alipay and WeChat made RMB familiar to the rest of the world. Outside of China, though, the RMB is not yet easily found in currency exchanges, which simply indicates the limitation of RMB's global use, in contrast to China's economic size and Chinese companies' global growth. Comparing the latest available statistics regarding the uses of RMB and the US dollar on two basic functions of an internationalized currency (trade settlement and foreign currency reserve), RMB internationalization is still in the embryonic stage.

China's RMB internationalization gained considerable momentum in the early 2010s by launching various promotion programs and collaboration with global partners led by the UK. Having joined IMF's SDR basket in 2015 became the most remarkable milestone of RMB's global strategy. However, most of that momentum started to fade in 2016 due to global geopolitical environment changes. As a result, minimal progress has been made in the following years until the US and China tension started in 2018 raised the urgency of RMB's internationalization. Given the escalating concern of RMB's risks due to its dependence on the US dollar, the focus on promoting RMB internationalization has ascended since then. As a result, international use of RMB significantly progressed in 2019 in trading settlements (an 18.2% increase from 2018), capital transactions[3] (a 26.7% increase from 2018), and securities investments[4] (a 49.1% increase from 2018), while Chinese domestic RMB financial assets[5] held by foreign entities increased 30.3% from 2018, according to a 2020 PBOC report.

RMB internationalization is undoubtedly important for China. What is its impact on the world? Why does it matter to China's corporate governance development? What then are the obstacles to its progress?

The Importance of RMB Internationalization

The 2008 global finance crisis highlighted global financial system risks due to its reliance on one currency. With China becoming one of the largest trading countries as well as a major economy, promoting international use of RMB will generate various positive impacts, with three important items listed below.

Strengthen Global Financial Market Resilience

According to a 2018 study by Nomura Institute of Capital Market Research, a Japan-based research institution specializing in financial and capital market studies and policy proposals, currency competition will stabilize the international monetary system, and "a tripolar system centered on the dollar, euro, and renminbi would serve as a safety net for the global economy should the dollar regime collapse". However, establishing a tripolar system requires that an RMB currency zone be recognized and supported by dollar and Euro zone dominated countries. In addition, trade settling with RMB can reduce the exchange rate cost and preserve transaction efficiency without using the US dollar or another global currency as mediating currency. Because of lessons learned from the 2008 global financial crisis, member countries in an RMB-centered currency zone (possibly forthcoming) can be protected from the external currency risks of a dollar or Euro zone. China's neighboring countries and global partners will benefit from China's stable economic growth and currency value.

However, the resistance from the US and other countries cannot be underestimated. There are many reasons for this, the simplest being the amount of US dollar debts and reserves held by countries during the US dollar's global expansion over the past several decades. Any potential for the US dollar to lose its stability and value could put those countries at significant currency and financial risks. Therefore, any significant progress of RMB's internationalization won't be possible without global collaboration.

Enhance China's Economic and Political Positions in the Global Community

With China's trading volume, increasing RMB use as trade settlement will reduce exchange rate risks and make Chinese trading companies more competitive in the global market. Moreover, developing a strong offshore RMB market will make China's economy more resilient.

The slow progress of RMB internationalization indicates that China has not found the opportunity to break through the bottleneck created by the domination of USD and EUR in international trade, investment settlement, and foreign currency reserve. Improvements are needed in many aspects: ascending the global value chain in order to acquire settlement currency leverage; establishing a China-centered economic zone with investment and trade opportunities to promote RMB use; having a strong financial institutions system that includes offshore financial markets to provide service for Chinese companies and other multinationals; and building a stable economy with access channels to attract foreign investment in RMB assets.

Improve China's Financial Regulation System

Further opening financial markets will accelerate China's integration with the global financial market, stimulate the improvement of Chinese financial regulation standards, and raise requirements for Chinese companies' corporate governance practice and information disclosure. The wholly owned Chinese subsidiaries of influential financial institutions such as BlackRock will offer more mutual fund products to the Chinese market, accelerate the development of Chinese mutual fund products, and encourage long-term investment; and will likely stir more ESG momentum with stakeholder communication in the Chinese market, coinciding with shareholder interest protection actions as discussed in early chapters of the book. Although the practice of shareholder engagements and shareholder interest protection is still very new in the Chinese market, further regulatory support from Chinese authorities and practical guidance from those international advocates will accelerate the establishment of more sophisticated corporate governance practice for Chinese companies, help build a trustworthy investment environment in China, and eventually support RMB internationalization.

China's RMB Internationalization Programs

The complexity of RMB's internationalization is continuing to increase, despite much potential and some uncertainties. What has the Chinese government done to promote it? How will China measure its progress? I found that three currency internationalization prerequisites proposed in the same study by the Nomura Institute of Capital Market Research can be helpful to understand three aspects of RMB internationalization: domestic regulation reform to allow unencumbered capital transactions of the domestic financial market for both residents and nonresidents; economic and currency zones establishment; and international recognition and comparable positions with other currency zones. Let us review a series of selected programs launched chronologically since the 2000s by Chinese authorities concurrently with the government's efforts on three dimensions: opening financial markets, promoting offshore RMB markets, and liberalizing capital control regulations. These three dimensions are also used to examine RMB's internationalization progress.

Qualified Foreign Institutional Investor (QFII)[6] and RMB Qualified Foreign Institutional Investors (RQFII)[7]

Qualified Foreign Institutional Investor (QFII) (launched in 2002) and RMB Qualified Foreign Institutional Investor (RQFII) (launched in 2011) are sibling programs containing quotas, and the latter offers fewer restrictions for participants' qualifications. Both QFII and RQFII enable qualified foreign investors to invest directly in mainland China's stock markets (the SSE and SZSE). Although the Chinese government has initiated a copious number of reforms to simplify rules and remove restrictions of both programs including eliminating the quotas in 2019, the restrictions and barriers for investors to move money from China have offset the effects of those two programs. Further reforms to relax fund outflow restrictions will encourage more investments through both programs.

Dim Sum[8] Bonds

Dim Sum Bonds are RMB-designated bonds issued outside of China as a channel to allow foreign investors to buy RMB-designated assets. Dim Sum Bonds issuers can be either Chinese or non-Chinese institutions. The bonds program was launched in 2007 and Hong Kong has been its primary market since then. Dim Sum Bonds emerged in 2010/2011 and its popularity has faded due to RMB's volatility in 2015/2016, which indicates that investors' appetites for Dim Sum Bonds are heavily focused on the stability of RMB's value.

Pilot Programs and Free Trade Zones[9]

To enable RMB international settlements, the Chinese government introduced a pilot program in four cities in 2008, then extended the program throughout the country a couple of years later. Today, all trade and investment transactions with other parts of the world can be settled in RMB. In addition, free trade zones have been established in nearly 20 provinces in China (including Shanghai, Guangdong, Tianjing, Fujian, and Hainan) since 2013 to stimulate RMB's flow between free trade accounts and foreign companies' onshore and offshore accounts.

Offshore RMB Markets and Bilateral Swap Agreements

In 2009, PBOC launched offshore RMB clearinghouses to encourage offshore RMB business. The establishment of offshore RMB markets accelerated RMB's use as trade settlement currency and also enabled direct currency trade between participating countries without using USD as a mediating currency. Hong Kong has been the major offshore RMB hub since then, followed by Singapore. In addition, China has engaged in currency swap agreements with 39 countries since 2009 to accelerate offshore RMB market development. At the end of 2019, the total offshore RMB deposit amount was RMB3.7 trillion (3% of onshore RMB totaled approximately RMB109 trillion). Compared to the ratio of the US dollar's offshore versus onshore deposit amounts listed in early part of this chapter, there is long way to go for RMB offshore market development.

Cross-Border RMB Cash Pooling[10]

A two-way, cross-border RMB cash pooling program was launched in 2014 to enable channels for qualified Chinese and foreign multinationals to move RMB across borders, providing the amount is within the quota's restrictions. The program also enabled RMB loan-granting abroad. The cross-border cash pooling program was extended to multiple currencies in 2019 with positive feedbacks. However, the cash pooling program has potential international tax issues (such as interest deductibility, transfer pricing, withholding tax, and value-added tax) when the taxing country differs from the cash location country. Therefore, it's essential that participants understand the possible tax repercussions. Particularly when cash pooling programs were offered by Chinese banks as loan arrangements with no specific regulations at national levels, addressing those tax issues has become challenging without unified regulatory guidance.

Stock Connections

In order to increase foreign investment accessibility to the Chinese capital market, China has established stock connection programs with other capital markets to further enable global investments in A-share markets. Some notable stock connections are Shanghai–Hong Kong and Shenzhen–Hong Kong Stock Connects were launched in 2014 and 2016, respectively; Shanghai–London

Stock Connect in 2019; Shanghai–Deutsche Stock Connect in 2020; and the 2022 expansion of Shanghai–London program to include SZSE and stock exchanges in Germany and Switzerland.[11]

Interbank Payment System (CIPS)[12]

CIPS is the Chinese alternative to the Society for Worldwide Interbank Financial Telecommunication (SWIFT), the main international financial transaction network based in Belgium. CIPS was launched in 2015 under the supervision of PBOC and is becoming the main channel of RMB cross-border transactions, aiming to gradually remove the barriers of RMB's overseas use. In 2019, CIPS processed RMB transactions across 96 countries and regions in Asia, Europe, Africa, and Oceania totaling RMB135.7 billion ($19.4 billion) per day. The amount is insignificant compared to the $5 trillion daily transactions processed through SWIFT. CIPS received increasing attention since the regional war between Russia and Ukraine in 2022 as the US sanctions cut off Russian banks from the international financial system.

Panda Bonds

In contrast to Dim Sum Bonds that are RMB-designated bonds issued outside of China (mainly in Hong Kong) by Chinese or foreign issuers, Panda Bonds are RMB-designated bonds issued in the Chinese market by non-Chinese issuers. The issuing of Panda Bonds in 2015 was an important step to promote RMB's international bond market's development providing low risk and stable returns. Since then, Panda Bonds' issued amounts and geographic area of issuers have not yet seen significant increases, but issuers have become more diversified. Out of the 40 Panda Bonds issued in 2019 with total amount of RMB59.8 billion, 23 bonds were issued by 12 non-Chinese-owned foreign entities, of which half were new issuers. Panda Bonds have gained more popularity among foreign companies and institutions since the COVID-19 outbreak in 2020. As a result, Chinese authorities launched a pilot program in November 2021 to encourage foreign issuers' sustainability-themed Panda Bonds in China's interbank market.

Removing the Cap for Foreign Ownership in Certain Financial Sectors

A remarkable milestone in China's financial market opening was the removal of the requirement for foreign financial institutions to have a local partner for certain financial sectors (e.g., mutual fund operations) in China. In July 2021, BlackRock submitted an application with the CSRC to launch its mutual fund product "BlackRock China New Horizon Mixed Securities Investment Fund" in China as the first foreign wholly owned mutual fund enterprise in China.

JPMorgan Chase and Morgan Stanley are currently planning to buy out their Chinese partners. Allowing sole foreign ownership in the financial sector will motivate more global funds to invest directly in the Chinese market.

Directions for Future Reforms

Further reforms to simplify application and operation procedures and improve regulatory guidance will enhance the effectiveness of the above programs, while liberating capital control will facilitate RMB internationalization.

In addition to the low percentage of RMB use in trade settlement and foreign currency reserve today that suggests a lack of those programs' effectiveness, feedback from participants also revealed the fundamental challenges that those programs face: a complicated processing procedure that includes less efficiency (e.g., the offshore RMB clearing process); a demand for further regulation reform (e.g., QFII and RQFII investors' concerns regarding barriers on moving money from China); and the concern regarding RMB exchange rate stability (e.g., Dim Sum Bonds' marketability fading out in 2015). At the same time, discussions regarding transforming from a controlled RMB exchange rate system to a market-oriented RMB exchange rate system were initiated in 2019 by PBOC, but well-structured reforms to move RMB to a floating exchange rate system and its interest rate liberalization are needed to free capital transactions and flow.

On the other hand, it is worth mentioning that the question regarding to what extent is liberating capital control necessary for a currency's internationalization, which has been an ongoing debate and research topic. Research and study of the US dollar's boost in the international monetary market of the 1960s and 1970s, combined with the US government's authorities' significant control of capital during the same time, further supports the argument that fully liberalizing capital control is not a necessary condition for a country's offshore currency market expansion, as long as the country establishes regulatory support to balance the potential risks of its offshore currency markets. However, I believe further study or practical experimenting is needed before any conclusions are reached on this topic. RMB internationalization may also become another testimonial in the coming decades. For the time being, most cross-border fund transfers in and out from China still need approval by the State Administration for Foreign Exchange.

Geopolitical Influences on RMB's Internationalization Progress

As we can see from the above, China's RMB internationalization initially gained momentum in early 2010s with the launching of many promotional programs to attract interest in the global financial market. The progress has slowed down since 2015 primarily due to global geopolitical influences, including global partners' reactions to those programs concurrently with these countries' internal political environments and the international economic and political policy relationships changed. Below are some notable events.[13]

Launching AIIB in 2014

Asian Infrastructure Investment Bank (AIIB) was proposed by China in 2013 and launched in 2014 as a complement to the US-led World Bank and Washington-based IMF. The AIIB was created mainly due to inadequate recognition China received from the IMF after years of investment with the organization. Echoing the launching of the BRI in 2013, the formation of AIIB aims to facilitate the BRI on promoting the RMB internationalization.

EU–China Relationship in 2014 and 2015

The 2014–2015 "honeymoon period" between the EU and China significantly promoted RMB's internationalization in those two years. In 2014, a milestone event of RMB's internationalization (the Dim Sum Bonds program) occurred when the UK treasury became the first advanced country to issue a sovereign bond denominated in RMB (RMB 3 billion [$490 million]) with the majority of investors from Asia and European countries. In January 2015, Switzerland's central banks signed as a designated RQFII participant, which made Zurich another RMB trading hub in Europe, in addition to the RMB hubs in London, Frankfurt, Paris, Luxembourg, and Prague. Also in 2015, led by the UK, other advanced countries (France, Italy, and Germany) joined AIIB, the US and Japan were the exceptions though.

RMB Strategy Adjustment after 2016 Brexit[14]

UK's decision to leave the EU in 2016 led to worldwide concerns regarding its viability, causing China's RMB growth to slow in Europe. While China's foreign direct investment (FDI) reached its peak in 2016, Brexit slowed China's free trade agreement negotiations with the EU and its FDI in the UK and was forced to adjust its global RMB strategy since London was the second-largest RMB offshore market after Hong Kong.

US–China Geopolitical Rivalry Started in 2016

China started to sell US debt in 2016 to save its own currency when it depreciated in 2015, after being the US' biggest foreign creditor since 2008.[15] In 2016, the formation of TPP in the Asia-Pacific region led by the US excluded China, prompting a US–China supremacy rivalry in the region.

Global Geopolitical Landscape Changes in 2017

In addition to the negative impact from Brexit, 2017 elections in the Netherlands, France, and Germany further slowed negotiations of the EU–China Bilateral Comprehensive Agreement on Investment. In the same year, China was placed on the US Treasury's Monitoring List of major trading partners whose currency required close attention.[16] The harmony between the emerging markets' "Rising Star" and those advanced countries entered into a different stage from those changes.

In the modern business world's interdependency among superpowers, the influence from global geopolitical changes on a country's currency internationalization is inevitable and unavoidable. Global partners' political policy changes from 2014 to 2017 significantly affected China's RMB's internationalization progress. The pause between 2016 and 2018 provided opportunities for the Chinese government to adjust its RMB strategy and fine-tune its monetary policy and promotion programs.

Signing the ASEAN-Centric RCPE in 2020

With the expectation of China taking an important economic leading role in RCEP member countries' post-pandemic recovery, the increase of RMB use in both trade settlement and financial products becomes promising. China Construction Bank's partnership with The Asian Banker produced a recent annual survey confirming the prediction that 81% of overseas companies believe the RCPE will promote or maintain the international use of the RMB.

China's Rapid Economic Recover from COVID-19 in 2021[17]

China's steady economic recovery from the pandemic made China the only major economy to attain positive growth in 2020, which motivated foreign investors' active allocation to RMB assets. By the end of June 2021, the amount of RMB-denominated financial assets held by overseas investors reached RMB10.26 trillion ($1.59 trillion), an annual increase of 42.8%. According to the People's Bank of China's 2021 RMB internationalization report: The cross-border use of the RMB gained record highs in 2020 and the first half of 2021; in 2020, RMB's cross-border payment and receipts settlement reached RMB 28.39 trillion ($4.40 trillion) with a year-to-year increase of 44.3%; in the first half of 2021, the RMB cross-border payment and receipts settlement reached RMB 17.57 trillion ($2.72 trillion), with a year-to-year increase of 38.7%.

The use of CIPS also shows a strong increase in 2021. The joint annual survey also identified global financial institutions which use CIPS for over 40% of their cross-border transactions increased in number from 29% in 2020 to 42% in 2021. The same survey also indicated that overseas RMB-denominated assets will continue their popularity with 64% of global financial institutions expecting to increase or maintain their holdings in 2021, while 34% of overseas companies and 33% of Chinese companies expect to increase their overseas RMB-denominated assets holdings during the same time period. Meanwhile, of those who indicated they would reduce their holdings, the total amount of those firms declined.[18]

What's Next?[19]

The annual survey conducted jointly by China Construction Bank and The Asian Banker also concluded that digital currency and sustainable finance will be the key drivers of RMB internationalization. Although I agree that both will be global trends in the coming years, the complexity of monetary policies and cross-country regulations, in my opinion, suggests differently based on my understanding of the short-term and long-term goals of RMB internationalization.

China's Digital Currency (e-CNY)

E-CNY is an advanced function that improves the efficiency of cross-border RMB transactions at the moment, but not a driver for RMB's internationalization in the short term. Distinguished from bitcoin, which is not regulated, digital RMB, China's central bank digital currency (CBDC), is issued by China's central bank, the PBOC. The Chinese government's strategy of e-CNY is identical to most other strategies and takes a gradualist approach. The development of e-CNY started in 2014; pilot programs in Shenzhen and Chengdu started in 2019, and another trial program in 2021 was set to release RMB40 million ($6.2 million) e-CNY to citizens in Beijing as a lottery to prepare for that currency's use by foreign visitors at the 2022 Beijing Winter Olympics. As a result, Reuters reported over RMB2 million ($315,000) e-CNY was used every day at the 2022 Winter Olympics,[20] which was labeled as China "showing off" by Bloomberg.[21]

During e-CNY's trial period, a cross-border CBDC trading platform was initiated by the Hong Kong Monetary Authority (HKMA) and the Bank of Thailand, eight Thai banks and two Hong Kong banks have joined the platform to test digital currency-based cross-border transactions between Thailand and Hong Kong. The PBOC and Central Bank of the United Arab Emirates (UAS) also joined the platform during its second phase. Presently, the CBDC trading platform has been exploring potential businesses with a desire to become a cross-border network for large financial institutions. In addition to the CBDC trading platform, Indonesia and China formed a partnership in September 2020 that allows direct exchange rates and interbank trading between the Chinese RMB and the Indonesian rupiah instead of using the US dollar as a reserved currency for transactions settlements. Direct exchange rates and interbank trading are essential and symbolic steps for the CBDC trading platform to work efficiently.

E-CNY can make foreign exchange transactions faster and less expensive, but the exchange rate will not be different from traditional RMB. The CBDC trading platform might offer competitive foreign exchange rates and convenient options such as short-term, cross-border borrowing, and transaction settling liquidity to attract more central banks to join. However, global adoption of the CBDC trading platform requires interrelated international legal and regulatory standards in digital currency, digital taxes, and anti-money laundering.

Sustainable Finance

Sustainable finance will become a significant driver for RMB internationalization in the new era. China's fast pace in the ESG movement has accelerated RMB's international adoption in the past couple of years and will continue serving as a key driver of RMB internationalization. Since the COVID-19 outbreak in 2020, Panda Bonds have gained popularity among foreign companies and institutions. In June 2020, the China-backed AIIB issued its first Panda Bonds in the amount of RMB 3 billion ($425 million) with the proceeds sent to support member countries during the outbreak, while also bankrolling AIIB's sustainable infrastructure project investment sector for the long term. According to data from China Chengxin International Credit Rating, 37 Panda Bonds were issued by 17 issuers in the first six months of 2021 totaling RMB 57.9 billion ($8.96 billion), representing a 42.6% increase compared with the same period in 2020. In March 2021, the Asian Development Bank raised RMB 2 billion ($282 million) from Panda Bond sales, followed by the BRICS (the acronym for the emerging economies in Brazil, Russia, India, China, and South Africa) New Development Bank's RMB 5 billion ($707 million) issuance.[22]

In November 2021, Chinese authorities launched a pilot program that allows foreign issuers to sell sustainability-themed Panda Bonds in China's interbank market. The new pilot program adds more options for foreign borrowers, which will most likely further boost Panda Bonds' issuance.

Russian–Ukraine Regional War Impacts[23]

The Russian–Ukraine regional war that started in early 2022 will be another key driver for RMB's international adoption.

In March 2022, several Chinese firms used RMB to buy Russian coal, marking the first commodity shipment paid with RMB since US sanctions were imposed on Russia, which cut off Russian banks from the international financial system as well as the SWIFT interbank messaging system. With the increasing adoption of RMB by more and more countries, RMB will most likely be used as the settlement currency for a part of Indian and Russian bilateral trade.

Since Russian banks have been removed from the SWIFT payment system and that country's central bank's foreign reserves have been frozen, many nations are seeking an alternative to the US dollar. Consequently, the progress of RMB's internationalization over the past two decades, combined with China's growing international influence, has allowed the RMB to be an alternative currency option for Russia and other countries.

Also in March 2022, the success of the RMB-based oil deal between Saudi Arabia and China signaled the potential for the RMB to advance its global use. The agreement reveals Saudi Arabia's strategy to mitigate potential currency risk due to the increased US dollar supply as a response to the COVID-19 pandemic crisis. RMB-based oil deal will expose the Saudis to a non-dollar currency and enable them to hedge against the RMB, while reducing China's vulnerability to potential sanctions from the West due to the regional war.

In May 2022, after its record-high growth of foreign exchange reserves, China is building an RMB reserve by teaming with Indonesia, Malaysia, Hong Kong, Singapore, and Chile for a $2.2 billion RMB Liquidity Agreement (each country contributes RMB15 billion). The RMB reserve will allow participating central banks access to additional funding through the collateralized liquidity mechanism, which signals a new chapter of RMB internationalization.

Although a fair judgment of the Russian–Ukraine regional war resides in a different arena, the global economic disruption caused by a regional war and the necessity of establishing regional economic zones that can protect a certain part of the world from a regional war reiterates the importance of a tripolar system centered on the dollar, euro, and RMB would serve as a safety net for the global economy should the dollar regime collapse.[24] On the other hand, to capture the momentum for further promotion of the RMB's international adoption, China needs to ensure the long-term stability of the RMB to enhance the trust of other nations.

Given the significant differences between the US dollar and RMB used for foreign exchange transactions (as of May 2021, RMB accounted for only 4% of global trade transaction settlements, in contrast to 88% using US dollars, according to 2020 IMF data), the increase of RMB international adoption in the past couple of years won't pose a serious challenge to the dollar's dominant role, at least in the short term. But the trend of anticipated and remarkable global geo-political and geo-economics structure changes in the future will likely be due to the RMB's influential role of as part of those inevitable changes.

The Ballooning US Debt[25]

The US' national debt has tripled in the past decade compared to 2009, when the amount was $10.6 trillion USD early that year, and an estimated debt of $50 trillion is projected by 2030. In 2021, the national debt reached nearly one and a half times of the US' annual GDP, which indicated a potential path consistent with Japan's anemic economic growth.

Moreover, the mounting US debts, together with a high inflation rate coming out from the pandemic, are shaking the US dollar's dominant position as the global reserve currency. To mitigate its domestic inflation and the US dollar's status erosion in global reserve currency, the US government started to lift interest rates beginning in 2022, which immediately pumped up the value of dollars in the global market, but also raised more questions regarding the government's ability to serve its debts, including the principal and growing interest.

The US' struggling economy stimulated discussions regarding the multipolar international currency system, for which RMB is viewed as the most important driver.[26] Moreover, IMF's adjusted percentages of the five primary SDR basket currencies in 2022 reflect the increasing recognition of the Chinese currency. However, in terms of global foreign currency reserve in 2022, the share of RMB remains small at 2.76%, while the share of the US dollar was 59.79%. While the ballooning US debt has increased the risk of a deep recession and stirred economic uncertainty in many countries,[27] the US dollar's dominant position as global currency remains strong.

Short-Term and Long-Term Goals

Although the existing programs discussed in this chapter did not significantly move RMB's internationalization forward at the expected pace, they made tremendous improvement toward enhancing China's financial regulation system. Corporate governance standards in financial and other sectors in China's domestic market have improved and become important parts of the foundation for China's future economic growth and the promotion of RMB's global use. Despite the hurdles, feedback of those programs has led to help identify areas for future progress toward continual reforms, as well as direct China's corporate governance development in government and corporations toward building *trust* – the *trust* in the stability of China's economic growth; the *trust* of stable Chinese monetary policy and RMB exchange rate; the *trust* in the government's consistent attempts at transparent regulation reform; and the *trust* of Chinese companies' commitment of fine-tuning their corporate governance practices.

Realistically, building *trust* by escalating the RMB in the international currency hierarchy should be the *short-term goal* of the Chinese government's RMB internationalization strategy.

Compared to the progress in the domestic market, the status of the RMB's regional and international recognition are still in very early stages. One important role of a regional currency zone is to protect member countries from exchange rate fluctuations from external influences. Japan previously led the Asia-Pacific region's economy for over four decades until China surpassed it in 2010. However, an Asia-Pacific regional currency zone has yet to be formed. RCEP is a great opportunity for China to lead the building of that zone due to its influential size combined with the remaining RCEP member countries' collective GDP, although most Asian countries today still tie their currency to the USD in order to acquire stable exchange rates. Will China be able to capitalize on opportunities from large-scale trading agreements with its RCEP partners to stimulate RMB's internationalization? A "seed has been planted", and China needs to demonstrate the stability of its economic growth and continuous improvement of the country's institutions, which are two fundamental elements needed to become the preeminent power in the region to build trust with RCEP member countries.

The BRI has created a platform for China to promote RMB internationalization and build an RMB-centered international currency platform. Partnering with the AIIB and Silk Road Fund – both were created to support the BRI – China has been trying to incentivize debt settlements using RMB and develop RMB reserves for settlements of future accounts. Since its launching in 2013, the BRI has successfully helped spread China's influence and offered RMB as a currency choice option, but the progress of RMB use on BRI projects is relatively slow. Consequently, a majority of BRI investments are still using USD rather than RMB at the moment. With the targeted completion of BRI in 2049, will China be able to accelerate RMB use in future BRI projects? Given the ESG issues raised from BRI partner countries and other challenges and competition from the West, perhaps putting together a comprehensive strategy is necessary and urgent for China to better utilize the platform to improve social and economic impacts, enhance its financial institutions' support, and leverage capital providers' power to promote RMB use.

Regardless of global geo-economics and geopolitical influence and pressure, the Chinese government will continuously explore more opportunities through the BRI and RCEP. The BRI has created many opportunities for RMB internationalization in investing, financing, and trading. The Chinese government could encourage China's institutions to set up overseas branches and provide policy support for those overseas branches to extend offshore RMB business. Also, opportunities with partner countries to increase RMB use in investment and financing, and encouraging innovation regarding financial products to enhance promotion on RMB internationalization, should be considered. China is now the leading country of RCEP so exploring opportunities with partner countries will undoubtedly better utilize sizable trade agreements. In addition, China should take advantage of global green economy transformation to explore better strategies for RMB's internationalization. The Chinese government's commitment to green energy, green infrastructure, and green economy transformation will hopefully capitalize on opportunities through the country's emboldened green finance system. Will China be able to extend its economic influence in global green economy transformation? Will China's global partners collaborate?

Last but not the least, the Russia–Ukraine war and the consequential financial market and economic disruptions alerted the world again (after the 2008 financial crisis) about the risk of relying on a single currency. Compared with 2008, both China and the rest of the world are more ready to accept and promote RMB's international usage. Since the war started, RMB has been considered the first alternative currency for international trade settlement by other countries, mainly due to the enhanced confidence in China's economic growth and currency stabilization. The establishment of RMB reserve with five other countries and regions is a breakthrough and the snowball will grow. Can China ride the momentum to escalate RMB internationalization? I believe the answer is yes. The only items unsure at the moment are as follows: To what extent will that momentum take RMB? What challenges and opportunities will be discovered in domestic and international markets?

As one of the Chinese government's long-term strategies, RMB's internationalization is time sensitive, and its pace will be affected by those of the above conditions relative to domestic, regional, and international implications. RMB's internationalization can help build a healthier global financial system and will need support and acceptance from global partners and dominant countries from other currency zones. The *long-term goal* for China's RMB internationalization should not be the replacement of the US dollar or euro, but to become one of the designated currencies in a tripolar system.

Takeaways

- **China's RMB internationalization will improve the resilience of the global financial market and China's economy.** Financial regulation reforms of RMB internationalization will also enhance China's corporate governance development infrastructure as well as Chinese companies' corporate governance practice.
- China's RMB internationalization's **short-term goals** should focus on increasing its influence in the international currency hierarchy, **long-term goals** should not be to replace the US dollar, but to become one of the designated currencies in **the "tripolar system"**. The progress will be influenced by global geopolitical changes and other superpowers' domestic and international political changes. That scenario will continue.
- **China's RMB internationalization still has a long way to go!** Capturing current opportunities and momentum will accelerate the process.

Notes

1 Chi Huan KWAN, "Issues Facing Renminbi Internationalization: Observations from Chinese, Regional and Global Perspectives," Public Policy Review, 14: 5, September 2018. www.mof.go.jp/english/pri/publication/pp_review/ppr14_05_03.pdf
2 Dong He and Robert Neil Mccauley, "Offshore Markets for the Domestic Currency: Monetary and Financial Stability Issues", *Bank of International Settlements*, September, 2010, www.researchgate.net/publication/46443438_Offshore_Markets_ for_the_Domestic_Currency_Monetary_and_Financial_Stability_Issues
3 Capital transaction includes Inward and Outward Direct Investment, cross-border RMB cash pooling transactions, and the issuing of RMB international bonds.
4 Securities investment including Bond investment, Shanghai–Hong Kong Stock Connect, and Shenzhen–Hong Kong Stock Connect, RQGII.
5 Domestic RMB financial assets include stocks, bonds, loans, and deposits.
6 Qualified Foreign Institutional Investor (QFII) is the first program to allow qualified foreign investors to invest in both SSE and SZSE. Although QFII has operated using specific quotas and certain prerequisites mandated for qualified investors, the program is China's first step to relax capital control and open its capital market.
7 RMB Qualified Foreign Institutional Investor (RQFII) program was established to allow foreign institutional investors' RMB investment funds to be set up in Hong Kong and invested directly in the Chinese capital market. RQFII is a sibling program of QFII, with fewer restrictions.
8 Dim Sum is a popular cuisine from southern China.
9 Dorcas Wong, "China's Six New Free Trade Zones: Where Are They Located?" *China Briefing*, September, 2019. www.china-briefing.com/news/china-free-trade-zones-six-provinces/
10 Anthea Wong, Linjun Shen, and Bo Yu, "Cross-Border RMB Cash Pooling Made Possible for Multinational Corporations in China," *PWC*, February, 2015. www.pwccn.com/en/china-tax-news/chinatax-news-feb2015-7.pdf
11 "China Stock Connect: Expanding the Shanghai–London Program to Germany and Switzerland", January 5, 2022, China Briefing. www.china-briefing.com/news/china-stock-connect-expanding-shanghai-london-program-to-germany-switzerland/ . "China Hints at Launching Shanghai–Zurich Stock Connect Program", April 29, 2021, China Briefing, August 18, 2021. www.china-briefing.com/news/china-hints-at-launching-shanghai-zurich-stock-connect-program/
12 CBN Editor, "Bank of China Report Calls for Shift from SWIFT to CIPS for Cross-Border Settlement Due to Concern over US Sanctions," *China Banking News*, July 15, 2021. www.chinabankingnews.com/2020/07/31/bank-of-china-report-calls-for-shift-from-swift-to-cips-for-cross-border-settlement-due-to-concern-over-us-sanctions/
13 Ryan, John. "Geopolitical Influences on the Future of Renminbi", Security Policy Brief, No. 82, March 2017, August 22, 2021. http://aei.pitt.edu/86887/1/SPB82.pdf
14 "Brexit" is the abbreviation of "British exit", that refers to the UK's withdrawal from the EU after the UK voting in June 2016.
15 "China Is No Longer the Biggest Foreign Holder of US Debt", December 16, 2016, CNN, August 22, 2021. https://money.cnn.com/2016/12/16/investing/china-japan-us-debt-treasuries/index.html
16 "Trading Partners of the United States", US Department of the Treasury, April 13, 2018, August 22, 2021. https://home.treasury.gov/news/press-releases/sm0348
17 PBOC, "2021 RMB Internationalization report", September 6, 2021. www.pbc.gov.cn/en/3688110/3688172/4157443/4433239/2021122809344466286.pdf

18 2021 Renminbi Internationalization Report, RMB pushes forward amid disruptions, China Construction Bank. www2.ccb.com/cn/ccbtoday/news/upload/20211022_163 4866375/20211022092955802527.pdf

19 Hugh Zeng, "Global Corporates and FIs See Digital Currency and Sustainable Finance as Key Drivers for RMB Use", The Asian Banker, November 22, 2021. www.theasianbanker.com/updates-and-articles/global-corporates-and-fis-see-digi tal-currency-and-sustainable-finance-as-key-drivers-for-rmb-use

20 Marc Jones, "Over $315,000 in Digital Yuan Used Every Day at Olympics, PBOC Official Says", Reuters, February 16, 2022, www.bloomberg.com/news/articles/ 2022-02-15/china-is-showing-off-its-central-bank-digital-yuan-currency-at-beijing-olympics#xj4y7vzkg

21 Joe Light, "China Is Showing Off the Digital Yuan at the Olympics. Can the US Compete?", Bloomberg, February 15, 2022. www.bloomberg.com/news/articles/ 2022-02-15/china-is-showing-off-its-central-bank-digital-yuan-currency-at-beijing-olympics#xj4y7vzkg

22 Wang Yushi and Han Wei, "China Opens Bond Market to Foreign Social and Sustainable Borrowers", November 12, 2021. www.caixinglobal.com/2021-11-12/ china-opens-bond-market-to-foreign-social-and-sustainable-borrowers-101803 699.html

23 Bloomberg News, "Russia Coal and Oil Paid for in Yuan Starts Heading to China", Bloomberg, April 6, 2022. www.bloomberg.com/news/articles/2022-04-07/russ ian-coal-and-oil-paid-for-in-yuan-to-start-flowing-to-china. Vishnuaravi, "China's Yuan Is Getting Attraction Because of Russia-Ukraine War", April 9, 2022, DataDrivenInvestor, https://medium.datadriveninvestor.com/chinas-yuan-is-getting-attraction-because-of-russia-ukraine-war-931e6e42b1bc

24 According to a 2018 study by Nomura Institute of Capital Market Research, a Japan-based research institution specializing in financial and capital market studies and policy proposals, currency competition will stabilize the international monetary system.

25 RBC analysis, April 2022, "Is the U.S. Dollar Losing Its Global Appeal?" www. rbcwealthmanagement.com/en-us/insights/is-the-u-s-dollar-losing-its-global-app eal. Alan Rappeport and Jim Tankersley, Oct. 2022, "U.S. National Debt Tops $31 Trillion for First Time", www.nytimes.com/2022/10/04/business/national-debt. html. Wen Sheng, Oct. 2022, "Ballooning US Debt a Ticking Time Bomb for World Economy", www.globaltimes.cn/page/202210/1276756.shtml

26 Zhou Lanxu, Dec. 2022, "RMB Internationalization Gets more Attention", https:// global.chinadaily.com.cn/a/202212/28/WS63aba467a31057c47eba68f9.html

27 Patricia Cohen, "The Dollar Is Strong. That Is Good for the U.S. but Bad for the World", www.nytimes.com/2022/09/26/business/economy/us-dollar-global-impact. html

Chapter 10

The Future of Hong Kong

In this chapter, I review

- Local Political Change and Global Geopolitical Pressure
  Local political issues
  Hong Kong national security law impacts
  Geopolitical pressures

- Hong Kong Embraces China's Economic Growth
  Hong Kong as the international financial center
  Hong Kong as the wealth management hub
  Hong Kong as an important RMB offshore center
  Hong Kong's roles in the Greater Bay Area (GBA)

Hong Kong, the "Pearl of the Orient", is one of the most beautiful cities in the world. What I love most about Hong Kong is its contrasting beauty of well-mixed Western and Eastern cultures, expensive Michelin restaurants and street gourmet food, worldwide brands and open-air markets. As one of the international financial centers and a world tax haven, Hong Kong has been considered the window to and from China that attracted many foreign banks, financial institutions, and corporations to establish regional headquarters and branches over the past several decades.

In 2015, I had an opportunity to join a Hong Kong company, a newly established subsidiary of a Chinese SOE. Due to China's "going global" wave in the mid-2010s, the SOE was planning to develop this Hong Kong subsidiary as its overseas headquarters preparing for future global growth. My main responsibility was to assist the SOE to establish its long-term business strategy and operations of this important subsidiary while simultaneously reporting to the Hong Kong company's chairman/CEO, who also held an executive position in the SOE. Despite being warned of the "housing space shock" by two college

DOI: 10.4324/9781003302919-15

friends who moved there for bank jobs from the US in the early 2000s, I moved to Hong Kong and expected opportunities to practice my Cantonese. However, for the two years I lived there, other than taxi drivers and street shop owners, most Hong Kongers spoke either Mandarin or English. I was impressed indeed by the number of Mandarin speakers who applied for the finance and investment opening positions while we were building the local team, most of whom studied Mandarin in mainland China.

The Hong Kong company I worked for was welcomed by local banking and investment communities. With influential support from top leaders of the SOE and several executives from corporate headquarters, we assembled a local team and devised some strategies and supported the SOE parent company to raise a significant amount of US capital at the Hong Kong Exchange (HKEX) through US bond issuances. We reviewed a number of investment opportunities, including pre-IPO and asset acquisitions, and established a joint venture company in the US. The fast pace of all those activities made my two-year experience in Hong Kong a life-changing journey filled with much excitement. It also opened my eyes and mind about Chinese companies' agile growth and regulatory guidance, both of which were evolving simultaneously, in contrast to my years of experience with US companies, where I observed their growth within a well-regulated business environment. I also had opportunities to attend meetings at the SOE's headquarters in mainland China, interact with the SOE's chairman, board directors, and different levels of executive managers, and participate in meetings with government officials in both Hong Kong and mainland China as the representative of the Hong Kong company. Those experiences exposed me to the inner workings of the SOE's board structure, board functions, board decision-making process, SOE executives' responsibilities, and the most sensitive matter – the government's intervention in the SOE. In addition, I had opportunities to communicate with certain Chinese authorities (including the State Administration of Foreign Exchange) and experienced some RMB internationalization programs, e.g., RQFII[1] and offshore RMB as a mediator of RMB exchange rates.

Once I had a chance to subsequently study Chinese SOE reform and corporate governance regulatory reform, I realized the importance of Chinese SOEs' evolving journey toward China's regulatory reform and corporate governance development. I also realized the value of my work experience at the Hong Kong company. Through those experiences, I witnessed China's fast economic growth as the powerful engine that enabled the SOE's access to domestic and international capitals, the SOE's influence in Hong Kong and other Asian regions, and its ability "to do business the Chinese way". Moreover, I had a profound feeling of native Hong Kongers' "sense of loss" through our local employees' words and behavior, and the paradoxical sensation they had working for a mainland China company.

Hong Kong's privileged economic position has been fading over the past couple of decades due to China's fast growth, and the economic wane has been accelerated since 2019 by political upheaval and foreign companies' concerns regarding new legislation. The unpredicted COVID-19 outbreak in 2020 accelerated those concerns resulting in many Western countries' expatriates returning to their home countries and a number of Hong Kongers migrating to Singapore or other countries. Moreover, thousands of street shops and luxury stores have shut down during the pandemic due to the absence of mainland Chinese shoppers and a significant reduction in international tourism. While Hong Kong's economy was negatively impacted, Chinese authorities officially declared that Hong Kong's inclusion in China's 14th FYP's dual circulation strategy and its vital role as part of GBA development are undeniable.[2] While the future of Hong Kong has become a concern of the entire world, that fear may be illusory.

Local Political Issues and Global Geopolitical Pressure

The complexity of the relationship between Hong Kong and the mainland contains many historical factors, in addition to 150 years of British Hong Kong's pathway that differs from the mainland,[3] such as British colonial passports issued to Hong Kong residents that caused a series of racial abuse accusations; mainland refugees who fled to Hong Kong after the establishment of P.R. China in 1949[4]; Hong Kong's legislative and chief executive election systems' transfers after the mainland's takeover; and the US-Hong Kong extradition treaty signed in 1996 preceding Hong Kong's return to the mainland. Therefore, the gaps between Hong Kong and mainland China – century-long systemic differences (including language dialect), external influences, and lifestyles – cannot be easily bridged merely because Hong Kong is part of the P.R. China. Hong Kong's political challenges today combine local and geopolitical matters. The development and progression of those matters will significantly impact Hong Kong's future.

Local Political Issues

Since Hong Kong was handed over to China in 1997, conflicts between Hong Kong's localism and China's nationalist integration strategy have transpired over the past two decades, notably in 2003, when a protest opposing a national security law occurred[5]; in 2012, when a protest against "Moral and National Education" was instilled in Hong Kong's public school curriculum[6]; in 2014, when a 79-day "Occupy Central" protest (also known as the "Umbrella Movement") against a decision made by Chinese authorities in August occurred regarding a selective prescreening of candidates for the 2017 election of Hong Kong's chief executive[7]; and in 2019, when a protest initially opposed to the extradition bill grew to wider demands for democratic reform[8] and ultimately became violent.

It's worth mentioning that those protests evolved from initially peaceful and being led by students and influential scholars, to heated confrontations by disorganized and frustrated young Hong Kongers with explicit political demands. The accumulated grievances from Hong Kongers were based on two primary complaints: Hong Kong's economic downturn over the prior two decades that led to detrimental changes in Hong Kongers' careers, notably, by increasing numbers of Hong Kongers who either worked for mainland-owned companies in Hong Kong or Hong Kongers who pursued job opportunities in other GBA cities; and, the increasing influence and demand of Mandarin to be spoken in a city where its citizens have always spoken Cantonese, resulting in Hong Kongers feeling pressured and as if they are a "stranger in my own town". In addition, young Hong Kongers have been raised in an atmosphere of political pressure and economic decline in recent years, so combining their sentiment with the lack of job opportunities in Hong Kong has caused them to be quite agitated and emotionally disconnected from the mainland. Paradoxically, the Chinese government's reaction to those protests evolved from negotiable to becoming more forceful despite not only the protestors' appeals and their objections to formality changes, but also because China was becoming increasingly stronger in global economic and political positions. The 2019 Hong Kong protest continued after the outbreak of COVID-19 in early 2020, and its impact on Hong Kong-mainland relations has extended to the global geopolitical contest.

Major Impacts of Hong Kong National Security Law (HK NSL)

The HK NSL, which was promulgated on June 30, 2020, stirred noticeable concerns regarding the risks for international business. A 2021 Harvard University Kennedy School of Government research paper[9] reviewed the fundamental changes in Hong Kong's legal system due to HK NSL and points to the core of those concerns: Hong Kong's legal system lost its autonomy and the Chinese central government exaggerated national security risks relative to its finance, energy, technology, and infrastructure sectors; additional new risks (including the potential for legal liability of violating national security laws); and the risks for international companies and those who operate them (as well as their families) operating in Hong Kong or mainland China. This paper warned international businesses to exercise considerable caution should they contemplate future business operations in Hong Kong and mainland China based on several factors:

First, the HK NSL has accelerated changes in Hong Kong's talent market, including potential international employees. Specifically, an increasing number of Westerners have left Hong Kong since 2020 or are considering leaving, concurrent with the restructuring of Hong Kong's economy.

Second, the HK NSL will expedite a global supply-chain relocation from Hong Kong. The broad range of national security matters will trigger strategic change considerations for international companies due to fears of potential breaches involving trade secrets and intelligent property transfers.

Third, the HK NSL affects Hong Kong's legal and regulatory system development. The Chinese central government's overarching national security provisions stipulated in the HK NSL may result in commercial disputes involving intellectual property that could potentially raise national security or state secrets concerns, while possibly targeting companies' merger and acquisition deals. The HK NSL reshapes the legal liability and enforcement mechanisms of commercial matters, which significantly impacts the compliance mindset and focus of corporate governance roles for business in Hong Kong.

Fourth, the intermingling of HK NSL with geopolitical tensions. Recent legal framework development in China has tightened national security scrutiny that led to further geopolitical tensions between China and Western countries led by the US. For example, the newly released Data Security Law provides the legal framework for a broader definition of "illegal transferring of data", allowing for punishment of companies and their employees, while geopolitical tensions have accelerated the application of HK NSL to national security scrutiny. The recently tightened scrutiny of mergers and acquisitions enacted by both China and US governments is an excellent example.

Global Geopolitical Pressure

After the HK NSL became effective on July 1, 2020, Canada, Australia, the UK, New Zealand, France, and the US suspended their extradition treaties with Hong Kong. Adding to the multidimensional tussle between the US and China, the former also suspended other commercial and diplomatic treaties with Hong Kong (including taxes, export-control, and passport controls in late 2020[10]). Losing those treaties erased many advantages Hong Kong possessed over other Chinese cities. In addition, the volatile atmosphere created by the escalation of US–China tension has spread to Hong Kong. Beijing issued new Anti-Sanctions Laws effective in June 2021 in response to US and EU sanctions, with plans to extend the laws to Hong Kong and Macau. Many international companies in Hong Kong will be caught between the West's sanctions and Beijing's counter-sanctions, while the US–China conflict will compromise those companies' compliance with Chinese and their home countries' laws and vice versa.[11]

Having been well-known as an international financial hub, the world's top tax haven, and its reputable legal and financial systems, Hong Kong has earned trust from global investors, banks, businesses, and wealthy individuals, so the impact on Hong Kong's business community from Beijing's counter-sanctions is serious but unpredictable. Although Beijing delayed its extended power plans due to its cautious measurement of Hong Kong's future, Hong Kong's local government and the Chinese central government are working closely on calculating the impact of the counter-sanction law and considering potential modification of certain terms or alternative implementation approaches.[12]

However, Hong Kong lost more people in 2020 than in any previous year for which records were kept. COVID-19, quarantines, and restrictions on travel are exacerbating its other problems. The city's lawmakers have pushed through a record number of legislative acts that could create obstacles to foreign commerce. Many firms are relocating functions to the mainland, Singapore, or elsewhere. Hong Kong has lost its luster over the past couple of years. Having lived in the "Pearl of the Orient" for two years, I internalized some of the contradictions experienced by the city and local professionals over their economic struggle, political transformation, and lifestyle changes.

Hong Kong Embraces China's Economic Growth

At the 14th Asian Financial Forum on January 18, 2021, Guo Shuqing, Party Secretary and Deputy Governor of PBOC, clearly defined Hong Kong's supporting roles in China's 14th FYP dual circulation strategy, and Hong Kong's important roles as an international financial center, major offshore RMB market for RMB internationalization, and part of GBA development. In May 2021, CSRS officially confirmed its plan to promote both Hong Kong and Shanghai as international financial centers by 2035,[13] with expectations of future reciprocal openings, improved international financial services, and further international alignment.

However, many believe the economic development of Shanghai and Shenzhen will affect Hong Kong's position in China's future economic growth. Let us zoom into some details.

Primary Changes in Shanghai and SSE

The most remarkable changes in this mega city and its stock exchange market are driven by three economic development factors: China's launching of a registration-based IPO system; China's green finance movement; the establishment of GBA.

Shanghai's financial status has been accelerating quickly within recent years due to the opening of the city's free trade zone, the launch of a STAR market, the recent opening of a climate bonds office (the Shanghai Office of the Climate Bonds Initiative), and a Chinese national carbon trading market. The Chinese authority's decision to promote two international financial centers will stir competition between those two cities focusing on legal and supervisory system improvements, investor interest protections, and systematic financial risk mitigation.

A remarkable reform of the SSE was the launch of a new "NASDAQ-style" STAR Market overseen by the exchange in the second half of 2019. In 2020, a total of 104 companies successfully issued IPOs on STAR's board, raising funds amounting to 52.5% of total SSE IPO that year. A flagship IPO on STAR's board was the secondary listing of HK-listed chip maker Semiconductor Manufacturing International Corp., which demonstrated a few major effects of SSE's reforms through its STAR board, such as a registration-based listing system that allowed for dual-class share issuance, and more importantly, a higher valuation potential for high-tech companies. Moreover, compared to SSE's regular IPO application processing time averaging six months, STAR's board showcased its 26-day, fast-track approval with Ant's expedited IPO application in September 2020, despite the fact that Ant IPO was suspended by Chinese regulators late that year. In early 2023, China rolled out a registration-based IPO system to all mainland stock exchange markets to encourage new listings and boost fundraising by simplifying the IPO process while also emphasizing information disclosure. With the IPO reform, the SSE, the fourth-largest stock market in the world and the largest in China, is expected to undertake the responsibility to mitigate corruption risk and help build a disciplined financial market.

In addition to the SSE's great potential with the IPO reform, Shanghai's international financial center lead role in green finance transformation became more evident in 2021 due to some late developments: a Climate Bonds Office in Shanghai.[14] In March 2021, CBI Shanghai's office[15] was launched in Shanghai Lujiazui Financial City that confirmed Shanghai's role as a green financial center to promote green bonds, green standards, and green transition finance, together with the establishment of a Sino-British two-city linkage platform between Lujiazui Financial City and London; and China's National Carbon Market based in Shanghai. The launch of a national carbon market in Shanghai planned to have the city administer all carbon trading transactions occurring in eight regional pilot exchanges, making Shanghai the center of China's carbon market.

Although China's green finance transition inevitably lifted Shanghai into the premier financial center position for China's economic growth over the coming decades, Shanghai is not the exclusive beneficiary in China's green finance movement. The CBI also released a report in June 2021 to address a GBA green infrastructure investment opportunity report, highlighting the significant amount of $299 billion green infrastructure investment in Guangdong province out of $777 billion budgeted for major infrastructure projects that were planned in China's 14th Five-Year Plan for the province. The report also emphasized

GBA's important roles in green finance development, such as promoting green asset-backed securities and issuance of local government green bonds, and discussed the roles of the Hong Kong capital market to support GBA's green infrastructure development. In the same month, Guangdong province also launched a renewable energy trading platform that contributed to GBA green economic transformation. As an important part of GBA, Hong Kong plays important leading roles in regulatory development needed for economic transformation due to its relatively mature capital market. The next steps will depend on actual action to capitalize on opportunities and plans.

Repositioning Hong Kong – International Financial Center and Wealth Management Hub

Hong Kong has been known for decades as an international financial center due to its sound legal system, effective financial regulations, and mature capital market. With market capitalization sized at $6.1 trillion, the HKEX was the third-largest in Asia and the fifth-largest in the world by the end of 2020, following the SSE (currently ranks second in Asia and fourth in the world). Although the HKEX was ranked below the SSE, there are some advanced features of the HKEX that will take some time for the SSE to develop and equal.

An Effective and Trustworthy Financial Regulation System

In addition to its registration-based IPO system, broader international exposure, sound financial infrastructure, and effective regulatory system, the HKEX has built a trustworthy investment environment over the past several decades that has been vitally important for HKEX's international reputation. The continuous regulation reform of the HKEX, including the creation of the Hang Seng Tech Index, has made the exchange more attractive for high-tech and biotech companies. In 2020, 154 companies raised $51.28 billion at the HKEX through IPO – offerings. Of those, nine were US-listed Chinese companies secondarily listed in Hong Kong with funds totaling $16.9 billion, which was nearly 30% of the total amount on the HKEX – placing the HKEX second in global ranking[16] in 2020 (NASDAQ was first with $57.3 billion, while the SSE was third with $49.42 billion). However, activity at the HKEX was reduced in 2021 due to various reasons, with 98 IPOs that raised over HKD328 billion ($41.8 billion).

First Choice of Chinese Companies "Homecoming Wave"

HKEX reform in 2018 allowed a dual-class shares structure that enabled Alibaba's secondary listing in 2019 to raise $11 billion, a 6.6% share price increase on the first trading date (Alibaba was not able to list on the HKEX before the 2018 reform due to restrictions on its dual-class share structure). Alibaba's HKEX IPO was the world's largest listing in 2019, surpassing Uber, who raised $8 billion through an IPO that year. Increased scrutiny and regulatory uncertainty (by default) from US stock markets permitted Alibaba's successful experience that made the HKEX the first choice location among Chinese companies' secondary listing. Chinese technology companies led by JD.com, Baidu, and Bilibili chose Hong Kong as their secondary listing in 2020 and 2021. In July 2022, Alibaba announced its plans to apply for a primary listing in Hong Kong, which will position it as the first Chinese tech giant company with primary listings in both New York and Hong Kong.

Continuous Leading Roles on ESG Regulation Reforms

In 2012, the HKEX was the first Chinese stock exchange to issue ESG reporting guidelines. Since then, the HKEX has played a role in facilitating ESG-reporting education by offering training courses and various consultation services, as well as several updated versions of ESG reporting guidelines within the past decade, the latest occurring in 2020 that included climate-related disclosure requirements to align with TCFD international standards.

Moreover, the HKEX issued its *2022 Analysis of ESG Practice Disclosure* based on its study of a sample group of 400 issuers. The study focused on those companies' corporate governance practices and board involvement on several ESG-related matters; companies' knowledge and disclosure on climate-related information and their compliance with TCFD and the newly published climate standards by International Sustainability Standards Board (ISSB); companies' consideration of social and governance related risk and training; and overall ESG-reporting quality based on four principles including materiality, quantitative analysis, balance, and consistency.[17]

The analysis report marked a new milestone in HKEX's leading role in ESG regulation development, validation, and enhancement of Chinese financial markets.

Boosting the International Asset and Wealth Management Hub Position

According to a November 2021 Forbes article,[18] Hong Kong is Asia's largest and the world's second-largest, cross-border private wealth-management hub, with the number of "institutional family offices" established in the Asia-Pacific region growing 44% from the end of 2017 to July 2019 (the worldwide growth rate was 38% in the same period) due to the trend of worldwide eastward wealth migration, growing complexity of wealth management, digital transformation, and vulnerability of family business from cyberattacks in 2017.

With its dynamic financial market, simple low-rate local tax system, comprehensive network of tax treaties, and robust regulation system on wealth management, most of the world's largest banks and money managers have a presence in Hong Kong.[19] The rise of a Chinese billionaire group in the last decade and Hong Kong's geographic location and important position within the GBA (a region with 20% of China's high net worth families) have become a natural resource for Hong Kong to boost its role as an international wealth management hub. Even with the pandemic crisis, total assets under management rose 21% with a 25% year-to-year increase in private banking and private wealth management, according to the Hong Kong Securities and Futures Commission (SFC).[20]

Hong Kong government and the financial community are actively catching this growth opportunity with new initiatives including:

In January 2020, the SFC issued "The licensing obligations of family offices", providing formal guidance for professionals to properly manage family offices' funds and other financial services in Hong Kong;

In July 2020, the Hong Kong Financial Services Development Council (FSDC) issued *Family Wisdom: A Family Office in Hong Kong*, a publication with recommendations to develop Hong Kong's family office hub on regulation, tax, talent development, and service;

In November 2020, the establishment of the Family Office Association with government support to foster the industry;

In November 2021, two local laws (the Securities and Futures amendment and the Limited Partnership Fund and Business Registration Legislation amendment) were issued in Hong Kong to enhance comprehensive mechanisms of investment vehicles known as the Open-ended Fund Company and the Limited Partnership Fund.[21] Those amendments intend to increase those products' popularity and adoption to challenge the Cayman Islands and the British Virgin Islands (BVI) as favored fund domiciles.[22]

Hong Kong has been the world's top wealth management hub for decades. The city intends to retain its strong growth momentum to further its development as the regional and international wealth management hub.

Hong Kong's Special Purpose Acquisition Companies' (SPAC) Debut

Special Purpose Acquisition Companies' (SPACs') listing regime has been around since the 1990s. In 2020, it experienced explosive growth in the US stock market, followed by a slowdown due to US regulators' tightened scrutiny. Singapore and Hong Kong both jumped on the SPAC bandwagon in 2021 during the slowdown, and the former hosted three SPAC listings in January 2022.[23] In March 2022, HKEX listed its first SPAC.[24]

HKEX is well-known for its problematic back-door listings over the past decades. The back-door listings are usually accomplished through a "reverse takeover", when opportunities for fraud occur due to the complexity of the asset swap process and a lack of regulatory requirements needed to determine accurate valuation. While SPAC and back-door listing share many similarities, a SPAC listing offers a transparent acquisition process guarded by regulations, with which investors are involved in the decision-making process. Although the second Hong Kong SPAC was been put on hold in April due to the high volatility of the market in 2022, the future of SPAC listing is arguable at the moment due to the underperformance of a significant portion of SPAC IPOs. Nevertheless, launching SPAC listings in HKEX indicates Hong Kong's determination to continue its international financial center roles.

An Important RMB Offshore Center

Hong Kong has been the largest RMB offshore center since 2003 and the largest market of RMB international bonds (both Dim Sum Bonds and Panda Bonds). According to Hong Kong Monetary Authority 2019 information, over 70% of world RMB settlements have been resolved through Hong Kong, and Hong Kong held the biggest RMB liquidity pool of over RMB632.2 billion outside of China ending in 2019, (that number decreased from its peak of RMB1,003 billion in 2014). The HKEX already identified the reasons for Hong Kong's offshore RMB deposit amount reduction from 2014 to 2019 and provided options to increase its offshore RMB liquidity pool in a HKEX 2019 report.

Over the past many decades, the sales of H Shares on the HKEX have been one of the most important channels for Chinese equities to access offshore capital. As the largest RMB offshore center subservient to Chinese capital controls, Hong Kong has been instrumental in its support of the authorities to guide the direction of offshore RMB exchange rates and interest rates. With its broad exposure to the international financial system, Hong Kong is the best measurement tool regarding monetary demand trends in the international market.

Although the amount of RMB cross-border transactions handled in Shanghai has been increasing according to a 2020 PBOC report, the experiences and financial market supporting system developed in Hong Kong have placed Hong Kong ahead of the game in the offshore RMB markets' future growth.[25] In addition, Hong Kong's lead role in a digital RMB cross-border trading platform also anchors the city's important position in RMB's internationalization.[26]

Potentials of Guangdong–Hong Kong–Macau GBA

The concept of the Guangdong–Hong Kong–Macau GBA was established in China's 13th FYP in 2016. The GBA covers nine cities in Guangdong (including Shenzhen and Guangzhou, the capital city of Guangdong province) together with Hong Kong and Macau that comprises 5% of China's total population and 12% of the country's GDP. With many well-known Chinese tech companies (e.g., Huawei and Tencent) headquartered in Shenzhen and the comprehensive supply-chain system in other Guangdong cities in the GBA, the concept has become the primary platform for the world's fast prototyping systems and low-cost engineering processes, by which it ostensibly gained its Asian "Silicon Valley" name. In addition, the GBA is part of China's BRI that encompasses a well-developed infrastructure system, with rich features from Cantonese culture that includes the official language, Cantonese, spoken in both Hong Kong and Macau. Therefore, the GBA is a national plan to integrate the Special Administrative Regions (SAR) of Hong Kong and Macau and the nine Guangdong cities across the Pearl River Delta.

The 2019 Outline Development Plan for the Guangdong–Hong Kong–Macau GBA developed by the Chinese government lays out two milestones for GBA's development: to establish the framework for a first-class international bay area (consisting of Guangzhou, Shenzhen, Hong Kong, and Macau) by 2022; and to attain that status by 2035.

Historically, Hong Kong's economy has been chiefly centered on four sectors (supply chain, financial, professional service, and tourism), which can no longer support Hong Kong's economic condition due to global economic environment changes. Hong Kong's GDP has slowed since the early 2000s; consequently, Hong Kong's economic restructuring will happen one way or another.[27] Being part of the GBA opens broader industrial opportunities for Hong Kong, offers diversified job opportunities for Hong Kongers, both of which will accelerate Hong Kong's economic restructuring. At the same time, Hong Kong can leverage its advanced financial and supply-chain systems and broad international accessibility to help achieve GBA's potential.

Other Opportunities for Hong Kong

Decades of distinct development inherent to Hong Kong that were required to build its effective and lucrative financial system as the Asian financial center has benefitted the global community. Although recent trends indicate the Chinese government's commitment and determination to improve the country's regulatory standards to align with international benchmarks, building a trustworthy society including a credible nationwide social credit system may take decades to construct to achieve those goals. It makes little sense to lose Hong Kong's global financial hub's position to spite China's long-term interest.

While China's central government is defining Hong Kong's roles for the future, Hong Kong is also trying to discover what the city can offer to China. In his September 2021 article titled "Hong Kong's Unique Role as China's Broker for the NewSpace Economy",[28] Professor Gregg Li elaborated on Hong Kong's unique position as an international trading hub and financial center, with the potential to bridge China with the West in order to align regulations for a future, digitally based economy. Additionally, establishing mutually beneficial cybersecurity and data protection infrastructures, bridging research and commercialization by building market-driven labs in space, urbanization, and an energy development sector to enhance the nation's technology ability and support China's 14th FYP are goals of becoming a leading innovative country by 2035. Also in September 2021, the International Conference on Rural Revitalization hosted by the University of Hong Kong gathered academic experts and influential business leaders from Hong Kong, mainland China, and other countries to share and collect ideas regarding how to utilize Hong Kong's international position and inquired of developed countries' successful experiences in rural modernization. The conference was a positive start to establish a suitable rural revitalization strategy for China with which to support the current green economy and trending digital economy transformation.[29]

Although the discussion regarding those new sectors in which Hong Kong can contribute to China's long-term strategy is still in an early stage, the initiatives of a joint effort from academic and industry sectors from Hong Kong and mainland China will stir further discussion regarding new business models, political policies, and economic regulation reforms to facilitate the progress. More importantly, the initiative demonstrates the intention of both sides to explore and optimize governance models containing corresponding responsibilities at the institutional level and from the business sector.

How will the Chinese government diplomatically handle the local political and geopolitical challenges to minimize damage to Hong Kong's economy? How will Beijing measure and balance the efficiency of Hong Kong's political and economic autonomy in order to retain Hong Kong's role as an international financial center? How will Hong Kong's government and other organizations collaborate with the Chinese central government to further explore and capitalize on Hong Kong's continued value in order to support China's long-term global strategy? Will all stakeholders collaborate for the betterment of Hong Kongers' livelihoods and the future of its businesses, instead of making Hong Kong the battleground of today's geopolitical contest among superpowers?

Understanding that it will take decades to overcome significant dimensional differences to unify Hong Kong and mainland China, Hong Kong's future will be written by both entities, as will the ongoing change of global geo-development strategies across the world.

The political power transition in Hong Kong becomes a perfect testimonial of the definition of China's corporate governance, "Corporate Governance is about power and responsibility".[30]

Takeaways

- The changes in Hong Kong's local political system and geopolitical position were escalated by the launching of HK NSL. Consequentially, Western businesses and individuals have been leaving. Future engagement between the city and mainland China will inevitably change the economic structure, talent pool, and the social and legal systems in Hong Kong. **Eventually, corporate governance practices for businesses operating in Hong Kong and mainland China will concurrently change**.

- Hong Kong's mature capital market, effective regulation system, broader international connection, and experience developing its RMB's offshore market are the foundation of **Hong Kong's future roles in supporting China's long-term strategy**.
- Considering its history in the international market, the current political challenges in Hong Kong indicate the delicate nature of the Chinese government's cautious approach to Hong Kong's future international position. However, the **joint effort of Hong Kong and mainland China to discover new areas utilizing Hong Kong's advantage is promising signs of its future**.

Notes

1 The RMB Qualified Foreign Institutional Investors (RQFII) program was established in 2011 to set up quotas for qualified foreign institutional investors to invest in the Chinese bond and stock markets. There are jurisdictional requirements and total asset under management thresholds for different groups of RQFII applicants.
2 At the 14th Asian Financial Forum on January 18, 2021, Guo Shuqing, Party Secretary and Deputy Governor of PBOC, clearly defined Hong Kong's supporting roles in China's 14th FYP "Dual Circulation" strategy, and Hong Kong's important roles as an international financial center, major offshore RMB market for RMB internationalization, and part of GBA development.
3 "British Chief Promises Hong Kong a Tight Check on China", The New York Times, March 5, 1996, August 22, 2021. www.nytimes.com/1996/03/05/world/british-chief-promises-hong-kong-a-tight-check-on-china.html
4 "How Hong Kong's Complex History Explains Its Current Crisis with China", National Geographic, August 7, 2019, August 22, 2021. www.nationalgeographic.com/culture/article/hong-kong-history-explain-relationship-china
5 "Key differences between Hong Kong street protests of 2014 and now," The Straights Time, June 13, 2019, August 21, 2021. www.straitstimes.com/asia/key-differences-between-hong-kong-street-protests-of-2014-and-now
6 "'National education' Raise Furor in Hong Kong", July 30, 2012, August 21, 2021. www.cnn.com/2012/07/30/world/asia/hong-kong-national-education-controversy/index.html
7 "Explainer: What was Hong Kong's 'Occupy' Movement All about?" Reuters, April 23, 2019, August 21, 2020. www.reuters.com/article/us-hongkong-politics-occupy-explainer/explainer-what-was-hong-kongs-occupy-movement-all-about-idUSKC N1S005M
8 "Why Are There Protests in Hong Kong? All the Context You Need," BBC News, May 21, 2020, August 21, 2021. www.bbc.com/news/world-asia-china-48607723
9 Dennis W. H. Kwok, "The Risks for International Business under the Hong Kong National Security Law", Harvard Kennedy School, July 2021. https://ash.harvard.edu/publications/risks-international-business-under-hong-kong-national-security-law

10 "US Becomes Latest Country to Suspend Extradition Treaty with Hong Kong", The Diplomat, August 20, 2020, August 22, 2021. https://thediplomat.com/2020/08/us-becomes-latest-country-to-suspend-extradition-treaty-with-hong-kong/

11 "China Prepares New Anti-Sanction Laws for Hong Kong and Macau", WSJ, July 28, 2021, August 22, 2021. www.wsj.com/articles/china-prepares-new-anti-sanct ion-laws-for-hong-kong-and-macau-11627475091

12 "China Delays Anti-Sanctions Law for Hong Kong', WSJ, August 20, 2021, August 22, 2021. www.wsj.com/articles/china-delays-anti-sanctions-law-for-hong-kong-11629460523?tpl=cb

13 Staff report, "China to Lift HK, Shanghai's Roles as Global Financial Hubs in Broad Plan for Capital Market," Global Times, May 9, 2021, June 12, 2021. www.globalti mes.cn/index.html

14 Leena Fatin, "Climate Bonds Opens Shanghai Office: Signs MoU with Lujiazui Financial City," Climate Bonds Initiative, March 29, 2021 www.climatebonds.net/ 2021/03/climate-bonds-opens-shanghai-office-signs-mou-lujiazui-financial-city

15 Climate Bonds Initiative (CBI) is a not-for-profit international organization launched in 2012. By providing annual studies on the evolution of the green bonds market and standards and guidance on green bonds, CBI advocates climate change consider-ations through financial institutions' investment and lending activities.

16 Staff report, "Hong Kong Ranks as 2nd Largest IPO Market in 2020," *Sovereign Resources*, March, 2021, www.sovereigngroup.com/news-and-views/hong-kong-ranks-as-2nd-largest-ipo-market-in-2020/

17 HKEX, November 2022, "2022 Analysis of ESG Practice Disclosure", www.hkex. com.hk/-/media/HKEX-Market/Listing/Rules-and-Guidance/Environmental-Social-and-Governance/Reports-on-ESGPD/esgreport_2022.pdf

18 Forbes, "Hong Kong Breaks New Ground in Wealth Management," Forbes, November 1, 2021. www.forbes.com/sites/hongkong/2021/11/01/hong-kong-bre aks-new-ground-in-wealth-management/?sh=3ca0418b1212

19 Bloomberg, "Hong Kong: A Growing Hub for Family Offices", Bloomberg, https:// sponsored.bloomberg.com/article/invest-hk/a-family-home-in-hong-kong

20 Forbes, "Hong Kong Breaks New Ground In Wealth Management" Forbes, November 1, 2021, www.forbes.com/sites/hongkong/2021/11/01/hong-kong-bre aks-new-ground-in-wealth-management/?sh=3ca0418b1212

21 ONC Lawyers, "New Legislation for Re-Domiciliation of Foreign Funds into Hong Kong", Lexology, June 28, 2022, www.lexology.com/library/detail.aspx?g=4918e b75-b938-49f8-a8a2-d18af563559c

22 Zhang Yukun and Wei Yiyang, "In Depth: Hong Kong's Strategy to Break Cayman Islands' Stranglehold on Offshore Funds", CaixinGlobal, October 21, 2021. www. caixinglobal.com/2021-10-21/in-depth-hong-kongs-strategy-to-break-cayman-isla nds-stranglehold-on-offshore-funds-101789869.html

23 Jing Yang, "Singapore Kicks Off New Era of SPACs in Asia with String of Listings", WSJ, January 20, 2022. www.wsj.com/articles/singapore-kicks-off-new-era-of-spacs-in-asia-with-string-of-listings-11642676640?mod=article_inline

24 Jing Yang, "Hong Kong's First SPAC Makes Its Debut", WSJ, March 18, 2022. www.wsj.com/articles/hong-kongs-first-spac-makes-its-debut-11647587585

25 Research report, "Leveraging Hong Kong as an Offshore Renminbi Centre for Advancing Renminbi Internationalisation," *HKEX*, March, 2021. www.hkex.com. hk/-/media/HKEX-Market/News/Research-Reports/HKEx-Research-Papers/2021/ CCEO_HKrmb_202103_e.pdf?la=en

26 Muneeb Jan, "The Rise of the Renminbi: Hong Kong's Role as an Offshore RMB Hub," *The China Guys*, April, 2021. https://thechinaguys.com/the-rise-of-the-renmi nbi-hong-kongs-role-as-an-offshore-rmb-hub/

27 Hongbin Cai, "The Path of Economic Restructuring of Hong Kong," HKU Business School, July 17, 2021. www.fbe.hku.hk/research/thought-leadership/hkej-column/the-path-of-economic-restructuring-of-hong-kong/

28 Gregg Li, "Hong Kong's Unique Role as China's Broker for the NewSpace Economy?" September 5, 2021, September 14, 2021. www.linkedin.com/pulse/hong-kongs-unique-role-chinas-broker-newspace-economy-gregg-dr-g-li/

29 "New Era, New Rural Community, New Opportunities – HKU International Conference on Rural Revitalization", The University of Hong Kong, September 24, 2021. https://mp.weixin.qq.com/s/e0kvkBnUTFcoYo_EUqBCSA

30 Peter Alexis Gourevitch and James J. Shinn, *Political Power and Corporate Control: The New Global Politics of Corporate Governance*, page 2 (Chapter 1), Foreign Affairs (Council on Foreign Relations), Princeton University, January, 2006, November 1, 2020. https://researchgate.net/publication/24117949

Key Recommendations

I am often asked questions by colleagues from the global community regarding practical strategies and tactics working with Chinese companies. However, like most complex issues, there's no one-size-fits-all answer to each challenge they have experienced or will encounter. Despite my multi-culture background and fluent language skills, I had struggled when navigating the governance system and decision-making structures of Chinese companies I worked for. After three years of study of Chinese corporate governance development including its connections with the country's culture, society and economic environment, and regulatory and legal systems, I am able to explain some of the root causes of Westerners' confusions regarding Chinese companies governance practices. Therefore, I hope my recommendations in this chapter can inspire more thinking and discussion that help you navigate solutions for your particular challenges and make rational business and professional decisions.

Guanxi – An Important Chinese Social Phenomenon

Guanxi (also spelled as "Guan Shi") is a familiar word for most people doing business in China. Although most people understand the importance of Guanxi when navigating Chinese society, Guanxi is often interpreted as a unique and mysterious phenomenon. Therefore, I believe revealing this mystery should be the first step when talking about common Chinese businesses, as the term Guanxi and some related information will be mentioned in my recommendations.

What Is Guanxi?

There are many attempts to translate Guanxi into English, such as "connection", "relationship", and "network". In my opinion, these translations are all appropriate, but none of them can perfectly reflect the underlying meaning of Guanxi as a societal phenomenon. One explanation I found precisely describes Guanxi: "Guanxi is the *OIL* that keeps the wheels of community, business and politics running in China". Therefore, Guanxi comes "first" when navigating Chinese society.

Chinese often say, "Guanxi is not about what you know, but *WHOM* you know". I often share this story to reflect this saying. Most times, when having a car accident in the US, we call the police to get a police report. Both parties exchange insurance companies' information and embark on their way if the vehicles are still drivable. The insurance companies then will coordinate with both drivers to solve the problem. When people in China have a car accident, the first phone call made by both parties usually goes to their friends or relatives working in the police bureau or insurance companies. Those friends or relatives then will coordinate with police and insurance companies to resolve the situation. Chinese people believe that not having friends in the police bureau or insurance company will most likely lead to unfair treatment.

I also found that the interpretation of Guanxi as the synonym of "back-door", "bribery", or "corruption" are pitfalls, or bad "Guanxi", which is part of the reason why Guanxi is considered a secret relationship that cannot be openly discussed. Good Guanxi paves the way for a successful journey in China – not just for business, but also for day-to-day life! Perhaps the following comparison table can help understand the similarities and differences between Western networking and Chinese Guanxi.

Table 11.1 Western Networking vs. Chinese Guanxi

Three Aspects	Western Networking	Chinese Guanxi
Way of thinking	Information-oriented -Seeking truth -Based on sequential -Argument and debate	Relationship-oriented -Collectivist -Hierarchical -Holistic
Way of action	Information-driven -Seeking truth -Based on sequential -Argument and debate	Relationship-driven -Long counting process -Formal meetings -Explanation first -Forging long-term relationships
Way of ENTER	Professional events/ organizations	Introduced by INSIDERS

Source: Compiled by the author.

As we can see from Table 11.1. the most crucial element in Chinese Guanxi is "relationship", and the most notable difference between Guanxi and networking is the way of entering – being introduced by insiders is the most common starting point of Guanxi. However, once you are in Guanxi circles, you have opportunities to build longtime, trustworthy relationships, which serve as a savings account from which a deposit can be withdrawn when needed. Building Guanxi takes time, but the benefit of having a good Guanxi can last a lifetime.

Guanxi Hierarchy and the Culture Roots

How can foreigners find this critical insider to build Guanxi in Chinese society then? Common-understanding channels include family relations, schoolmates, current or previous colleagues, home towners, current or previous business ties, and acquaintances. However, the level of trust and the magic power of Guanxi are different with each channel. In principle, family relationships reside at the highest hierarchy of Guanxi; for other channels, the closer to family relationships, the better quality of Guanxi. The Guanxi hierarchy comes from China's thousands of years history as an agricultural society, when families had to work together to survive natural disasters. Therefore, traditional Chinese families prefer several generations living together, which makes family the strongest social tie.

When socializing with Chinese colleagues, one will find it's widespread for them to call each other "brother" or "sister", even with superiors. Those titles imply a close relationship, and the leaders are often called "big brother" or "big sister" as matters of respect. Also, in most privately owned Chinese companies, different business circles exist around the founder, reflecting the culture of family ties. The closest circle consists of those individuals who have been working with the founder(s) from the early stage of the business; most of them are still holding key positions in the company or serving as the founder's advisors. The relationship between founder(s) and those within the closest circle is family-like comprising the highest level of trust. The family-like culture makes founder(s) to consider themselves responsible for taking care of those closest – and expect followers' loyalty in return. Therefore, the most important decisions are made by those groups, regardless of their individual positions in the company. Moreover, the closest circle usually extends to those individuals' relatives and friends, making the relationship within Chinese companies complex and mixed. The nuance of those complex and combination relationships ties the organizations across multiple disciplines, including business, personal, emotional, and psychological.

As those companies grow in the global market, certain executive positions that require particular expertise will be filled by professionals from the talent pool. However, most of those professionals are considered outsiders or consultants who won't be part of decision-making for years until trust is built between them and the founder(s) or the closest circles. In traditional Chinese companies, outsider professionals are unlikely to enter the founder's most intimate inner circle and earn the same level of trust.

Evolving of Guanxi

New-generation business leaders are changing the context of Chinese Guanxi and how Chinese companies operate. The trend is that many Chinese companies are transferring leadership from the founder generation to a younger generation, who most of the time receive a Western education. Those young generational leaders would like to behave like their Western friends or run businesses with Western professional standards. A good example is Wahaha Group, China's top beverage-producing company (a case study of Wahaha's leadership transfer was in Chapter 3). The founder of Wahaha is a traditional Chinese entrepreneur who considers taking care of employees as part of his responsibilities. The new-generation leader, Fuli Zong, the founder's daughter, received a business degree from the US, lived there since high school, and managed the company using Western professional standards. As a result, employees with poor performance were fired by the daughter, later rehired by the father. Wahaha's example demonstrates a fundamental business mentality difference between the founder and second generation. It indicates that Guanxi might evolve but will never disappear from Chinese companies and society. One can contend that the daughter's professional management style will make the company more effective, while others might argue that with family-like Guanxi, a traditional Chinese entrepreneur cares more about employees, which aligns with today's ESG movement.

Chinese companies' globalization and fresh business minds from an increasing number of Chinese returnees with overseas education are changing the context of Guanxi while extending Guanxi to the international community. The rise of the middle class in China in the past couple of decades has enabled those families to support their children's Western education. The young generations are influenced by Western culture and professional business standards. Many have returned to China with different business mindsets that will change Chinese companies' business practices. Moreover, those young professionals will influence the context of Guanxi and become channels for global professionals who want to build Guanxi in China. It's worth mentioning that in Chinese cities with more developed economies and international connections, business styles are more professional, and the context of Guanxi is changing faster than in inland China cities.

Guanxi is a societal phenomenon embedded with deep Chinese cultural roots. As Chinese society changes and its economic environment continues to improve, Guanxi will abet those transformations, evolve within its own context, and expand to the international community. Not only will Guanxi not disappear, but it will also become professionalized and refined to accommodate global demand. When working with Chinese partners, it's essential to understand Guanxi and seek paths to build it when opportunities coincide. However, there's no need to be afraid of the challenges of working with Chinese partners without depending on Guanxi!

Six Tips to Work with Chinese Parent Companies

The last decade was marked as the golden period of Chinese companies' global expansion, with Chinese foreign direct investment reaching its peak in 2016. As a result, many companies across the world are now owned by Chinese corporations. How should those companies work with their Chinese parents? Western companies are used to their home countries' well-established institutional environments, sophisticated governance systems, and standardized business practices. However, successful collaboration with Chinese parent companies not only accelerated Western companies' China access and Chinese market share growth but also enabled "freedom" for product development, as pointed out by a senior manager of Volvo,[1] a Swedish luxury automobile brand.

In early 2023, 13 years after their merger in 2010, Volvo and its parent company, Geely, (an 82% shareholder[2]) jointly launched a new Luxury EV Brand, Geely Yinhe (Galaxy in Chinese, and referred to as Galaxy by most American media), with plans to build seven new models in the next 2 years.[3] With the urgency of EV evolution as a critical part of the global climate movement, the launching of Galaxy demonstrates the success of the Volvo and Geely merger after 13 years of integration between these two businesses involving culture, management, operation, and branding strategy. Volvo's advanced technology was empowered by Chinese capital, while Chinese ownership accelerated Volvo's product development, both of which maximized the synergy between these two businesses and resulted in their success.

It is common understanding that an acquisition deal is just the beginning of a merger, because to ensure that one plus one becomes greater than two, there is so much to learn, do, and work together in the post-acquisition process to overcome differences and maximize synergy. The process is complex and challenging. How did Geely and Volvo handle their post-acquisition challenges and make one plus one greater than two? How did the Chinese unique corporate governance style contribute to the process? Let us zoom into the Geely/Volvo acquisition for some details.

Case Study   Geely/Volvo Acquisition – Mutual Learning Drives Synergy Maximization

Geely – meaning fortune and luck in Chinese (吉利) – was founded in 1986 by Shufu Li as a home appliance manufacturing company. Geely then began manufacturing motorcycles in 1993 and became the first privately owned Chinese automobile manufacturing company in 1997, having received the Chinese central government's approval. By 2010, Geely was positioned within China's top 500 firms with a full range of automobile manufacturing capabilities including R&D, production, distribution, and service.

Because of Li's belief that technology provides a competitive advantage for automobile companies, Geely established an R&D team with nearly 2,000 Chinese and international engineering experts, that number representing over 13% of Geely's total employees in the early 2000s. Also at the time, Geely acquired over 1,200 patents (30% of which are internationally registered) and became a price leader and an energy-efficient leader in China due to its ability to manufacture most components in-house. In the first decade of 2000, Geely entered the international market, established its first joint venture with a British automaker, and made an overseas acquisition in Australia. However, all these success stories cannot offset the safety and quality concerns regarding Geely's products.

Acquiring Volvo Car Corporation, a premier European luxury brand, was a big step for Geely, not only to facilitate its international expansion but also to upscale its global branding value. In the case of Geely/Volvo, the acquirer was much smaller and less experienced in the international market, while the target company was a well-established global brand. Challenges of the merger contained many significant differences in culture, global branding recognition and strategy, management style – including top executives' background – and technology sharing and transfer. A 2020 study analyzed the complexity of the Geely/Volvo post-acquisition process and concluded mutual learning was the key to their success.[4] Below is an analysis to illustrate the primary challenges of the Geely/Volvo merger and the corresponding win-win solutions as the outcome of mutual learning and close collaboration.

Table 11.2 Synergies and Challenges Analysis of Geely/Volvo Merger Case[5]

Short-Term Challenges	Conflicts	Potential Opportunities	Win-Win Solutions
Global branding Geely is a much smaller, less experienced acquirer/Volvo is a sophisticated automobile manufacture with existing global markets and brand recognition	**Branding strategy** Geely wanted Volvo to develop larger, flashier luxury cars to meet Chinese consumers' ostentatious tastes/Volvo wanted to retain small, safe, fuel-efficient cars to keep its reputation for safety and environmental friendliness	**Global branding** Volvo is a premium luxury global brand	**Consumer driving brand strategy** Volvo developed a new model to meet Chinese luxury segment demand – Geely and Volvo agreed to build new larger scale plants to develop larger and more luxurious cars

Short-Term Challenges	Conflicts	Potential Opportunities	Win-Win Solutions
Culture integration Chinese company's predominant culture/Sweden has a proud Scandinavian tradition	**Management style** Early-stage company management style dominated by founder/ sophisticated and professional management style	**Culture integration** Volvo's collaborative relationship with internal and external stakeholders is valuable to Geely	**Respect culture differences** Volvo kept its Swedish heritage, including its own management team, board of directors, and headquarters in Sweden
Technology sharing Some of the Volvo technologies were still held by Ford Motor Co. after the merger		**Technology sharing** Volvo's cutting-edge technology in safety, quality, and environmental technology	
Profitability To restore Volvo to long-term profitability (Volvo had no profit since 2006, with a $2.6 billion USD accumulated loss two years before the merger)			**Profitability** Volvo: 20% sales increase, 36% Chinese market share increase, and creation of over 5,000 jobs in Belgium and Sweden Geely: 43% revenue growth from 2009 to 2010; RMB900 mill ($130 mil USD) working capital increase from 2009 to 2010

Source: Compiled by the author.

Moreover, like many other privately owned Chinese companies as discussed in this book, Geely founder's influence played an essential role in mutual learning that started by identifying challenges and potential opportunities in the early stage of post-acquisition integration. Shufu Li, a farmer's son, is now one of the most successful entrepreneurs in China, having recognized the important relationship of Swedish culture to the success of Volvo, while also acknowledging the inherent value of his counterpart, Stefan Jacoby, Volvo's CEO. Jacoby's successful track record in the automobile industry was of intangible value to Volvo and Geely. Therefore, instead of deploying Chinese companies' predominated culture with 82% ownership after the acquisition, Li decided to keep Volvo's executive management team and board of directors, which ensured the continuity of Volvo's Scandinavia culture and relationship with various stakeholders. Although Li has been firm on consumer-centered product development and branding strategy, his respect for Volvo's culture and management style and his willingness to compromise set the tone for mutual respect, learning, and collaboration, which ultimately led to the long-term success of Geely/Volvo.

Li represents a different mindset from many founders of privately owned Chinese companies, although the company culture and governing styles could be significantly different in those companies. Also, the complexity of post-acquisition integration has many contextual dimensions. Therefore, many processes of the Geely/Volvo case might not be repeatable. However, Geely/Volvo's successful experiences demonstrated the very basic principles of working with Chinese parent companies: to foster mutual respect and mutual learning while appreciating the diversity of corporate cultures and governance styles.

Having worked in Chinese multinational companies' headquarter and overseas subsidiary, below are six tips summarized from my own experiences.

Adjust Expectations

Many Western multinational companies established global operations beginning in the middle of the twentieth century. Back then, multinational companies typically handed over well-established, Western-style, turnkey operation systems (including requirements for group policy compliance, business conduct guides, group accounting menus, transfer prices, and global travel policies) to their overseas subsidiaries. In the past several decades, Western companies have been refining their internationalization model and global operations. In contrast, many Chinese companies are relatively new to the global market (most Chinese multinational companies started global operations in the early 2000s), with limited experience operating in many host countries as well as the lagging of comprehensive operation systems compared with Western companies' standardized global expansion. In addition, most Chinese multinational companies are young and are still optimizing their internal operations and governance systems. Therefore, it's essential to understand the early stage nature of Chinese parent companies.

Prepare for Over-Communication

As much as Chinese holding companies want to support their overseas subsidiaries, they might not understand the expectations of overseas subsidiaries, as some of the routine process in Western business practice might never be heard in Chinese companies. Therefore, I recommend over-communication – explain in detail when asking for support and guidance, find counterparts in the Chinese parent company, and ask for help when navigating the organization's system. When visiting Chinese parent companies, please plan to spend additional days there to talk with more people in the facility and operation. You will be surprised about what you can learn from small conversations and dinner time with local employees during your visit. Even if your Chinese friends are not in the same discipline, they will appreciate your interest in their work and life stories. That is one of the channels of building Guanxi.

Be Open-Minded

In Western business practices, we are used to and often expect best practices. However, how often have we questioned whether those best practices limit our creativity in problem-solving? Although there might not be a well-established operation system in most Chinese multinational companies, working closely with Chinese parent companies to establish a new collaboration system can be an excellent opportunity to develop an effective communication channel, explore different options, and even learn from Chinese companies. Creativity is an essential feature of Chinese companies' business practices. As most companies worldwide are seeking the most suitable approach for their corporate sustainability development, could PingAn and Xiaomi's ESG strategy as discussed in the book inspire innovative ideas for sustainable solutions?

Meeting Room Manners

Two most notable meeting room manners differ between Chinese and Western companies: First, where to sit? Please be aware that there are rules for sitting in Chinese organizations. Most Chinese multinational companies use name tags as part of meeting arrangements, which helps considerably. But, where should one sit when there are no name tags in the meeting room? Please ask the meeting host or Chinese colleagues for suggestions rather than randomly picking a seat. Second, what should be said? In Chinese companies' meetings, very few people argue or debate with superiors, especially if the superiors' bosses are also in the same meeting. Different opinions or disagreements are normally discussed before or after the meeting privately. Some claim that the Chinese business culture lacks diversity, while understanding meeting manners can also be viewed as a cultural respect.

The next two items apply to overseas subsidiaries of Chinese SOEs.

Differences in Types of Chinese SOEs

Some SOEs are owned by the central government, and some by local government (at the province and city levels). In the past decades, most central government-owned SOEs have expanded the business into the international market and recruited different levels of professional managers with international experience. Therefore, central government-owned SOEs' governance systems and business practices are more standardized across various industries. The governance practice of local government-owned SOEs varies according to the geographic region of the local government. The Chinese coastal area (especially the Yangtze River Delta area) consists of 41 cities, including Shanghai and three provinces with a total population of 230 million as of 2019, and the Great Bay Area, consisting of 9 cities including Shenzhen and two Special Administrative Regions – Hong Kong and Macao, with a total population of 70 million as of 2020. China's coastal area has the most developed economy and historic international connection. The governance practice of local government-owned SOEs in the coastal area is closer to Western tradition. Significant gaps exist among local SOEs in the coastal zone and inland China regarding relation-oriented business practices, the differences in professionals seeking director positions, executives, and middle-level managers, and average English communication skills.

Government Officials versus Entrepreneurs

Most board directors and executives in Chinese SOEs are government officials, whose top priority is safeguarding the countries' assets and ensuring that SOEs' operations comply with regulations and the country's development strategy. They are not compensated as Western companies' CEOs, nor are they accountable for companies' performance. However, these government official business leaders ensure SOEs' business strategy aligns with China's Five-Year Plans. Therefore, to understand Chinese parent companies' strategic directions and decisions, it's essential to stay updated with the Chinese government's development goals (such as China's 14th Five-Year Plan) and critical economic regulation reforms.

Do You Know the Different Contents of Board Mechanisms?

China's "Compressed Journey" as it has successfully expanded its economic growth over the past four decades, the country's regulation system, including corporate governance code, is still being fine-tuned. As a result, many regulatory concepts, standards, and terminologies are imported from Western models and then mechanized in Chinese companies to showcase implementation without substantial process. Therefore, business interpretations can vary. Several board mechanisms fall into this category.

Board Committees

The prevailing adoption of the US unitary board governance structure by many countries around the world today has provided a common understanding that a company's board should establish at least three essential board committees: audit committee, nomination and governance committee, and remuneration committee.

These three board committees are regulatory requirements for Chinese companies. Most Chinese companies have established committee charts to document the functions and roles of each committee. However, the actual practice might not be the same as those operating in Western companies, mainly due to Chinese companies' controlling shareholder structure. In Chinese SOEs, most board directors and CEOs are appointed by SASAC, and the SASAC also decides the compensation of CEOs and board directors. Therefore, the functions of the nomination committee and remuneration committee in Chinese SOEs are not as commonly understood as those in Western companies. And in founder control companies, board members and CEO selections and their compensation are most likely influenced by the controlling shareholder. Therefore, the roles of nomination committees and remuneration committees are primarily theoretical and documentary-based.

Independent Directors

Independent directors have been the "Christmas tree decorations" of Chinese company boards for quite some time. Having independent directors on the corporate board is one element of compliance for Chinese companies. But many independent directors are not invited to decision-making and are unaware of business operations. After the Kangmei case debacle, improving independent directors' professional skills and their ability to offer qualified and independent opinions have been a priority for Chinese companies' board governance development. However, there are two major challenges that will take time to overcome.

First, a limited pool of qualified candidates. The detrimental wave of directors who resigned after the Kangmei case revealed a significant challenge that Chinese companies faced to fill those directors' seats. Serving on a company's board is obviously prestigious, but individuals have now realized that implies fiduciary duty and exposure to legal liability. Independent directors will have to carefully measure their responsibility and liability versus their qualifications, then safely analyze their companies' reporting transparency that allows them to access necessary information for decision-making. More directors may resign upon careful evaluation. As a result, will the number of qualified candidates be able to satisfy the demands of Chinese companies?

Second, the definition of independence. How a country's corporate governance system defines independent directors' independence determines their contribution and roles. In the US boards, with a dispersed shareholder structure, independent-mindedness and the freedom to offer independent opinions matter most. The Chinese companies' shareholder structure is very concentrated and different from the US. Moreover, recent research in the West further defines the measurement of board directors' independence from two dimensions: formal independence and social independence. Formal independence requires no other business and/or family relationships between directors and companies, other than the directorship, which is obvious and straightforward. Social independence refers to the information connection between directors and managers, such as shared educational experiences or other shared social experiences or connections. Today's China inherits many relation-based phenomena from Chinese ancient culture, such as Guanxi. How will these two dimensions affect Chinese companies' definition, and what criteria will be used to measure their directors' independence? These answers are not yet known.

Board Diversity

Discussions regarding board diversity in Chinese companies are primarily concentrated on gender diversity at the moment. According to Oriental Finance Choice data, as of February 2017, 17.44% of A-share companies' board directors and executives are women. Among that amount, 5.18% of A-share companies (a total of 162 companies) have a female board chair, and 6.50% of A-share companies (a total of 203 companies) have a female CEO.[6]

However, it's worth mentioning that gender and other board diversity characteristics have not yet become part of China's corporate governance code provisions. Globally, the gender equality movement advances and the trend toward boardroom gender diversity has been led by Western countries. Many of those countries have mandated gender diversity or provided recommendations, e.g., Norway, Spain, France, and the US. As China furthers its involvement in the global market, additional Chinese companies will face compliance and supervision requirements by other countries' regulatory systems. Therefore, we can foresee gender diversity becoming a required part and measurement factor within Chinese companies' corporate governance structure, while other board diversity dimensions (such as age, function, and the diversity of opinions in the boardroom) that are widely discussed in the global community will have to come in the future.

Corporate Board Secretary

A corporate board secretary is a key officer in a company and its board and consists of four traditional roles: record keeper for all meeting minutes, board meeting planning and arrangement, corporate advisor on governance practice and compliance issues, and the orientation trainer of new board directors. Most corporate board secretaries in US and UK companies have an academic background in corporate law or corporate governance, which ensures the professional skills necessary to conduct corporate board secretary responsibilities.

The Chinese Corporate Board Secretary comprises a broader range of professional backgrounds, and their responsibilities are beyond the traditional four roles. For example, Chinese companies' board secretaries represent the board to the media or certain government authorities, and they also undertake significant responsibility for investors' relationship management. Some board secretaries were promoted internally from other critical positions within the business, which has allowed them to be well acquainted with the business' operations.

It's commonly understood that each board is unique due to many factors, including board members' professional backgrounds, experiences, and personalities, the corporation's culture and boardroom dynamics, decision-making process, and power distribution within the boardroom. Therefore, interpretational or practical differences between other board mechanisms are to be expected, which, while not listed here, could be crucial. Pointing out these board mechanisms here does not mean criticizing, as we should respect the achievements Chinese companies have made with their compressed journey and allow time for them to improve and fine-tune the system and practice. However, I believe understanding those differences will help us adjust our expectations, which is vital for rational judgment and effective communication.

China Speed – Any Inspirations for Future Business Models?

In June 2022, I had a chance to speak with John, a partner of a fast-growing venture capital firm in the US that is aggressively investing in early-stage companies utilizing cutting-edge technology. When asked about the next strategic plan for one of the ventures, a China-focused supply-chain system with great market potential in China, he has led the investment. John replied, "to compete in today's market, we need to grow with 'China Speed.' To a certain extent, I want the team to think as if we are building a Chinese company". I kept thinking about John's comments and realized the potential of the new trend of young professionals and entrepreneurs in Western countries recognizing the advantages of China Speed, and that they are willing to adopt the concept for future success. In this section, I would like to share my opinion regarding China Speed, particularly its current strengths and weaknesses.

China Speed has been demonstrated by China's fast-growing economy since the country opened its door to the world in 1978. The compressed journey of China's corporate governance development discussed in this book is a perfect example of China Speed. It took China three decades from legalizing corporations in the early 1990s to actively enact reforms to fundamentally improve the country's regulation system, after realizing potential systematic risks due to some Chinese companies' belief in the "too big to fail" myth.

China Speed also applies to other aspects of Chinese economic growth. Table 11.3. below provides some comparison data.

Table 11.3 China Speed Compared to Selected Countries

	China	The US	Germany	Japan	India
No. of Fortune 500 companies 2010–2021	46/135	139/122		71/53	8/7
% of top 500 brands 2010–2021	4.0%/16.8%	39.4%/32.8%			
No. of top 500 brands 2010–2021	20/84	164/197	34/22	54/34	8/12
Outbound cross-border M&A 2001–2010/2011–2020	5%/11%	29%/29%	5%–11%	12%/8%	
FDI inward flow (billion USD) 2010–2020	115/149	198/156	66/36		27/64
FDI outward flow (billion USD) 2010–2020	69/133	278/93		56/116	<1/12

Source: Compiled by Author from EMR Report 2021 (Emerging Markets Institute, "Merging Market Multinationals Report 2021: Building the Future on ESG Excellence", Cornell University, https://ecommons.cornell.edu/handle/1813/110935).

Trade-Offs and Prerequisites of China Speed

However, The fast pace of economic growth certainly comes with trade-offs, namely, environmental deterioration, food safety concerns, labor rights issues, IP protection, and product quality control challenges. Without timely reduction or converting them to synergy, those trade-offs will become significant business and ESG risks. Western investors and companies could consider several approaches to mitigate the trade-offs and risks: first, clearly define requirements for return on investment or loans; second, establish specific criteria for products delivery; third, clarify the reasonableness of milestones; fourth, standardize the operational process to scale up China Speed toward global operation.

Moreover, there're some prerequisites needed to achieve China Speed in business operation, namely, a China Speed agile business mindset, a China

Speed-ready team, and, more importantly, a corporate culture governance system that encourages and appreciates China Speed with a suitable incentive system and failure tolerance mechanism. Western companies considering implementing China Speed for their supply chains and operations are highly recommended to benchmark those prerequisites on team building and business model optimization.

The Evolving of China Speed

China's newly launched 14th Five-Year Plan is designed to switch the country's next stage of economic development strategy from high speed to high quality, which indicates that the Chinese government acknowledges the shortage of China Speed and is thus determined to fine-tune it concurrently with the ongoing ESG revolution. Therefore, implementing China Speed implies opportunities for Western business practices to improve and evolve toward higher standards in product quality control, environmental and social considerations, and reporting requirements.

The Inspiration for China Speed

The China Speed of which John referred insinuates Chinese companies' fast-track growth in various aspects, including business expansion, digital transformation, ESG integration, and strategy formation for sustainability and implementation. However, that fast track typically comes with the possibility of skipping specific protocols or simplifying the process, which might generate new risks that we need to be aware of. However, before judging the possible negligence of China Speed, maybe implementing China Speed will offer the best opportunity for global companies, particularly those from advanced countries, to reevaluate the effectiveness and efficiency of existing protocols that have been applied to the business for years or decades, or to try an alternative option with fresh energy.

Because of its 150-year history with the development of corporations, Western business has established a mature system that respects and sustains best practices as a paradigm. However, the quick transformations of new technology and digitalization do not allow adequate time to establish best practices, notwithstanding the unpredicted pandemic. What do we do when there's no best practice? China Speed will certainly offer insight regarding quick reactions to unexpected changes.

Moreover, the constant urgency for global sustainable development and the more imperative elements pertaining to corporate responsibility (strategies, effective and germane business models) asks "what can we do to establish the first best sustainable practices to compete with our current best practices models?" Perhaps inspiration from China Speed will foment more thinking regarding the paths taken for global sustainable development.

So, are we ready to implement **China Speed**? Are we ready to forgo the changes of sustainability without best practices? Are we ready for upcoming global changes with a different role played by China? I hope you find this book helpful for your journey.

Notes

1 Alysha Webb, December 2022, "Executive Says Chinese Ownership Gives Volvo More Freedom", www.wardsauto.com/industry-news/executive-says-chinese-ownership-gives-volvo-more-freedom

2 Norihiko Shirouzu, February 2023, "Exclusive: Volvo readies EV blitz in biggest product revamp under Geely", www.reuters.com/business/autos-transportation/volvo-readies-ev-blitz-biggest-product-revamp-under-geely-2023-02-02/

3 Perry Stern, February 2023, "Volvo and Polestar Owner Geely Launched Luxury EV Brand", https://cars.usnews.com/cars-trucks/features/geely-launches-luxury-ev-brand

4 Anna Jonsson and Jan-Erik Vahlne, "Complexity Offering Opportunities: Mutual Learning between Zhejiang Geely Holding Group and Volvo Cars in the Post-Acquisition Process," Global Strategy Journal, 1–32, November 2020.

5 Xinran Wang and Michael Young, "Geely Automotive's Acquisition of Volvo," Asian Case Research Journal, 19, 183–202, June 2015.

6 www.hntqb.com/resfile/2017-03-10/A14/hntqb20170310A14.pdf

Conclusion

The rise of the China Model has been challenging the corporate governance best practices and development approaches of the West. The ongoing criticisms regarding Chinese companies' corporate governance practices, China's lagging regulations, and government interference, are mystically contradictory to the continual increase in the number of global investors and their appetites for the Chinese market. As a result, multiple research projects have been conducted on corporate governance development and alternative streams of ideas beneficial to understanding China's planned economy and politicization of its corporate governance amelioration.[1] Debates and discussions continue regarding whether the government's involvement in China's corporate governance development will serve as effective and viable facets of China's banal regulation system. As this book is being written, China's wide range of pandemic lockdowns in the first half of 2022 raised more questions and debates regarding a nationalistic swing and China Speed of getting things done, while we all believe the former incident will depart along with the pandemic.

In this concluding chapter, let us start by revisiting China's unique, but not abnormal, corporate governance structure as a result of its "compressed journey".

Unique, but Not Abnormal

Following the "crossing the river by feeling the stone" strategy coined by China's then-leader Deng Xiaoping, Chinese corporate governance development took a unique path identical to the country's economic development route. Moreover, unlike most Western countries, which spent over a century on industrialization (from the middle 1800s to the middle 1900s) before establishing a comprehensive regulatory system, China quickly moved from an agriculture-based economy into a modern-model economy, squeezing industrialization and regulatory system development into a few decades.

During this compressed journey, there were no best practices nor adequate time for solid analysis before some regulations were issued, so there was no adequate regulatory guidance for business practices. As a result, Chinese companies enjoyed regulatory flexibility and became creative in their governance structure and business practices. In the meanwhile, the Chinese government constantly interfered with businesses without clearly defining and disclosing its roles; despite that, large Chinese companies rapidly expanded to the global market without a mature governance structure. The pros and cons of those common characteristics have made Chinese corporate governance unique when viewed through the lens of international standards.

The Chinese government is now determined to switch its development strategy from high speed to high quality and establish a trustworthy social system and a high-quality regulatory system, and some of those characteristics will slowly evolve. For example, while the Chinese regulation system was well-known for its laggardness compared to the nation's business practices, recent ESG regulation reforms took a proactive approach. Regulators not only issued new rules ahead of time to guide financial and business participants but also aligned those new rules with international standards. At the same time, Chinese companies' continuous experiences in today's complex global market will help those companies become resilient and sophisticated in strategic decisions and stakeholder relationships.

A nation's corporate governance system needs to serve the country's economic development strategy in order to align with its culture, history, social, economic, and political systems. In Europe, the Netherlands integrated the two-tier board structure to accommodate its unique tightly knit political culture, accomplish harmony among major stakeholders in the society, and make the Netherlands Europe's model economy in the 1990s with a low unemployment rate and relatively high standard of living. Today, most EU countries have adopted a US-style board structure in order to attract US institutional investors, although the shareholder primacy principle does not align well with those countries' stakeholder-oriented cultures and histories. In Asia, the stakeholder-focused Japanese corporate governance model enabled Japan's post-war economic miracle to proliferate due to its government-directed, corporatist capitalism system that relied heavily on implied and interrelated contracts among strategic industries and banks.[2] However, Japanese corporate governance reforms in recent decades are moving toward the US-style, one-tier board structure for the same reason as European countries. In South Africa, the first issuance of the King Report on Corporate Governance in the 1990s helped stabilize the country's economy after notable political changes. Although the King Report was deeply influenced by the UK model, the first and three updated versions of the report each created provisions as reflections of the country's economic and social concerns at that time and aimed to guide South African companies' growth while interacting with the international market.

The Chinese corporate governance system started by learning from the US model and the German two-tier board structure and has evolved over time to serve and support the Chinese economic development strategy. Therefore, the path of Chinese corporate governance development is *unique, but not abnormal*!

Moreover, given the complexity of today's global interdependency among nations, a country's governance structure and practice are inevitably affected by global geopolitical landscape changes and its global partners' domestic and international political changes. While Chinese legal framework reforms such as new anti-corruption policies, data security, and personal information protection have interfered with Chinese companies' governance practices and corporate governance functions, other countries' policy changes have also affected China's regulation adjustment and corporate governance development, such as US regulatory scrutiny of US-listed Chinese companies and political involvement in global financial markets to reduce US investment in certain Chinese companies.

The Chinese government's support of Chinese companies' global growth in Africa and other Asian countries has created unfair competition, while the lack of adequate supervision from government authorities has nourished some business behaviors that cause local environmental and social issues. Obliged to the global ESG movement, those issues have been challenged by local and international standards, which ensure compliance with business standards and practices regardless of political and geopolitical ambitions. The same counterbalance applies to global concerns regarding the Party's involvement and government's control in Chinese companies, whose transparent disclosure of the Party's roles has been catalyzed, and whose recognition of shareholder interest protection has been encouraged by the worldwide trend of regulatory requirement for E, S, and G information disclosure.

A half-century ago, many of today's emerging market countries were fighting famine and pestilence to survive, while the West continued industrializing. Today, climate change and sustainability have become the biggest global risks with a looming long-term battle that requires immediate attention and reaction from all advanced and emerging market countries. The economic strength of the emerging market world is increasing, and the traditional geographic North/South divide is evolving. The worldwide pandemic beginning in 2020 alerted sustainability considerations, and the regional war between Russia and Ukraine has caused severe economic disruptions across the world, accelerating a rebalance between advanced and emerging market economies, signaling a "new normal" in the post-pandemic era. All of those will directly affect the economic, social, political, diplomatic, and monetary policies of China and its global partners and, eventually, influence the international and domestic governance systems of those countries, including China.

The US–China Relationship in the New Era

The US–China relationship will continuously influence Chinese corporate governance development in the new era, with three critical tasks on the agenda.

First, inconclusive attempts between PCAOB and Chinese regulations still leave most US-listed Chinese companies in limbo of delisting risks, in addition to "chilling the temperature" between the US and China due to US regulators' scrutiny of Chinese companies. The American Securities and Exchange Commission's (SEC) announcement of planned new disclosure requirements for Chinese IPOs and Chinese regulators' increasingly restrictive crackdown on cybersecurity review and pre-approval rules for Chinese companies seeking overseas capital in the past couple of years have exacerbated tension between both countries. However, it's not easy to reverse the deep economic interrelationship and considerable cross-investments between the US and China; instead, both are further expanding in vertical (economic depth) and horizontal (economic width) directions in the business arena. According to the US SEC's data, there are approximately 586 US mutual funds currently investing in China A-shares totaling $37.2 billion. With BlackRock releasing its wholly owned mutual fund products in the Chinese financial markets, those numbers will most likely increase. On the other hand, the US market has become the second-most popular listing destination for Chinese companies over the past several decades. Although some Chinese companies have been or will be delisted from the US market, many new companies are getting ready for pre-approval from China and restricted compliance requirements from US stock markets. For the betterment of both countries' economic development and people's lives, improving US–China collaboration using better manners and attitudes is a *when* and *how* matter that requires an icebreaking moment.

Second, emerging global risks such as the climate crisis create urgent demands for those countries to effectively collaborate. Although a US–China joint climate action agreement was reached in November 2021 as the most remarkable achievement of COP26, details are still pending. As the world's two largest nations that collectively produce over 40% of the world's carbon emissions,[3] substantial actions taken by them will impact the global effort to slow the deterioration of climate conditions. As I discussed in this book, climate change urgency already stimulated some initiatives for the US and China to establish esprit de corps, which is undoubtedly promising. Although both countries have not taken lead roles in climate change abatement or the ESG movement, healthy competition between them will further the formation of global connectedness to erect a platform toward global ESG reporting and measurement standards, climate-related information disclosure and strategy implementation, and the establishment of international carbon trading pricing.

Third, both countries' strategies and roles toward a diplomatic solution to end the current regional war and promote diplomatic attitudes in future global leaders are warranted. In addition to the humanitarian crisis and economic disruptions, the regional war between Russia and Ukraine has produced remarkable amounts of air and water pollution, revealing the negative impact of military incursions and the use of armaments on climate change, according to a recent Hesper Herald article.[4] As the world's two leading economies, the US–China relationship affects not only them. Under extreme situations such as the regional war, the entire world is looking to those two countries for solutions.

With China's rising influence in the global community and the US attempting to maintain its superiority, their mutual tension has exacerbated global anxiety across economic, political, cultural, military, and perhaps individual emotional dimensions. Despite that tension, perhaps it's more important for both countries to put sustainable development, climate, and humanitarian issues at the top of their global superpower agendas. Acknowledging that the US–China clash will continue, leading the global sustainability transformation movement should be the top priority for both countries in the next era!

Chinese Corporate Governance System versus Sustainability Transformation

The concurrent development of the Chinese corporate governance system and the country's sustainability transformation progressed during my three years of research. Although I am not in a position to comment on the antecedents and consequences of the two, I would like to point out a few developments for more discussion and debate.

Corporate Social Responsibility (CSR) is the Essential Ingredient in the Chinese Corporate Governance System. CSR has been an essential topic in the West since the 1960s and was introduced to Chinese companies by their Western business partners after China started its economic reform in 1978. Compliance with CSR standards became the precondition for conducting business with Western multinational companies. From the late 1990s to the early 2000s, exports with mostly labor-intensive manufacturing goods drove China's economic growth, which made embracing CSR a competitive advantage for Chinese companies to compete with companies from other emerging market countries. The Chinese government also realized the importance of CSR and included CSR recommendations in China's first Corporate Governance Code in 2002. In 2006, upon amending the nation's Company Law and Security Law, CSR became a regulatory mandate for Chinese companies. The Shenzhen and Shanghai Stock Exchanges released social responsibility instructions for listed companies in 2006 and 2008, respectively, while the State-Owned Assets Supervision and Administration Commission (SASAC) requires CSR implementation for all Chinese SOEs and provides companies with social responsibility guidance updates, most recently in 2008 and 2015. The Chinese government's active regulatory guidance injected social responsibility into the blood of Chinese companies. Embracing CSR accelerated the growth of China's export-oriented economy in the 1990s and early 2000s.

Most Chinese companies utilize CSR as a basis for philanthropy and have frequently focused their efforts on poverty alleviation, including providing donations to build infrastructure and education projects in poverty-stricken areas and also to help save endangered wild animals. Some companies even expanded their donations to help other countries during the pandemic outbreak, including Jack Ma and Alibaba Foundation, who contributed COVID-19 medical equipment to African countries in early 2020.[5] Chinese companies' philanthropic activities have stirred a like mindset and roused a social responsibility attitude in the Chinese public and the entrepreneur community. In 2021, through Tencent's online charity platform established in 2007, 150 million donations were made by Chinese citizens totaling RMB5.4 billion ($845 million), the largest amount ever contributed globally to an internet charity fundraising cause. In addition, many Chinese entrepreneurs and celebrities are personally involved in philanthropic activities, such as sponsoring children from low-income families for education needs and initiating various environmental protection campaigns. Although philanthropy is not the only purpose of the CSR movement, Chinese companies' philanthropic activities accentuate social responsibility that initiate and encourage a broad range of stakeholder engagement, in addition to creating a collective business mindset change in the Chinese business community.

From being required to comply with Western CSR standards to actively leading CSR regulatory development, China and Chinese companies brilliantly switched their positions from international standard followers to global CSR regulation reform pioneers. Moreover, the business mindset set up by CSR will assist the quick adoption of ESG by China and Chinese companies.

Building the Chinese Environmental, Social, and Governance (ESG) Model. When ESG was introduced to Chinese companies concurrent with the rise of Social Responsible Investing in the early 2000s, many Chinese companies were well familiar with CSR and understood ESG to be a measurement system of their CSR and sustainability performances. As discussed in Chapter 4, Chinese companies understand that high ESG rating scores are welcomed by institutional investors, so they are diligently improving their ESG ratings within the global ESG rating system. Like CSR, the Chinese government has been the primary driver of the ESG revolution in China, actively pushing ESG transformation from China to the rest of the world. It's worth mentioning a couple of changes in how the Chinese government approaches ESG adoption.

China is building a specific ESG model that aligns with the international framework and reflects Chinese economic and social situations. In this book's early chapters, I discussed how new ESG regulations released in the past couple of years have been aligned with international standards. Pondering upon the unique Chinese economic and social environments will lead one to consider the Chinese ESG evaluation systems as excellent examples. Although the Chinese ESG model is in its early stage and the Chinese ESG rating systems have not been used by international investors, integrating Chinese culture, its economic environment, Chinese companies' governance styles, and the nuances of the relationship between the Chinese government and business within the Chinese ESG rating system makes the system more meaningful and useful for business leaders and investors' decision-making.

As the emerging markets world is looking to establish economic growth models that better suit the economic, social, and cultural contexts of those countries, the Chinese ESG model might pioneer the trend of new ESG models for other emerging market countries.

Sustainability Mindset is Reshaping the Chinese Social and Regulatory Systems. Governance is the core of ESG integration and sustainability transformation. While we urge companies to enhance their governance practice, improve stakeholder consideration, and boost business morale, having appropriate external incentives and violation enforcement systems to build a trustworthy business environment is all equally essential. Global sustainable development is an intergenerational mission that requires the collaboration of all participants, including countries, businesses, and individuals. A higher standard institutional system helps position China as a global leader and connects the nation to worldwide markets and Chinese companies to the international business community.

Moreover, the fact that the Chinese government has actively adopted CSR and endorses the ESG movement indicates a sustainability mindset, which strengthens China's determination to build a high-quality regulation system and achieve its 2060 carbon neutrality goals!

However, reviewing China's active regulation reforms that have occurred within the past couple of years, as discussed in this book, is relevant, mainly because most of those reforms occurred without portent. Many of those reforms may appear to be draconian compared to those in the West, whose countries' well-established regulation systems and regulatory methods can be arduous due to comprehensive study. Therefore, while we discuss room for improvement in China's regulatory system reform process due to those shocks and surprises, maybe it's also time to reevaluate the efficiency of Western regulation systems and their complexity, given the views of today's dynamic environment.

It is difficult to say whether the Chinese government's determination to build a higher standard regulation system and trustworthy society is the outcome or the driver of China's involvement in worldwide sustainability development. Regardless of the cause and effect, improving its regulation system to enhance the **core** of the Chinese ESG model will certainly increase China's global position.

Future Studies

Professor Gregg Li once said that to understand corporate governance in China, we need a series of books to explain the fast pace of China's growth, Chinese companies' internal development, and the ongoing changes in China's global influence and its effect on the global geopolitical landscape.

Upon completing the manuscript, many new questions continue to appear that will lead to interesting research and discussion regarding Chinese corporate governance and sustainability development, such as:

- How will the improvements in China's social and regulatory systems facilitate Chinese companies' sustainability strategy in the new era?
- Will China and Chinese companies be able to integrate sustainability factors into the China Model? How will advanced and emerging markets countries adapt to the China Model?
- Will China Speed be optimized and fine-tuned by integrating it with Western high-standard business practices, and will it become the next fashion in the business world?
- Can China and Chinese companies outperform their counterparts in the ever-urgent sustainability journey? If so, I am sure they will become true leaders in the global arena.

I welcome your comments and suggestions on those questions or other topics for my future books.

Notes

1 Tami Groswald Ozery, "The Politicization of Corporate Governance – A Viable Alternative?" Harvard Law School Forum on Corporate Governance. June, 8, 2020. https://corpgov.law.harvard.edu/2020/06/08/the-politicization-of-corporate-governance-a-viable-alternative/
2 Andrew Kakabadse and Nada Kakabadse, *The Geopolitics of Governance: The Impact of Contrasting Philosophies*, Pages 53–55, Palgrave, 2001. https://searchworks.stanford.edu/view/4672494
3 "Chart of the Day: These Countries Create Most of the World's CO2 Emissions", World Economic Forum, June 7, 2019, August 30, 2021. www.weforum.org/agenda/2019/06/chart-of-the-day-these-countries-create-most-of-the-world-s-co2-emissions/
4 www.hesperherald.com/news/3768/war-fuels-climate-change-and-only-diplomacy-can-save-us/
5 https://africacdc.org/news-item/jack-ma-and-alibaba-foundations-donate-covid-19-medical-equipment-to-african-union-member-states/

Appendix 1

China's Corporate Governance Regulation Reform Timetable

Year	China SOEs Regulation and Reforms	China's Corporate Governance Regulation Reforms	Purpose of the Regulation or Reforms
1981	Introduces a "dual-track" system – an intermediate price system from a State price control system to a free-market price system		To allow some enterprises to sell their surplus products at market prices, while the planned quota product was to be sold at State-set prices
1985	Launches a "responsibility contract system"		To establish accountability mechanisms for SOE managers
1990	Reopening of the SSE and establishment of the SZSE		The first milestone of SOE reform. To build a foundation for corporate governance development by diversifying SOE share structures, allowing SOEs to raise funds in the stock market, and transferring partial SOE shares to investors
1992		Establishment of the China Securities Regulatory Commission (CSRS)	To form the CSRS as a government body to regulate the new stock market

(Continued)

Year	China SOEs Regulation and Reforms	China's Corporate Governance Regulation Reforms	Purpose of the Regulation or Reforms
1993	Establishment of the first set of Company Law		The second milestone of SOE reform. To set up a legal foundation for the establishment of a corporate governance structure for Chinese SOEs
1999	Establishment of the first set of Security Law		The third milestone of SOE reform. The first economic law drafted by State legislatures, not government departments
2001		The CSRC publishes guidelines for listed companies regarding independent directors	To require at least one-third of the board members be independent directors
2002		The CSRC issues its first set of Corporate Governance Code	To establish Corporate Governance Code
2002		Introduction of Qualified Foreign Institutional Investors	To allow foreign capital entrance to China's stock market via institutional investors
2003	Establishment of the State-Owned Assets Supervision and Administration Commission (SASAC)		SASAC as a government institution to manage and transfer state assets to the market
2005		The CSRC introduces split-share structure reform and begins converting non-tradable shares of the 1,000-plus listed SOEs into tradable shares	To diversify the SOEs' shareholder structure
2006		Establishment of new Company Law and Security Laws	To increase the liability exposure of directors, improve the management structure of listed companies, and make CSR a requirement for companies
2006		The SZSE issues social responsibility instructions to listed companies	To define CSR as a mandate for listed companies

Year	China SOEs Regulation and Reforms	China's Corporate Governance Regulation Reforms	Purpose of the Regulation or Reforms
2007	The issuance of China's first Labor Contract Law		To protect workers' legitimate rights and interests
2007	New Corporate Bankruptcy Laws		To regulate the bankruptcies of SOEs, foreign investment entities, and domestic companies
2007		Partial adoption of International Financial Reporting Standards and International Standard on Auditing	To align China's accounting and auditing standards with international standards
2007	SASAC issues a new directive in Enterprise Risk Management		To provide guidance for SOEs regarding risk management
2007	Enterprise Income Tax Laws enacted		To establish a uniform tax rate of 25% for all types of enterprises operating in China (before this tax reform, income tax for SOEs was 33%, and for foreign-invested companies 17%)
2008	SASAC issues guidelines to SOEs directly managed under the central government to fulfill CSR standards		To make CSR required for all central government-controlled SOEs
2008		CSRC requires leading firms to have annual board reviews	To improve corporate governance practice
2008		SSE releases notice of improving listed companies' assumption of social responsibilities; SZSE releases social responsibility instruction to listed companies	To require CSR for listed companies
2009	The SASAC mandates all SOEs under its supervision develop CSR mechanisms in their corporate governance		To require CSR for all SOEs
2012	The SASAC mandates all SOEs under its supervision publish their first CSR report by the end of 2012		To require CSR reporting mandates for all SOEs

(Continued)

Year	China SOEs Regulation and Reforms	China's Corporate Governance Regulation Reforms	Purpose of the Regulation or Reforms
2012		HKEX releases the first ESG Reporting Guide	To encourage ESG information disclosure
2014		China's State Council issues the Planning Outline for the Construction of a Social Credit System	To initiate China's social credit system including Corporate Social Credit System (CSCS)[1]
2015		SASAC issues Guidance on Social Responsibility, Guidance on Social Responsibility Reporting, and Guidance on Classifying Social Responsibility Performance	To emphasize CSR requirements
2015		The HKEX issues a consultation paper increasing the requirement of ESG reports from "suggested disclosure" to "comply or explain"	To encourage ESG information disclosure or require explanation
2017	State Council mandates the majority of external directors be established in wholly owned SOEs		To improve corporate governance for SOEs and emphasize SOE ERM
2018		The CSRC requires companies on the Ministry of Environment and Ecology's list of heavy polluters to disclose details of their pollution and pollution control measures	To mandate ESG information disclosure
2018		Revised Corporate Governance Code for listed companies (Revised Code)	To improve corporate governance practice
2018		The SSE and SZSE issue the ESG Disclosure Guide	To encourage ESG information disclosure

Year	China SOEs Regulation and Reforms	China's Corporate Governance Regulation Reforms	Purpose of the Regulation or Reforms
2019		The HKEX issues an updated ESG Reporting Guide with mandatory disclosure requirements	To mandate ESG information disclosure
2020		The HKEX issues updated ESG Reporting Guidance and E-training	To better standardize and improve the effectiveness of ESG reporting and align with international climate change disclosure standard[2]
2020		The HKEX launches the Sustainable and Green Exchange (STAGE), an online platform that addresses issues such as data availability, accessibility, and transparency	To provide investors with information for investment decisions and provide issuers visibility of sustainable standards and the issuers' compliance status
2001		The new Corporate Governance Rules of Banking and Insurance Institutions	To consolidate the existing separate regulations and immediately supersede the Corporate Governance Guidelines on Commercial Banks (2013) and the Guiding Opinions Regulating Governance Structure of Insurance Companies (2006)[3]
2021		The CSRC issued new ESG reporting guidelines with a set of risk disclosure rules	To require companies to disclose protecting procedures and measurement systems for environmental factors (e.g., pollution and waste management), and to encourage disclosures of social factors (e.g., poverty alleviation and rural revitalization)

Source: Compiled from Leng, Jing, *Corporate Governance and Financial Reform in China's Transition Economy*, Hong Kong University Press (2009); Tricker, Bob, and Gregg Li, *Understanding Corporate Governance in China*, Hong Kong University Press (2019), and other resources for regulation updates after 2018.

Notes

1 Alexander Chipman Koty, "China's Corporate Social Credit System: What Businesses Need to Know," China Briefing, November 5, 2019, May 21, 2021. www.china-brief ing.com/news/chinas-corporate-social-credit-system-how-it-works/
2 David Liu, "HKEX ESG New Reporting Regimes Effective on July 1, 2020," Kroll, March 24, 2020, May 21, 2021. www.kroll.com/en/insights/publications/apac/hkex-esg-new-reporting-regimes
3 Norton Rose Fulbright, "CBIRC Issues New Corporate Governance Rules", July 2021. www.nortonrosefulbright.com/en/knowledge/publications/a84293ea/cbirc-iss ues-new-corporate-governance-rules

Appendix 2

Beautiful China ESG 100 Index Table 2020–2021

Top 10 Portfolio Weighted Constituents of Beautiful China ESG 100 Index (June 2020)

Rank	Code	Issuer	2020 Portfolio Weight (%)	Sector
1	601398.SH	Industrial and Commercial Bank of China	18.18	Financials
2	601288.SH	Agricultural Bank of China	12.67	Financials
3	601988.SH	Bank of China	9.35	Financials
4	601166.SH	Industrial Bank Co Ltd	3.96	Financials
5	000002.SZ	China Vanke Co	3.20	Real Estate
6	000001.SZ	Ping An Bank Co Ltd	3.20	Financials
7	00066.HK	MTR Corporation	2.85	Manufacture
8	600104.SH	SAIC Motor Corporation Limited	2.68	Consumer Discretionary
9	601668.SH	China State Construction Engineering Corp Ltd	2.67	Manufacture
10	02007.HK	Country Garden	2.52	Real Estate

Source: Author's based on data from Sina Finance, June 30, 2020, retrieved in September 2020.

Top 10 Portfolio Weighted Constituents of Beautiful China ESG 100 Index (June 2021)

Rank	Code	Issuer	2021 Portfolio Weight (%)	Sector
1	0941.HK	China Mobile Ltd.	15.64	Telecommunication
2	601318.SH	Ping An Insurance (Group) Co.	11.54	Finance
3	000858.SZ	Wuliangye Yibin Co.	9.18	Consumer Discretionary
4	2388.HK	BOC Hong Kong Holdings Ltd.	5.11	Finance
5	601012.SH	Longi Green Energy Technology Co. Ltd.	4.58	Information Technology
6	0960.HK	Longfor Properties	4.40	Real Estate
7	1109.HK	China Resources Land Ltd.	4.19	Real Estate
8	2007.HK	Country Garden Holdings Co. Ltd.	4.06	Real Estate
9	00294.SZ	BYD Company Ltd.	3.25	Consumer Discretionary
10	0981.HK	Semiconductor Manufacturing International Corporation	4.52	Information Technology

Source: Author's based on data from Sina Finance, June 21, 2021, retrieved on June 30, 2021.

Appendix 3

List of Acronyms

AGM	annual general meetings
AMAC	the Asset Management Association of China
Ant	Ant Group
ASEAN	Association of Southeast Asian Nations
BRI	Belt and Road Initiative
BUI	Bui Dam Hydroelectricity
CASVI	the China Alliance of Social Value Investment
CBDC	China's central bank digital currency
CBI	the Climate Bonds Initiative
CCDI	Central Commission for Disciplinary Inspection
CGTN	China Global Television Network
CICC	China International Capital Corporation
CIPS	Interbank Payment System
CPTPP	Progressive Agreement for Trans-Pacific Partnership
CSCS	Corporate Social Credit System
CSI	Chinese Securities Index Co., LTD
CSR	corporate social responsibility
CSRC	the China Securities Regulatory Commission
EM	Emerging Markets
ESG	environmental, social, and governance
FDI	foreign direct investment
FEILO	Feilo Acoustics Co., Ltd.
FOCAC	Forum on China-Africa Cooperation
FYP	China's 14th Five-Year Plan
G7	group of seven industrialized countries
GBA	the Greater Bay Area
GRI	Global Reporting Initiative
HFCA	Holding Foreign Companies Accountable Act
HKEX	Hong Kong Stock Exchange

HKMA	Hong Kong Monetary Authority
IMF	International Money Funds
IP	intellectual property
IPCC	Intergovernmental Panel on Climate Change
IPO	Initial Public Offering
ISSB	International Sustainability Standards Board
NAFMII	the National Association of Financial Market Institutional Investors
NAFTA	North American Free Trade Agreement
NYSE	The New York Stock Exchange
OECD	Organization for Economic Cooperation and Development
OLOE	the Overseas Listed Offshore Entity
PBOC	the People's Bank of China
PCAOB	Public Company Accounting Oversight Board
PRI	Principles for Responsible Investment
QFII	Qualified Foreign Institutional Investor
RCEP	Regional Comprehensive Economic Partnership
RQFII	RMB Qualified Foreign Institutional Investors
SAR	Special Administrative Regions
SASAC	State-Owned Assets Supervision and Administration Commission
SASB	Sustainability Accounting Standards Board
SDG	Sustainability Development Goals
SDR	Special Drawing Rights
SEC	Securities and Exchange Commission
SMEs	small and middle enterprise
SoCS	China's social credit system
SOEs	State-Owned Enterprises
SSE	the Shanghai Stock Exchange
STAR	Shanghai Stock Exchange's Science and Technology Innovation Board
STGF	SynTao Green Finance
SWIFT	Society for Worldwide Interbank Financial Telecommunication
SZSE	the Shenzhen Stock Exchange
TAL	Tomorrow Advancing Life
TCFD	Task Force on Climate-Related Financial Disclosures
TPP	Trans-Pacific Partnership
UAS	United Arab Emirates
VIE	variable interest entity
WFOE	the Wholly Foreign Owned Enterprise
WHH	Wahaha Group
WIPO	World Intellectual Property Organization

Appendix 4

More Readings

Casanova, Lourdes, Fernanda Cahen, and Anne Miroux, *Innovation from Emerging Markets: From Copycats to Leaders*, Oxford University Press, 2021.

Casanova, Lourdes, and Anne Miroux, *The Era of Chinese Multinationals – Competing for Global Dominance*, Elsevier Academic Press, 2019.

Clarke, Thomas, *International Corporate Governance – A Comparative Approach* (2nd Edition), Routledge Press, 2019.

Gore, Al, *The Future – Six Drivers of Global Change*, Random House, 2013.

Hu, Yong, and Yazhou Hao, *Haier Purpose: The Real Story of China's First Global Super Company*, Infinite Ideas, 2017.

Jawad, Ali Qassim, and Andrew Kakabadse, *Leadership Intelligence – The 5Qs For Thriving as A leader*, Bloomsbury, 2019.

Kakabadse, Andrew, and Nada Kakabadse, *The Geopolitics of Governance – The Impact of Contrasting Philosophies*, Palgrave, 2001.

Kakabadse, Andrew, and Nada Kakabadse, *Leading the Board – The Six Disciplines of World-Class Chairmen*, Palgrave, 2008.

Larcker, David, and Brian Tayan, *Corporate Governance Matters*, Pearson Education, 2016.

Lee, Kuan Yew, One Man's View of the World, *The Straits Times, Singapore Press Holdings Limited, 2013*.

Leng, Jing, *Corporate Governance and Financial Reform in China's Transition Economy*, Hong Kong University Press, 2009.

Normal, Paul, *Net Positive*, Harvard Business Review Press, 2021.

Tian, Tao, and Chunbo Wu, *The Huawei Story* (1st Edition), Sage Publications Pvt. Ltd., 2015.

Tricker, Bob, *Corporate Governance* (4th Edition), Oxford University Press, 2019.

Tricker, Bob, *The Evolution of Corporate Governance*, Cambridge University Press, 2021.

Tricker, Bob, and Gregg Li, *Understanding Corporate Governance in China*, Hong Kong University Press, 2019.

Wucker, Michelle, *The Gray Rhino*, St. Martin's Press, 2016.

Wucker, Michelle, *You Are What You Risk*, Pegasus Books, 2021.

Appendix 5

List of Interviewees

This list includes brief biographies of individuals who have participated in interviews and shared their opinions and experiences of various topics. While some of interviewees have respectfully requested they remain anonymous, their contributions are nonetheless genuinely appreciated.

Professor Andrew Kakabadse – Professor Kakabadse is Professor of Governance & Leadership, Programme Director of The Board Director's Programme, and Chairman of the Henley Directors' Forum. Professor Kakabadse has undertaken global studies spanning over 20,000 organizations in the private, public, and third sectors encompassing 41 countries. His research focuses on board performance, governance, leadership, and policy. Professor Kakabadse is listed in Who's Who and is a life member of the Thinkers50 Hall of Fame.

Professor Lourdes Casanova – Professor Casanova is a Senior Lecturer and Gail and Rob Cañizares Director of Emerging Markets Institute, S.C. Johnson School of Management, Cornell University. An accomplished researcher and author of many books, in 2014 and 2015, Professor Casanova was selected as one of 50 of the most influential Iberoamerican intellectuals by ES Global, an influential Hispanic executive training organization. Then in 2017, Professor Casanova was named as one of only 30 Iberoamerican intellectuals by the same organization.

Professor Edward Freeman – Dr. Freeman is a philosopher and professor of business administration at the Darden School at the University of Virginia. Dr. Freeman has been recognized since the 1980s for his stakeholder theory and his work on business ethics.

Christine Raynaud – Ms. Raynaud is a board director of the European Chamber of Commerce in Hong Kong and a senior executive with various world-class talent management consulting firms. Ms. Raynaud has advised Western and Asian companies with their global talent strategies since the 1980s and lived in Hong Kong for ten years.

Thomas Estines – Mr. Estines is the Co-CEO of Groupe Investissement Responsable Inc., a Canadian-based global firm specializing in sustainable development, responsible investment, and finance. As the Co-CEO, Mr. Estines ensures that the votes cast on behalf of GIR clients comply with their proxy voting policies, as well as the quality of the analyses produced by the team. Mr. Estines is also in charge of client relations, business development, and the creation of partnerships with other members of the industry.

Vivian Lin Thurston, CFA – Ms. Thurston is a partner and portfolio manager at William Blair Investment Management, co-managing various emerging markets and Chinese equity strategies. Previously, she worked at UBS Global Asset Management and Calamos Investments as a consumer analyst specializing in investment research and stock selection in the global consumer sector. She is also the founder and Chairman of the Board of Chinese Finance Association of America. Vivian received a B.L. in Sociology from Peking University and an M.A. in Sociology and M.S. in Finance from the University of Illinois at Urbana-Champaign.

Agnes K. Y. Tai – Ms. Tai is the Director of Great Glory Investment Corporation (a family-owned firm) and a responsibility officer for an Asian asset management company.

Fedor Heijl – Mr. Heijl, a native of the Netherlands, transformed his family's automotive business into an international success, sold his company to a leading US corporation, then established a consulting firm specializing in advising family-owned business entrepreneurs with their long-term business strategies. He also serves as a board member for numerous family-owned businesses.

Ernst Gylfe – Mr. Gylfe is the owner and Vice Chairman of Novita Ltd., a family-owned yarn manufacturer founded in Finland in 1928. His company is one of the largest of its kind in Europe. Mr. Gylfe is also the Chair of Board of Directors of a Zurich-based boutique investment company that manages wealth for UHNWI, and the founding partner of EMC Advisors Ltd. in Zurich. Mr. Gylfe has a master's degree in Business and Finance.

Lynda Kahari – Ms. Kahari is a business executive with extensive banking experience in large and startup banks in Africa and the Pacific. Lynda holds a master's degree in Finance and Investments and a master's in Business Administration. She is a graduate of the Australian Institute of Company Directors program and is also a Balanced Scorecard Professional.

Selebalo Ntepe – Mr. Ntepe is a board member of the biggest milling company in Lesotho and Chair of its Audit and Risk Committee, the Deputy Chairman of the Institute of Directors Lesotho, member of Mohlomi Governance Code Drafting Committee, and an IoD South Africa Member. He was the youngest ever member of Lesotho's Premier League Board (Committee) that operates under the auspices of the Lesotho Football Association.

Jacqueline Musiitwa – Ms. Musiitwa is a lawyer with experience as a company secretary, governance trainer, and non-executive director with experience on boards in the UK, US, and Africa. She has chaired governance and risk committees and has experience on audit and finance, and safeguarding committees.

Marie-Josee Pivyk – Marie-Josée is a member of CFA Montreal's ESG Committee, CPA Canada's Value Creation Working Group (Foresight Initiative), The Enterprise Data Management Council's ESG Working Group, and leader of the Quebec SASB FSA Credential Group. She also participates in the CCLI's Canadian Climate Governance Experts Initiative.

Clint Bartlett – Clint Bartlett is a professional impact investment consultant and strategy advisor. He has worked across Sub-Saharan Africa, the US, UK, and Europe on projects related to impact strategy and sustainable finance. Clint has an MBA from the University of Cape Town and a Master's in Advanced Management from Yale University.

Nawar Alsaadi – Mr. Alsaadi is a sustainable investment professional with more than ten years of experience in capital markets and corporate engagement. He has been involved with a number of high-profile activist encounters with TSX and NYSE-listed companies on issues pertaining to corporate governance and corporate strategy. Mr. Alsaadi holds a sustainable investment professional certification from Concordia University, an ESG Investing certification from the CFA Institute (UK), and an FSB credential from the Sustainability Accounting Standards Board (SASB).

Mukesh Butani – Mr. Butani is the Founder and Managing Partner of BMR Legal. With specialization in corporate international tax and transfer pricing, he has significant experience in advising Fortune 500 multinationals and large Indian business houses on a wide range of matters relating to FDI policy, business reorganizations, cross-border tax structuring, tax controversies, and regulatory policies across a range of sectors.

Madhura Bhat – Ms. Bhat is the Senior Associate at BMR Legal. She has a strong background in corporate, commercial, and insolvency law and provides tax advice and litigation services, as well as policy prescriptions proposals on a wide range of subjects including capital markets, foreign direct investments.

Kwan Kew Lai – Dr. Lai is a Harvard Medical School faculty physician specializing in infectious diseases. She is a disaster relief medical volunteer and has volunteered her services all over the world. While volunteering, Dr. Lai encountered governance challenges between international NGOs and those countries' local governments' medical operation facilities.

Rosa Zeegers – Ms. Zeegers is a partner with Newport LLC. Throughout her 30-year corporate career, she has successfully led global Fortune 500 brands and businesses in various industries to new growth levels. Ms. Zeegers has also served as an independent board director of non-profit and for-profit organizations.

About the Author

Lyndsey Zhang is a researcher, consultant, and lecturer on corporate governance and corporate sustainability. Before performing independent research on global corporate governance and ESG integration-related topics that resulted in this book, she had extensive experience working for Western and Chinese multinational companies in clean and renewable energies, high-tech, and automation manufacturing sectors. Lyndsey's frontline experiences leading Chinese companies toward global strategic expansion, through fundraising success in Hong Kong's stock exchange, and cross-border M&A and post-acquisition integrations in US and European countries, have uniquely positioned her to understand the opportunities and challenges of Chinese multinationals and their global partners and provided Lyndsey with a solid foundation for research and consulting.

Lyndsey has been a licensed CPA in the US since 2007 and earned certification as an Independent Board Director from Harvard University in 2019. She received her Master of Science in Accountancy from Illinois State University, and Bachelor of Science in Economics from Xiamen University in China.

Lyndsey is a Ph.D. researcher at Henley Business School at the University of Reading. Her doctoral research focuses on board directors' roles in business sustainability, a separate project from this book.

Index

Printed in the United States
by Baker & Taylor Publisher Services